Publications

of

# The Colonial Society of Massachusetts

VOLUME LXXI

# Reinterpreting
# New England Indians
## *and the*
# Colonial Experience

# Reinterpreting New England Indians *and the* Colonial Experience

Edited by

Colin G. Calloway & Neal Salisbury

*Boston*   THE COLONIAL SOCIETY OF MASSACHUSETTS   2003
*Distributed by the University of Virginia Press*

*Dedicated to the Memory of*

*Our Fellow Member*

RUSSELL PETERS

Printed from the Income of the Sarah Louise Edes Fund

# Contents

# Foreword

EVERY BOOK IS A JOURNEY, and this particular journey began with a long drive west along Route 2 to Deerfield, Massachusetts. Russell Peters, who lived just outside Boston, had agreed to pick me up near my home in Groton, Massachusetts. Towns like Groton and Lancaster had been the far edge of Puritan settlement in the 1670s and, consequently, had been abandoned during King Philip's War. Everything from the Nashua River west to Deerfield and the string of English settlements along the Connecticut River Valley would have been the uncontested territory of its First People, just as it had already been.

I had not met Russell before and was feeling nervous and self-conscious. What would the head of the Wampanoag Tribal Council have to say to me, a descendent of a Roxbury militia captain who had played a leading role in the Great Swamp Fight, one of the most notorious massacres of King Philip's War? To make matters worse, I was representing the Colonial Society of Massachusetts, an organization (until recent decades) so brahminical its blood ran blue. Over the first century of the Colonial Society's existence, many authors in its publications had contributed to the misimpression that Native Americans had simply vanished from the New England landscape, greatly complicating the struggle by contemporary native peoples for tribal recognition from the Federal government. I had a bad case of liberal guilt.

Yet Russell had a talent for putting people at their ease. During the long drive out to Deerfield, our conversation focused more and more on the positive things a conference on recent scholarship in Native American history could accomplish. At such gatherings in the past, Russell observed, academics and Native Americans had a way of talking past each other. Because scholars necessarily focused on written evidence, native peoples often went away angry from academic conferences, believing their past had been appropriated by presenters who showed insufficient respect for oral tradition, a source of knowledge to which Native Americans alone held the key. Russell wanted a conference where tribal historians and university professors would participate as respected equals in their exploration of the past.

Ultimately, the conference fully vindicated Russell's vision, but that never would have happened without the imagination and hard work of the other members of the Program Committee, whom we first met that day at lunch in Deerfield: Neal Salisbury had been an early leader in the revival of seventeenth- and eighteenth-century Native American studies; Colin Calloway was a young scholar of remarkable energy whose many titles on New England Indians had already won him a considerable reputation; and Barry O'Connell had brought passionate commitment and keen analysis to his writings about William Apess, an outspoken early nineteenth-century Indian preacher. Absolutely crucial to the whole endeavor was Marge Bruchac, an Abenaki woman, who conveyed a deeper understanding of Indian culture to students and tourists through her first-person interpretations at Old Sturbridge Village. Without Marge's extensive connections in the Native American community and her skill at peacemaking, the conference could never have happened as it did. Jean O'Brien, an Ojibwe scholar teaching at the University of Minnesota, made a number of important contributions to the committee's work through the miracle of email.

One of the most prolonged points of discussion during that first meeting of the Program Committee at Deerfield concerned where the conference should take place. We were fortunate that in the end the choice fell upon Old Sturbridge Village, which not only gave us access to its superb meeting facilities but also brought us the enthusiastic support of its Director of Research, Collections, and Library, Jack Larkin, and the managerial talents of Ed Hood, who joined the program committee as OSV's representative.

The choice of Sturbridge placed us squarely in Nipmuc territory and inevitably drew us into the controversy over that tribe's battle for federal recognition (which Colin Calloway and Neal Salisbury describe more extensively in their introduction). The kind of conference we wanted could only happen with the blessing of the Nipmuc people, but which of the various bands would be represented in the opening ceremonies? In the end, we invited them all, and thanks to Marge Bruchac's diplomatic talents, all attended. In fact, native people came from all over New England: well over 50 percent of registrants were Indians, a first for an academic conference of this sort.

It's hard to put into words what made the conference so special. Perhaps it was the large number of native faces? Perhaps it was the care with which the Program Committee had worked to ensure a variety of voices among the presenters? Perhaps it was the warm sunshine at the cusp of early spring in Massachusetts? Discussion was certainly spirited, but it was respectful. And there was excitement in the air about being part of a new, cooperative endeavor in Native American studies.

The Colonial Society is clearly proud of its role in the conference. From the beginning, the effort enjoyed the enthusiastic patronage of its president, Frederick Ballou, and the fact that proceedings of such a conference would make a good book fully justified the foresight of its Publications Committee, who should rightly be regarded as the initiators of the whole project. A bundle of sacred herbs (intended to bring "good mind" to any deliberations), presented to the Society at the conference by the Northeastern Representative of the American Indian Movement, now enjoys a place of honor in the Society's Beacon Hill headquarters.

Not every paper given at such a gathering adapts itself well to a volume of proceedings, but all enriched the discussion. I would like to take this opportunity to thank the presenters whose wise words do not appear in this volume: Emerson W. Baker, Kathleen Bragdon, Wendi Starr Brown, Catherine Ann Corman, Thomas L. Doughton, Jessie Little Doe Fermino, Bernice Forrest, Maurice Foxx, Kim Houde, Thomas Kelleher, Joan Luster, Kevin McBride, Ann McMullen, Alice Nash, Mark A. Nicholas, Chief Wise Owl, Carole J. Palavra (Red Sunset), R. Todd Romero, Deborah A. Rosen, Faren R. Siminoff, Tobias Vanderhoop, Chief Walter Vickers, Michael A. Volmar, and Frederick Wiseman.

Colin Calloway and Neal Salisbury carefully watched over the journey from conference to book. They are both the sort of expeditious, fair-minded editors any publisher dreams about. Kate Viens resolutely took on the painstaking job of copy-editing, and Jeanne Abboud is responsible for the book's handsome design, as she is for so many Colonial Society publications.

Unfortunately, Russell Peters's ill health prevented him from attending the conference he envisioned, and he died before the proceedings could appear in print. From the outset, his hopes shaped our whole endeavor, and the editors have chosen to dedicate this book to his memory.

Groton, Massachusetts
JOHN W. TYLER, April 2003
*Editor of Publications*

# Introduction:

## *Decolonizing New England Indian History*

COLIN G. CALLOWAY AND NEAL SALISBURY

IT IS OFTEN SAID WE CANNOT ESCAPE THE PAST, and that is particularly true in Indian country. At the same time, as any student of history knows, we cannot escape the present in looking at the past. For the indigenous peoples of New England—the Abenaki, Mohegan, Mohican, Narragansett, Nipmuc, Passamaquoddy, Penobscot, Pequot, Schaghticoke, Wampanoag and other tribal nations—the colonial period has not yet ended. The contemporary struggles of native peoples to defend their resources, shape their futures, safeguard their health, and provide for their families may seem to render the academic study of history of limited relevance to "real life." Yet, the manner in which that history is reconstructed and interpreted has very real effects on very real struggles, in a climate and society where Native rights are closely tied to political status and ethnic identity.

History is contested ground. Who tells it, who "owns the past," can leverage significant power. Colonialism *entailed*, indeed required, controlling how history is told. Colonial writers depicted Indians not as people who made history, but as people who stood in history's way.

Indians also stood between the colonizer and valuable resources and land. Writing was an instrument of dispossession that also exercised "conceptual violence" on Indian peoples, their world, and their ways of knowing. Indians were dehumanized and demonized as "savages," while their conquerors were ennobled as "civilized"; natives' homelands became "frontiers" or "wilderness," and their history was written according to colonial constructs.[1]

The legacies of colonial invasion—dispossession, racism, and ethnocide—are inextricably linked to loss of land, loss of political sovereignty, and loss of control over the telling of native histories. Native peoples have their own ways of understanding and recording history, and Indian communities and individuals are repositories of historical knowledge. Until recently, however, Indians were rarely consulted by non-native scholars and what little information they shared was usually accorded second-class status, subordinated to the researchers interpretations and academic purposes. The dominant approach to writing and interpreting New England colonial history has tended to obscure native experiences, native perspectives, and oral histories.

For most Americans, "colonial" conjures up images of Puritan settlers, powdered wigs, and tricorn hats—Plimouth Plantation and Colonial Williamsburg. It suggests a specific period predating the American Revolution. In New England, Indian people step briefly onto this colonial stage: they meet the Pilgrims, die of disease, lose their lands, and go down in defeat in the Pequot War and King Philip's War. Their part in America's history is limited to a colonial era that serves as prelude to the history of the United States. But for native people, colonialism lasts longer and reaches well beyond the moment of American independence.

Understanding colonialism in native New England requires looking beyond Indian-European contacts and conflicts. It requires seeing how colonial mechanisms of power and control were established and perpetuated, and how colonial attitudes continue to influence modern ways of thinking about race and gender, family and community, authority and power, culture and identity. It requires that we ask how and why Euro-American ways of recording history and scholarship have dominated the study of American Indian histories. Many native people point out that enduring colonial structures and attitudes curtail, deny, and distort their voices, and still allow non-native academics to monopolize the telling of their histories. They insist on greater intellectual and cultural sovereignty: knowledge from Indian communities should stay in the communities; native people should tell their own stories and write their own histories using native sources of knowledge. Many non-natives have reacted with alarm at these demands and at the support natives have received from some members of the non-Indian public. Some scholars worry that the increasing insistence of native nations on telling their own histories threatens to undermine academic standards as well as Americans' memory of their nation's history.[2] As a result of this mutual mistrust, native and non-native scholars have been telling histories of New England Indians that for the most part run parallel to one another, with no intersection.

Despite so much writing and talking past one another by scholars, a growing number of them have recognized that intersection is not only possible but desirable if we are to gain a fuller understanding of the region's history. The intersection, overlapping, and conflict of the scholar's past and the native present were very much in the minds of the committee that John Tyler, Editor of Publications of the Colonial Society of Massachusetts, assembled to plan a conference on Indian history in New England. Marge Bruchac (Abenaki), Jean O'Brien (Ojibwe), the late Russell Peters (Mashpee Wampanoag), Colin Calloway, Barry O'Connell, and Neal Salisbury, each, in her or his own way, understood the complexities of "doing Indian history." These scholars recognized that a full and accurate portrayal of native peoples and their past requires true collaboration by Indian and non-Indian historians, and that native perspectives are vital to reevaluating, deconstructing, and reinterpreting colonial ideologies, attitudes, and methods of recording history. They were adamant that the Colonial Society of Massachusetts, not known for its inclusion of Indian perspectives on New England's past, must do more than just invite academic papers.

Instead, the conference tried to do what the best scholarship in recent years has done: combine scholarly research and inquiry with native testimony and insight; strive for dialogue rather than definitive delivery. Titling the conference "Reinterpreting the Indian Experience in Colonial New England," the organizers understood that the rethinking could and should apply to "colonial" as well as to Indian experiences. They invited native participants to comment upon and to challenge the continuing colonial structures that constrain their lives and limit their opportunities. They selected Old Sturbridge Village, a place located in the center of Nipmuc homelands yet best known for portraying nineteenth-century white Yankee culture, as the appropriate site for this dialogue to take place.

That past and present are one was apparent in the opening session. The Nipmuc speakers who opened the conference had no doubts about who they are or about their history in their central Massachusetts homelands, but at the time of the conference they were awaiting a decision on their political status as a sovereign nation in the eyes of the federal government. President Bill Clinton had awarded the Nipmuc Nation federal recognition as an "eleventh hour" measure before leaving office. George W. Bush put their recognition on hold when he took office. The recognition Clinton had extended was subsequently withdrawn.

# *Introduction*

The Nipmuc experience is all too familiar in New England, where the status and identity of longstanding native communities have often been debated, decided and denied by outsiders. Federal recognition policies, popular attitudes, and decades of Eurocentric scholarship alike have failed to make sense of New England's Indian country and communities. Four hundred years of contact, conflict, and cautious coexistence have produced complex and mutlilayered webs of identity that defy consistent bureaucratic categorization and popular stereotypes. The images and one-dimensional histories generated during those centuries make it difficult for most Americans to understand the depth and persistence of Native American presence in New England.

In recent decades native and non-native scholars have whittled away at old attitudes and assumptions that denied Indian people a meaningful place in New England's past. Much work remains to be done to breach the still-formidable defenses against according Indian people a place in New England's present. Conversations such as those that took place at Sturbridge help to break down such barriers; scholarship such as the selection of papers published here represents the continuing needs and opportunities for deeper and fuller understandings of the shared colonial past that has shaped, and continues to shape, New England's present.

It proved impossible, in a volume like this, to include the full range of presentations and dialogue that comprised the conference. There were many short presentations, "non-papers," statements from the floor, and spontaneous remarks that enriched the conference but did not lend themselves to reproduction as part of the published proceedings. One or two short presentations addressing explicitly contemporary issues would not have fit well in a volume dominated by longer historical essays. Even as the editors tried to assemble representative papers from a conference designed to include native voices, they recognized that, in the published volume, some voices would yet again be absent. In the end, it was decided to publish a selection of ten essays from those submitted for consideration. The sample does reflect the conference in that it includes works by younger as well as established scholars, works by natives and non-natives, and collaborative efforts by Indian and non-Indian scholars. It includes essays on new topics, and essays that ask new questions of old topics. Collectively, the essays suggest some of the new directions scholars are pursuing, as well as some ways of thinking about history that are new to academia but very old in native communities. The volume concentrates on southern New England as the area on which the presentations were solidly focused. It does not offer a narrative history of such familiar topics as colonial-Indian encounters, Puritan missions, King Philip's War, and the French and Indian wars. Instead, the authors peer beneath the surface history of events to understand how non-Indian peoples projected and perpetuated colonialism and how Indian peoples in southern New England experienced and responded to it.

Virginia DeJohn Anderson examines a first meeting between New England Indians and an Old World domesticated animal. The incident was part of a huge encounter that had momentous ecological consequences, but Anderson explores it as a cultural encounter: how did the Indians make sense of the new creature? The English colonists' own failure to understand the complex world of Indian-animal relationships and the inability of their language to convey Algonkian spiritual concepts make this a challenging task for a historian working with seventeenth-century written records. Anderson resorts to studies of modern Cree to better understand the reciprocal and ritual relations that native hunters maintained with animals that possessed significant spiritual power. The cow that Chickwallop and his people discovered challenged their world view not only because it was a new creature but also because it was, to Englishmen, property.

Joshua Bellin takes a new look at some old sources and asks how we can treat the written texts created by a Puritan missionary. In John Eliot's tracts, Bellin finds "the unsettling power of encounter.... present in a variety of forms." He points out that Indians and missionaries alike lived in "contexts of translation," and that any documents created in such contexts bear the marks of both cultures as they adjust to and interpret the other. The very act of translation was an act of colonialism, even of colonial violence. The words expressed by Indian people in John Eliot's *Dialogues,* for example, belonged entirely neither to the Indians nor to Eliot. While such texts cannot be accepted at face value as representing the views or voices of native people, translation "enables us to see that the Indian presence is at once more elusive and more decisive than scholars of colonial texts typically allow."

Ann Marie Plane takes the issue of translation to another level, exploring the place of dreams in Puritan English and Algonkian Indian cultures. Analyzing an English missionary's written account of an Indian woman's dream, she attempts to "eavesdrop on an unusual conversation" between them about the meaning of dreams. Though Plane recognizes that she is working with "a highly compromised piece of historical evidence," her essay nonetheless suggests the potential for the uses of dreams as evidence for understanding cross-cultural encounters and colonization.

Scholars are also paying more attention to the scope of the Indian slave trade throughout colonial North America, locating Indian slaves in French colonial towns, Spanish silver mines, and British sugar islands, and finding that New Englanders bought, sold, and employed Indian slaves. Charles Town, South Carolina, was notorious as a port of exit for Indian slaves captured in the interior and shipped to the Caribbean, but Charles Town also exported Indian slaves to New England, while New England sent Indian captives to the Caribbean.[3] Margaret Newell focuses on Indian slavery in New England during the half century following 1670 and reconstructs the experiences and legal position of Indian slaves. New Englanders were prohibited from enslaving Indians unless they were captives taken in war; however, no such restrictions prevented Indians from being sentenced to involuntary servitude for non-payment of debt or other offenses, and the distinction between slavery and involuntary servitude was often slight.

Many, if not most, Indian servants were children. As part of an ongoing scholarly collaboration that has already produced important work, historian Ruth Wallis Herndon and Narragansett medicine woman and tribal historian Ella Wilcox Sekatau discuss the servitude of Indian children in eighteenth-century Rhode Island. Looking at the period 1750–1800, when the system of "pauper apprenticeship" was at its height, Herndon analyzes town records while Sekatau draws on Narragansett oral traditions to reveal the experiences of young Indians who, from illegitimacy, loss of parents, or poverty, found themselves servants. Racial labeling often proved fluid, and it was not uncommon for Indian slaves and servants to be identified as blacks in the official record.

Understanding Indian responses to colonialism requires us to look beyond epic struggles like King Philip's War and to avoid placing people in simple "for and against" categories. Natives developed multiple ways of resisting and surviving colonialism, even in such little acts as going to church, learning to read, telling a story, or making a basket. In another collaborative project involving a native and a non-native scholar, Trudie Lamb Richmond and Amy Den Ouden examine forms of resistance at the local level. Richmond reconstructs how native women tested the limits of colonial authority that intruded on their lives and tried to define their roles and identities; Den Ouden relates how the Mohegan community in the eighteenth century resisted the colony of Connecticut and tried to retain some autonomy not by going to war but by going to court.

Tammy Schneider, a member of the Sac and Fox Nation of Missouri and a graduate student at the time of the conference, also considers how a Mohegan struggled with the colonial power structure. She looks at the correspondence of Mohegan Indian preacher Joseph Johnson with Eleazar Wheelock, teacher and founder of Dartmouth College. Johnson used the language of the colonialist, and his writing tended to be conventional in form and confessional in content. But Schneider reads more deeply for insights into the complex relations that existed between Wheelock and his native students, and for evidence of how one person managed to construct an identity that allowed him to survive as an Indian in a colonial English world.

Indians in coastal Massachusetts likewise struggled to remain as Indians, and remain on their homelands, in a colonial world. David Silverman demonstrates how the "multifunctionality" of native churches allowed Wampanoags on Cape Cod and the islands to do just that. Though the church was a colonial imposition, Wampanoags turned it into an Indian institution that, in no small measure, contributed to the survival of the Indian communities. Daniel Mandell focuses on the Mashpee Wampanoags of Cape Cod. He shows how their participation in the American Revolution and their interpretation of revolutionary ideals shaped their ongoing struggle for autonomy vis-a-vis non-Indian outsiders.

Finally, Nan Wolverton explores the marginalized lives of Indian and non-Indian basketmakers and the world they inhabited. In seventeenth-century New Mexico, Pueblo women expressed veiled resistance to Spanish colonial oppression in the pottery they made, manipulating symbols such as cross motifs to convey their own meanings. In a similar vein, Indian women in eighteenth-century New England likewise saw basket-making as a form of cultural resistance, a mark of being Indian, against all the odds, as well as a means of making a bare living. They shared many experiences with non-Indian basketmakers. Like the strands of the baskets these people made, Indian and non-Indian lives were at once interwoven and separate in the New England created out of the centuries-long colonial encounter.

These essays represent but a sampling of the many approaches and topics that are contributing to what might be termed the "decolonization" of New England Indian history. Much more of such scholarship is on the way, both from these authors and others. Although differences in emphasis and interpretation will continue to characterize their works, the authors share a recognition that their critiques of colonialism and their attentiveness to the historical experiences of native peoples are compatible with, indeed strengthened by, the critical observance of academic scholarly conventions. In so doing, they are transforming our sense of the New England past, as lived and as written about, and the ways it continues to shape the present.

# Notes

1. José Rabasa, *Writing Violence on the Northern Frontier: The Historiography of Sixteenth-Century New Mexico and Florida and the Legacy of Conquest* (Durham, N.C.: Duke University Press, 2000).

2. Devon A. Mihesuah, *Natives and Academics: Researching and Writing about American Indians* (Lincoln: University of Nebraska Press, 1998).

3. Ron Welburn, "The Other Middle Passage: The Bermuda-Barbados Trade in Native American Slaves," in his *Roanoke and Wampum: Topics in Native American Heritage and Literatures* (New York: Peter Lang, 2001), 25-32; Alan Gallay, *The Indian Slave Trade; The Rise of the English Empire in the American South, 1670–1717* (New Haven: Yale University Press, 2002), 7. For a guide to the sources and literature on Indian slavery, see Russell M. Magnaghi, *Indian Slavery, Labor, Evangelization, and Captivity in the Americas: An Annotated Bibliography* (Lanham, Md.: The Scarecrow Press, Inc., 1998).

# Chickwallop and the Beast

## *Indian Responses to European Animals in Early New England*

VIRGINIA DEJOHN ANDERSON

ONE WINTER'S DAY IN 1635 OR 1636, a band of Norwottuck Indians noticed a strange creature floundering in deep snow near the Connecticut River. Advancing cautiously, they came upon a small, horned animal, which they later described as "poor and scarce able to rise." They had never seen anything like it before. Unsure of what to do next, they traveled back to their sachem, Chickwallop, and a few days later he accompanied them to view the beast for himself. The men lifted the animal up, but it quickly collapsed under its own weight. Soon it "died of itself with hunger and cold," leaving the Indians thoroughly puzzled. Where had this creature come from? Were there more of them nearby?[1]

Had an Englishman been present to witness this encounter between the Norwottucks and the strange beast, he might well have laughed at the Indians' bewilderment, for the animal would have been utterly familiar to him. The creature was nothing more than a young cow that had wandered away from one of the new English settlements in the Connecticut Valley. But the Norwottucks' confusion was perfectly understandable: they had never seen a cow, and there was no colonist at the scene to explain that it was an English animal. Never before had they come across a creature that none of them recognized. The Indians' careful examination of the beast suggested much curiosity on their part, yet their decision to fetch Chickwallop also testified to their concern and, perhaps, fear.

The first and only description of this incident appeared more than thirty years after the fact—in March 1669—in a scant few lines in a letter from one Englishman to another. It may seem to deserve the obscurity in which it has hidden for well over three hundred years. But as an exceedingly rare account of a first encounter between Indians and an Old World animal, it deserves close attention. We now know that the movement of European livestock across the Atlantic was no less momentous for the future of America than that of the European peoples who brought them. For the most part, however, examinations of this topic have concentrated on the ecological impact of the imported animals. Even as cattle, swine, horses, and sheep provided food and muscle power for English colonists—and, eventually, for some Indian peoples—they also competed for space with indigenous animals, altered forest composition, compacted the soil, and introduced diseases. In so doing, they threatened Indian subsistence regimes and even, as Jared Diamond has suggested, helped establish European hegemony in the New World.[2]

Without denying the importance of ecological developments, this essay shifts our attention toward the cultural impact of European animals on native peoples.[3] What follows is a case study of the ways in which New England Indians tried to incorporate the new animals into their mental world, and of how, and why, Indian ideas about the creatures changed over time. For, as the story of the Norwottucks and the strange beast demonstrates, European livestock first presented Indians with a conceptual puzzle long before subsistence and ecological problems emerged. Determining how the Indians grappled with that puzzle reveals a great deal about how well they could adapt to new conditions. In the end, however, their inability to pursue their own solutions without interference from the English exposed the uneven balance of power that characterized the process of colonization.

# I

We can never know, of course, exactly what Chickwallop and his men thought that day about the creature they had found. But one way to begin seeking an answer is to investigate what New England Indians thought about the animals with which they were familiar, on the assumption that they would have reasoned by analogy from the creatures they already knew. The task of recovering native ideas about animals is complicated, however, by the fact that Indians may not have conceived of the generic category of "animals" in the same way that the English did—as all non-human creatures capable of sensation and voluntary motion. Colonists like Roger Williams and John Eliot, who made an effort to record native vocabularies, noted that both the Narragansett and the Massachusett languages included a word for "beasts" (*penashímwock* in Narragansett and *puppinashimwog* in Massachusett), but this may have connoted—as it does in English—a four-footed mammal as opposed to all non-human creatures.[4]

Even if Indians did not think of "animals" as a general category, they certainly recognized individual species of animals. Moreover, their conception of those animals' place in the world differed markedly from the understanding of the colonists. Indians viewed animals as different from people, but not necessarily subordinate to them. When Indians spoke of animals, they employed grammatical constructions that implied that animals were specially linked to people and the spiritual world. All words in the Massachusett language that referred to humans, spirits, or animals belonged to the category of animate nouns. In the case of plants, however, only certain nouns (such as those for "cedar tree" or "pine tree") were animate, which indicates that the quality of being alive did not, at least in a grammatical sense, place plants in the same grouping as people and animals. Since other Eastern Algonquian languages, including Narragansett and Mohegan-Pequot, shared common features with Massachusett, they probably included a similar grammatical characteristic.[5] Such linguistic evidence is at best only suggestive, but it accords with other information that reveals a distinctive native understanding of animals as significant beings with spiritual connections.

English colonists recognized that Indian ideas about the nature of human-animal relations differed from their own, but even the most sympathetic commentators struggled to explain what they observed. Some of them, acknowledging the spiritual component of those relations, simply asserted that Indians believed that animals were gods. Not long after he arrived in Rhode Island, for instance, Roger Williams reported that the Narragansetts "have plenty of Gods or divine powers: the Sunn, Moone, Fire, Water, Snow, Earth, the Deere, the Beare etc. are divine powers." The inclusion of celestial and natural phenomena might possibly have made sense to Williams, at least insofar as he could draw analogies from his knowledge of other, more familiar cultures. The Ancients had worshiped nature gods, after all, and even the Puritans considered such things as comets or fires or floods to be providences, or manifestations of divine power (though not powers in and of themselves).[6] But animals?

In fact, the evidence was more equivocal than Williams's statement suggested. In the early 1620s, Wampanoags who told Plymouth colonists about their creator deity Kiehtan (or Cautantowwit) declined to describe him at all. They merely informed Edward Winslow that "[n]ever man saw this Kiehtan; only old men tell them of him." Culture heroes in New England Indians' oral traditions—Maushop and his wife Squant in the south and Gluskap in the north—appeared not as animals but as giant humans who shaped the landscape and worked miracles. At the same time, however, Edward Johnson reported in the early 1650s that Indians told him that Hobbamock (or Abbomocho), a deity linked to the underworld, appeared to people in visions and dreams in the shape of a deer, an eagle, a snake—or even, though Johnson's informants may have been enjoying a joke, "sometimes like a white boy." And in the same vein, John Josselyn claimed that some Indians in northern New England told him a "story of the *Beaver*, saying that he was their Father."[7]

If animals were perhaps not gods as such, supernatural beings or guardian spirits evidently could assume the shapes of animals at will. Spirits of prey animals appeared in hunters' dreams on the night before an expedition. One shaman from Martha's Vineyard admitted to having many animal-shaped guardian spirits, including "Fowls, Fishes, and creeping things." Spirits might appear in the guise of animals during times of crisis, as in the reported instance during King Philip's War when—as an Englishman described it—warriors "had a Pawaw when the Devil appeared in the Shape of a Bear walk[in]g on his 2 hind feet." Indians, who drew no sharp division between natural and supernatural phenomena, easily incorporated such experiences into their mental world in ways that Christian English colonists could not.[8]

If Indian comments on animals and spirits left many colonists confused, at least one Englishman edged closer to a better understanding of native ideas. After five years' residence near the Narragansetts, Roger Williams composed *A Key into the Language of America* in 1643, recording what he had learned about their customs and beliefs. One of his more notable discoveries was the fact that among the Narragansetts there was "a generall Custome . . . at the apprehension of any Excellency in Men, Women, Birds, Beasts, Fish, &c. to cry out *Manittóo* A God . . . ."9 By distinguishing between animals themselves and the particular quality of "excellency" that indicated *manitou*, Williams had made an intellectual leap, no longer directly equating beasts with gods. Yet he still struggled to explain in English terms what he had observed. His translation of the word *manitou* to mean "a god" was at best an awkward attempt to connect an alien idea with Christian sensibilities. "Spirit" might have been a better, though still imprecise, choice, for there is no direct Christian analogue to the concept of *manitou.*10

Algonquian peoples, including the Indians of southern New England, generally conceived of *manitous* as other-than-human beings capable of assuming a variety of physical forms—including animals—and exerting spiritual power in a number of ways. As far as Williams could discern, *manitous* among the Narragansetts most often took shape as deer, bears, black foxes, and coneys (rabbits). These creatures' elusiveness seems to have been a marker of their special status. Black foxes—but not red or gray ones—"are *Manittóoes*" which the Narragansetts "have often seene, but never could take any of them." Narragansett hunters had to take care in setting their traps "for they say, the Deere (whom they conceive have a Divine power in them) will soone smell and be gone." And although Williams offered no explanation, Narragansetts may similarly have "conceive[d] there is some Deitie" in rabbits because of their ability to evade humans.11

Indians may also have detected *manitou* more frequently in animals that were crucial to native subsistence as sources of food and raw materials for tools, clothing, and shelter. For instance, deer and bears—two creatures described by Williams as "divine powers"—figured prominently in the Indian diet. Native peoples who lived in northern regions and subsisted primarily through hunting were especially disposed to perceive spiritual value in animals. Micmacs,

Ojibwas, and Crees, among others, believed that benevolent spirits protected game animals. Abenakis personalized their relationships with animal *manitous* by addressing them as grandmother, grandfather, sister, and brother.[13] And even though various southern New England peoples, like the Norwottucks, practiced horticulture to a greater extent than their northern neighbors, they too hunted extensively in the autumn and early winter, and this may help account for their perception of spiritual power in their prey.[14]

But utility to humans was not in itself sufficient to confer spiritual power on animals. There is no evidence that Indians perceived *manitou* in game birds, such as ducks and geese, or in fish. More to the point, while wampum beads used in ritual ceremonies were held sacred, the shellfish that supplied the raw material for the beads apparently held no particular spiritual significance. And many Algonquian peoples feared two *manitous* that few, if any, persons had ever seen: a giant horned underwater serpent and a sacred thunderbird that occupied the sky world.[15]

What colonists found particularly striking were not so much the ways that Indians talked about *manitous* and animal spirits, but how they acted in accordance with their beliefs. John Josselyn had lived in Massachusetts less than a year when he learned something about local Indians' regard for the powers of certain animals. One June day in 1639, a group of "Gentlemen" visited Josselyn's house and proceeded to entertain their host with a strange tale. Not long before, in the harbor at Cape Ann, two Indians traveling in a boat with several English sailors had passed a rock on which "a *Sea-Serpent* or *Snake* . . . lay quoiled up like a Cable." The sailors wanted to shoot the animal, but the Indians "disswaded them, saying, that if he were not kill'd outright, they would be all in danger of their lives." The Indians may have mistrusted the marksmanship of the Englishmen (they were, after all, in a boat) and worried about how they would evade the thrashings of such a large wounded animal. But if that were the point of the story, it hardly merited retelling, for the foolhardy English sailors would have been the butt of the joke. Josselyn's guests clearly saw this instead as an example of *Indian* foolishness. The Indians' response was represented as all out of proportion to the provocation: the English sailors were not in the least afraid of this snake or serpent. Josselyn did not elaborate on what either he or his guests thought was the cause of the Indians' reaction, but they may well have concluded that it somehow reflected the Indians' odd ideas about animal powers. If so, they may have been on the right track. The Indians may have feared offending such an unusual animal's guardian spirit. It is also possible that they identified the creature as the Great Serpent, which in Algonquian cosmology represented potentially evil powers. Extreme caution around such a dangerous being, then, was the only sensible course.[16]

According to Roger Williams, Narragansetts exercised similar care in dealing with another creature with special spiritual connections. Although crows fattened themselves in Indian cornfields, "yet scarce will one *Native* amongst an hundred kil them." Children were assigned the task of chasing crows away, but not destroying them. Such forbearance stemmed from a "tradition, that the Crow brought them at first an *Indian* Graine of Corne in one Eare, and an *Indian* or *French* Beane in another, from the Great God *Kautántouwits* field in the Southwest, from whence they hold came all their Corne and Beanes." Other birds—ducks, geese, swans, cormorants, pigeons—were fair game and Narragansetts killed an "abundance" of them, but the crow's mythological link to the origins of horticulture protected it from hunters. The crow's special status may also have reflected the common knowledge that shamans' familiar spirits often took the form of crows.[17]

Nowhere is the distinctive relationship between Indians and animals better seen than in hunting rituals. Since *manitous,* or guardian spirits, could help animals avoid an arrow or a trap, hunters had to address those supernatural protectors and, in effect, receive permission to take game. Algonquians accordingly adopted practices that recognized a reciprocal relationship between hunters and the spirits of their prey. The precise forms these rituals took, let alone their full significance, have been largely obscured by the imperfect descriptions of colonists, who usually saw them as evidence of Indian superstition. But one rare seventeenth-century account of the ritualized treatment of a dead animal suggests something of a lost world rich in symbolic connections between hunters and prey.[18]

John Josselyn barely hid his distaste when he described the butchering of a moose killed by a party of northern New England Indians, suggesting that it was nothing more than an opportunity for gluttony when native peoples "stuft their paunches" to the limit with meat. In fact, his description of the treatment of the moose bears a remarkably close resemblance to modern-day practices of Cree Indians, who have preserved much of the symbolic context which gave meaning to the way their ancestors killed game and which continues to inform their own exertions. These parallels between past and present practices offer a way of interpreting the seventeenth-century incident that goes beyond Josselyn's bare description.

Josselyn began by describing "young and lustie" Indian hunters pursuing the moose through deep snow. Once they "tyred him," the hunters approached the beast "on each side and transpierce[d] him with their Lances." After it collapsed "like a ruined building," the men moved in to cut its throat. It was obviously in the hunters' interest to dispatch such a huge animal quickly, but the severing of the moose's carotid artery may have been more than purely functional. Like the Cree hunters who similarly kill their prey expeditiously, Josselyn's Algonquians may have felt an obligation to minimize the animal's suffering. The Crees believe that prolonging an animal's death, or inflicting unnecessary cruelty in any way, demonstrates a lack of respect for its guardian spirit that could jeopardize the success of future hunting.[19]

Once the moose was dead, the Algonquian hunters skinned it and then the women in their hunting party began the heavy work of butchering. First they removed the heart "and from that the bone." Cree women do not butcher game, but the men who perform the task, like Josselyn's Indians, start by taking out the heart and a thin layer of fat located across the rib cage, to be brought back to camp as "tokens" of their kill. The Algonquian women then removed the "left foot behind"; among the Crees, the posterior legs of large mammals are considered women's food and are prized for their marrow. Next, the Algonquian women drew out the leg sinews and cut out the tongue. Cree hunters do likewise, having for centuries considered the tongue a "medicine piece" with sacred connotations. (Josselyn himself, in another context, described smoked moose tongue as "a dish for a *Sagamor*," or chief.) Only then did the Algonquian women begin removing the meat, in a place where the men "with their snow shoos shovel[ed] the snow away to the bare Earth in a circle." Modern Crees similarly prepare a clean surface before cutting up game.

Josselyn did not mention how the moose hunters disposed of the animal's bones, but other seventeenth-century Algonquian hunters considered this activity to be another spiritually charged ritual that had to be performed properly. Indians in the Hudson Valley, according to one observer, "always burn the beaver bones, and never permit their dogs to gnaw the same; alleging that afterwards they will be unlucky in the chase." Modern Crees also treat bones in a special way—by hanging them in trees, or boiling or burning them—to show respect for the animal's soul. Treating the bones in a ritually-prescribed way propitiated the guardian spirit that might otherwise withhold game from even the most skilled hunters.[20]

Along with tales of animal spirits and observations of hunting rituals, the very appearance of New England native peoples alerted colonists to the Indians' distinctive relationship with animals. English commentators described in detail how Indians imprinted their skins with animal-shaped images, perhaps seeking to invoke the spiritual power of animals through body decoration. William Wood described Massachusetts Indians who bore "upon their cheeks certain portraitures of beasts, as bears, deers, mooses, wolves, etc.; some of fowls, as of eagles, hawks, etc." There were other motifs available for personal adornment—Wood indicated that some non-representational designs were also used—but Indians apparently exhibited a distinct preference for animal-shaped images. Many of the specific designs were of creatures commonly identified with *manitous* and shamanistic spirits, a correspondence that suggests that their decorative significance derived from the spiritual powers associated with these animals. This spiritual connection may explain why the Indians who wore such images intended for them to be indelible. Wood noted that Indians applied animal images not by "a superficial painting but [by] a certain incision, or else a raising of their skin by a small sharp instrument under which they convey a certain kind of black unchangeable ink which makes the desired form apparent and permanent." These were tattoos, not temporary applications of paint such as might accompany certain rituals or preparations for war, and Indians expected to wear such images for life.[21]

Algonquian peoples employed animal motifs in the creation of material objects as well. William Wood glimpsed Indians with "pendants in their ears, as forms of birds, beasts, and fishes, carved out of bone, shells, and stone." Roger Williams described Narragansett tobacco pipes made "both of wood and stone . . . with men or beasts carved" on them. Corroborating these seventeenth-century accounts, archaeologists have unearthed amulets in the shape of birds, and stone fetishes resembling bears and seals. They have found stone pestles topped with animal-shaped effigies and brass spoons—made from fragments of European kettles—decorated with cut-out images of bears. Native peoples also etched pictures of thunderbirds and serpents on rocks. Animal symbolism, then, was important enough to seventeenth-century Algonquians that they surrounded themselves with animal-shaped objects even as they inscribed their very skins with the images of non-human creatures.[22]

It was precisely because New England Indians perceived spiritual power in animals that the Norwottuck men could not ignore the creature they had found near the Connecticut River or treat it like any other game animal. Did the unusual beast have a *manitou*, and if so, how should they address it? These concerns doubtless explain why the men returned to their village to fetch Chickwallop, leaving it to him to figure out what to do. The very fact that the animal had been seen in the frozen marsh near the river could only have heightened their apprehension, for they deemed places such as deep woods and swamps to be sacred. These were regions where spiritually significant encounters between humans and other-than-human beings were more likely to occur. William Bradford reported that Wampanoag religious leaders near Plymouth preferred to conduct their "conjurations" in "a dark and dismal swamp" rather than out in the open. The Norwottucks' forbearance in dealing with the cow surely stemmed from the animal's very strangeness, but it may also have reflected their concern that they did not know the right way to treat it. Rather than do the wrong thing and invite retaliation from its guardian spirit, they did nothing at all.[23]

If the Norwottucks' understanding of animals as spiritually powerful creatures at first governed their approach to the cow, this response would be tested in the coming years. Encounters with cows and other English livestock soon became commonplace as the numbers of such creatures grew, requiring Indians to develop a more systematic approach to their presence. Not surprisingly, Indians initially employed familiar conceptual categories as they did so, fitting livestock into native understandings of what animals were, rather than altering their conception of what animals were to fit the new creatures. Just as predictably, the colonists intervened to redirect this process of incorporating new animals into the New World to suit their own purposes.

## II

Native peoples first attempted to incorporate the new creatures into their world literally on their own terms. Instead of using English vocabulary or giving livestock newly-invented names, which would have emphasized their alien origins, Indians assigned them the names of the indigenous wild creatures they most closely resembled in appearance and behavior. Thus Roger Williams reported that when the Narragansetts noticed that an *ockqutchaun*, or woodchuck, was "about the bignesse of a *Pig*, and root[ed] like a *Pig*," they decided to "give this name to all our *Swine*." They similarly assigned a native name to a horse—*naynayoûmewot*—although Williams neglected in this case to explain the word choice.[24]

This naming technique represented one part of a broader strategy whereby Indians emphasized similarities between familiar objects and European goods as a way of easing their incorporation into native society. Williams offered numerous examples of this practice at work. Noticing "a consimilitude between our Guns and Thunder," the Narragansetts called a gun "*Péskunck*, and to discharge [it] *Peskhómmin* that is to thunder." The Narragansett word for "red copper kettle" (*míshquokuk*)—an English trade item—combined the terms for "red earth" (*míshquock*) and "kettle" (*aúcuck*). The word for "letter" became *wussuckwhèke,* derived from the verb "to paint" (*wussuckwhóm-min*), because, Williams explained, "having no letters, their painting comes the neerest." They called a shallop *wunnauanoûnuck* and a skiff *wunnauanounuckquèse,* using variations of a generic term for "carrying Vessells." Identifying Englishmen by their distinctive possessions, Narragansetts called them *chauquaquock* ("knive-men" in Williams's translation) or *wautaconâuog* ("coatmen"). At other times, they simply called Englishmen *waútacone,* or "stranger."[25]

Which items the Narragansetts chose to name is just as revealing as the way in which they went about naming them. Not all English goods received native names, at least in 1643 when Williams recorded Narragansett vocabulary. In addition to the terms mentioned above, Narragansetts had words for cloth, gunpowder, box, key, and iron— but not for a variety of English foods, tools, or buildings with which they had almost certainly come into contact.[26] Evidently the most impressive or desirable goods—and, of course, the colonists them-selves—first required Narragansett names, for the Indians coveted the objects and had to deal with colonists in order to get them. Little wonder that livestock figured so prominently on the list as well. They were unusual, numerous, and, unlike any of the other goods the English brought with them, capable of initiating contact with native people on their own.

Much as native language at first shaped the Indians' identification of English creatures, native ideas about animals as spiritually power-ful beings governed early encounters with the unfamiliar beasts. In applying those ideas, New England Indians may have cautiously employed the concept of *manitou* to describe domestic animals' strange and as yet imperfectly understood powers. This, at least, would explain a curious incident recorded by John Winthrop in 1642. That summer, New England was awash in rumors of a Narragansett conspiracy against the colonists. Three Indian informers came forward in August to confirm the colonists' worst fears, and one of them had been inspired to do so by an ominous encounter with an English animal. The Indian had recently been "hurt near to death" by a cart drawn by an ox. Assuming that this was no ordinary accident, he sent for Connecticut's governor, John Haynes. It was clear that "Englishman's God was angry with him," the injured man explained, for that God "had set Englishman's cow to kill him, because he had concealed such a conspiracy against the English." Thus the injured man felt compelled to make a confession.[27]

Puritan believers in divine providence—including both Winthrop and Haynes—would have been just as likely to detect a godly admonition in such an accident. But they would have been less prone to focus on the ox as God's instrument of punishment. For an Indian thoroughly accustomed to the idea of animals' spiritual agency, however, the ox's behavior attracted specific attention. Its spiritual protector—which either the Indian himself or, more likely, his English interlocutors identified as "Englishman's God"—had demonstrated quite clearly its power to harm and a desire for propitiation that the Indian ignored at his peril.

This assimilation of new creatures and objects on Indian terms was hardly unique to New England, and probably typified North American Indians' responses to contact with Europeans and their possessions. Just as they accepted imported copper and glass beads as equivalents of native copper and quartz crystals, Indians seem to have initially conceived of English animals as variants of indigenous beasts. And, as the incident with the ox suggests, the notion that certain substances and creatures might have ritual significance or spiritual power could readily be transferred to imported objects and animals. The flexible idea of *manitou*, applied to new creatures and things, may have offered a particularly effective way of incorporating them into native cultures without requiring any significant changes in Indian beliefs or behavior.[28]

In seventeenth-century New England, however, the Indians' freedom to think about English animals as they wished diminished over time as the numbers of colonists and their herds multiplied. Linguistic changes revealed the Indians' growing understanding that English livestock were not really like indigenous creatures. The Narragansetts abandoned analogies to local fauna and created new names for livestock that employed English words and thus recognized the animals' alien character. Swine were no longer woodchucks but *hógsuck* or *pígsuck*; cows became *cówsnuck*, and goats, *gôatesuck*. As Roger Williams explained, "This Termination *suck*, is common in their language; and therefore they adde it to our *English* Cattell, not else knowing what names to give them."29

This decision was not as arbitrary as Williams suggested. John Eliot's study of Massachusett grammar revealed that the suffix *og* (which may have been pronounced *uck* by the Narragansetts) formed the plural of any noun representing an animate being. Eliot then echoed Williams's observations by noting that Massachusett Indians called oxen *oxesog* and horses *horsesog*. When some Indians began learning English, they continued to combine English terms with native linguistic forms. William Wood, for instance, heard native hunters call a mare caught in a deer trap an "Englishman's squaw horse." He proceeded to ridicule them for having "no better epithet than to call her a woman's horse" even though they probably used the word "squaw" as an adjective simply to indicate that it was a female animal.30

The invention of neologisms and English-language phrases symbolized the way in which Indians increasingly viewed livestock on English terms—an adaptation that was scarcely voluntary. But changing names was only one small step in the process whereby Indians lost the ability to incorporate domestic animals into their world in their own way. The colonists cared less about what the Indians called the animals than how they treated them. Most of all, they insisted that

Indians recognize livestock as nothing more (and nothing less) than property. Prior to the colonists' arrival, New England Indians regarded animals as property only after they were killed.[31] And even then—as Josselyn's description of the moose hunt indicates—successful hunters shared their bounty with members of the hunting party and their kin. There was no equivalent in the natives' world (with the possible exception of dogs) to the animate property that accompanied English colonists from the Old World to the New. Their thinking about livestock, and not just their names for them, would have to change.

From the moment in the spring of 1631 when the Massachusett sachem Chickataubut paid a beaver skin in recompense for a pig killed by one of his men, New England Indians discovered that English ideas about livestock as property would overshadow whatever natives might have thought about the animals. They learned that cattle, horses, and swine should no more be killed than English goods should be stolen from colonists' houses. Indians who hurt livestock, even inadvertently, faced prosecution in colonial courts. They could not retaliate directly against domestic animals that damaged their planting fields, but had to seek retribution through legal channels and learn to build fences to protect their crops. With English owners acting as such powerful human protectors, it may have seemed to Indians that livestock hardly needed spiritual guardians. Never before, in their experience, had "property" proven so troublesome or property owners so indifferent to keeping it under their control.[32]

Ironically, the colonists' lax supervision of their domestic animals—a practical response to a scarcity of labor—strengthened their insistence that Indians recognize livestock as property. Because the animals ranged freely, it was all the more important that Indians learn to leave them alone. As far as the English settlers were concerned, the status of domestic animals as property dated from time out of mind and had nothing to do with methods of husbandry. The connection was evident in the word "cattle" itself, which shared etymological roots both with "chattel" and "capital."[33] The colonists' intransigence on this point only intensified when they learned how efficiently their free-ranging animal property furthered the cause of imperial expansion. The English, more than other European colonizers, conceived of their New World empire as the extension of dominion over land, more than control of indigenous peoples or resources. Colonial livestock, foraging freely in woods and meadows, enlarged the compass of English occupation far beyond the bounds of towns and villages. And because the colonists believed that grazing livestock "improved" the land, domestic animals legitimized their claim to tracts where Indians only hunted—an activity that did not, as far as the English were concerned, secure their rights to property. John Winthrop spoke for many of his fellow colonists when he asserted that the Indians had no legitimate title to land "for they inclose no ground, neither have they cattell to maintayne it." The fact that the colonists, at least during much of the seventeenth century, "inclosed" relatively little ground themselves and scarcely used their animals to maintain it went unremarked.[34]

Livestock wandered off into fields and woods, but colonists insisted that an invisible tether still connected them to their owners. A missing animal was missing property, and since Indians frequented the fields and woods, they were the likeliest suspects when creatures disappeared. The lack of corroborating evidence offered no obstacle to prosecuting native people who were known to harbor superstitions about animals rather than a respect for them as property. Thus in 1668 the Plymouth Colony court ordered Mekamoo to pay fifty shillings to William Pointing merely "on suspicion" of killing Pointing's cow. Only if evidence later demonstrated Mekamoo's innocence could he have "the said sume returned to him againe." This inversion of the usual assumptions about guilt and innocence was surely not unique, at least where Indians were concerned, and testified to the colonists' readiness to entertain doubts about Indians' honesty without reasonable proof.[35]

The expansion of the colonists' dominion within New England only encouraged greater boldness in the making of such accusations. Jeremy Adams of Springfield, at least, did not let the lack of proof hinder him in lodging a particularly audacious complaint in 1669. Without so much as a shred of hard evidence, he insisted that Chickwallop and his men *more than thirty years earlier* had killed one of his cows—none other than the strange beast the Indians had found near the Connecticut River. Now Adams wanted justice, or at least compensation. Unable to make his word a sufficient defense against this outrageous charge, Chickwallop appealed to John Pynchon, the most influential Englishman in the valley, for support. In protesting his innocence, the sachem recalled his men's surprise at finding the unusual beast so many years earlier and offered a description so detailed that Pynchon could identify it as a two- or "at the most" three-year-old cow. Convinced that Chickwallop was telling the truth, Pynchon defended him in a letter to Connecticut's governor, John Winthrop Jr., and offered his own opinion about the errant cow. "[B]e it what it will or whosever it was," Pynchon declared, "I have already heard that it died of itself."[36] The intercession of Pynchon and Winthrop apparently protected Chickwallop from further harassment, but their support—as much as Adams's accusation—upheld the colonists' view that cows were property. Adams's charge failed to stick because he could not prove that the cow was his or that Chickwallop had killed it. Had Adams managed to substantiate both of these claims, Chickwallop—no matter what he had thought about the cow—would have been in trouble.

The story of Chickwallop and the beast reveals the extent to which English livestock helped to reshape the cultural, and not just the physical, environment in which New England's Indians lived. Indians and colonists had deeply-embedded—and quite different—ideas about what animals were and how they should be treated, which guaranteed that encounters over livestock would become opportunities for cultural exchange. The Indians' initial response—an ability to accept the new creatures and even to perceive in them evidence of *manitou*—indicated their willingness to negotiate the terms under which livestock might be incorporated into the New World. But the colonists showed none of the flexibility necessary for such an exchange. Their understanding of domestic animals as property only grew firmer in the context of colonization. Because colonists believed that their livestock helped establish English claims to Indian land and thus furthered the cause of English dominion, their status as chattel—as proxies for English occupants—could not be negotiable. The seemingly inexorable growth in the number of English settlers and English animals eventually tipped the balance in the colonists' favor, ensuring that their views would prevail. As Chickwallop came to understand only too well, that initial encounter with the cow was a fateful one indeed.

# Notes

1.  John Pynchon to John Winthrop Jr., March 5, 1668/69, in Carl Bridenbaugh, ed., *The Pynchon Papers,* 2 vols. (Boston: Colonial Society of Massachusetts, 1982-85), 1:79-80. I thank Kevin Sweeney for this reference and for his identification of Chickwallop as the Norwottucks' sachem.

2.  Key works in this area include two books by Alfred W. Crosby Jr.: *The Columbian Exchange: Biological and Cultural Consequences of 1492* (Westport: Greenwood Press, 1972) and *Ecological Imperialism: The Biological Expansion of Europe, 900–1900* (New York: Cambridge University Press, 1986), as well as William Cronon, *Changes in the Land: Indians, Colonists, and the Ecology of New England* (New York: Hill and Wang, 1983); Carolyn Merchant, *Ecological Revolutions: Nature, Gender, and Science in New England* (Chapel Hill, N.C.: University of North Carolina Press, 1989); and, more generally, Jared Diamond, *Guns, Germs, and Steel: The Fates of Human Societies* (New York: W. W. Norton & Co., 1997).

3.  Much new work in environmental history has also begun to examine the cultural impact of ecological change. See, for instance, the essays in William Cronon, ed., *Uncommon Ground: Rethinking the Human Place in Nature* (New York and London: W. W. Norton & Co., 1995).

4.  Roger Williams, *A Key into the Language of America* (1643), ed. John J. Teunissen and Evelyn J. Hinz (Detroit: Wayne State University Press, 1973), 173; John Eliot, *The Indian Grammar Begun . . .* (Cambridge, Mass: Marmaduke Johnson, 1666), 9. On the difficulty in recovering Indian ideas about the natural world, see Richard White, "Indian Peoples

and the Natural World: Asking the Right Questions," in *Rethinking American Indian History*, ed. Donald L. Fixico (Albuquerque: University of New Mexico Press, 1997), 87-100. I thank Jim Drake for this reference.

5. Ives Goddard and Kathleen J. Bragdon, *Native Writings in Massachusett*, 2 vols., *Memoirs of the American Philosophical Society*, no. 185, (Philadelphia: American Philosophical Society, 1988), 2:486-87; Ives Goddard, "Eastern Algonquian Languages," in Bruce G. Trigger, ed., *Handbook of North American Indians*, vol. 15, *Northeast* (Washington, D.C.: Smithsonian Institution Press, 1978), 70-77.

6. Roger Williams to Gov. John Winthrop, February 28, 1637/38, in Glenn W. LaFantasie, ed., *The Correspondence of Roger Williams*, 2 vols. (Hanover and London: Brown University Press/University Press of New England, 1988), 1:146. For Puritan beliefs in eclipses and other "wonders," see David D. Hall, *Worlds of Wonder, Days of Judgment: Popular Religious Belief in Early New England* (New York: Alfred A. Knopf, 1989), esp. chaps. 2, 5.

7. Edward Winslow, "Good Newes from New England . . . " [1624], in Alexander Young, ed., *Chronicles of the Pilgrim Fathers of the Colony of Plymouth, from 1602 to 1625* (Boston: C. C. Little and J. Brown, 1841), 356-57; William S. Simmons, *Spirit of the New England Tribes: Indian History and Folklore, 1620–1984* (Hanover: University Press of New England, 1986), 38-41, 172-234; Edward Johnson, *Johnson's Wonder-Working Providence 1628–1651* [1654], ed. J. Franklin Jameson (New York: Charles Scribner's Sons, 1910), 263; Paul J. Lindholdt, ed., *John Josselyn, Colonial Traveler: A Critical Edition of Two Voyages to New-England* (Hanover: University Press of New England, 1988), 97. See also Kathleen J. Bragdon, *Native People of Southern New England, 1500-1650* (Norman, Okla., and London: University of Oklahoma Press, 1996), 188-90 and, more generally, William S. Simmons, "Cultural Bias in the New England Puritans' Perception of Indians," *William and Mary Quarterly*, 3d ser., 38 (1981): 56-72.

8.  Merchant, *Ecological Revolutions,* 49; Henry Whitfield, "Strength Out of Weaknesse; or a Glorious Manifestation of the Further Progrese of the Gospel among the Indians in New England" [1652], in *Collections of the Massachusetts Historical Society,* 3[d] ser., 4 (1834): 187; Simmons, *Spirit of the New England Tribes,* 51. Virtually every study of Native American spirituality emphasizes the lack of a sharp boundary between the natural and supernatural worlds. See, for instance, James Axtell, *The Invasion Within: The Contest of Cultures in Colonial North America* (New York: Oxford University Press, 1985), 16; Colin G. Calloway, *New Worlds for All: Indians, Europeans, and the Remaking of Early America* (Baltimore: Johns Hopkins University Press, 1997), 72-73; Clara Sue Kidwell, "Science and Ethnoscience: Native American World Views as a Factor in the Development of Native Technologies," in Kendall E. Bailes, ed., *Environmental History: Critical Issues in Comparative Perspective* (Lanham, Md.: University Press of America, 1985), 277-87.

9.  Williams, *Key into the Language of America,* ed. Teunissen and Hinz, 191.

10. Variations in modern definitions of *manitou* suggest that scholars today share Williams's difficulty in trying to find a precise translation that would be meaningful to non-Indian readers. See, for instance, Bragdon, *Native People of Southern New England,* 184-90; Simmons, *Spirit of the New England Tribes,* 38-41; Neal Salisbury, *Manitou and Providence: Indians, Europeans, and the Making of New England, 1500–1643* (New York: Oxford University Press, 1982), 37-39; John A. Grim and Donald P. St. John, "The Northeast Woodlands," in *Native American Religions: North America,* ed. Lawrence E. Sullivan (New York: Macmillan, 1989), 118; Elisabeth Tooker, ed., *Native North American Spirituality of the Eastern Woodlands: Sacred Myths, Dreams, Visions, Speeches, Healing Formulas, Rituals and Ceremonials* (New York: Paulist Press, 1979), 11-30.

11. Richard White, *The Middle Ground: Indians, Empires, and Republics in the Great Lakes Region, 1650–1815* (Cambridge and New York: Cambridge University Press, 1991), 25; Williams, *Key into the Language of America,* ed. Teunissen and Hinz, 173, 174, 225.

12. M. K. Bennett, "The Food Economy of the New England Indians, 1605-75," *Journal of Political Economy* 63 (October 1955): 387-88.

13. Perhaps the best known historical study of the spiritual element in human-animal relations in Indian society is Calvin Martin, *Keepers of the Game: Indian-Animal Relationships and the Fur Trade* (Berkeley: University of California Press, 1978). Martin's thesis about the effects of European contact and the fur trade on the Indian-animal relationship has sparked considerable criticism, but his description of pre-contact relations remains useful. For Martin's critics, see Shepard Krech III, ed., *Indians, Animals, and the Fur Trade: A Critique* of Keepers of the Game (Athens, Ga.: University of Georgia Press, 1981). There are numerous examples of Indian conceptions of animal spirits in Trigger, ed., *Handbook of North American Indians,* vol. 15, *Northeast*; see, for instance, 84, 139, 192, 319. See also Colin G. Calloway, *The Western Abenakis of Vermont, 1600-1800: War, Migration, and the Survival of an Indian People* (Norman, Okla.: University of Oklahoma Press, 1990), 49-50; Ruth Underhill, *Red Man's Religion: Beliefs and Practices of the Indians North of Mexico* (Chicago: University of Chicago Press, 1965), 41-46.

14. M. K. Bennett estimated that southern New England Indians derived 65 percent of their daily calories from grain products, and 10 percent from meat; see "Food Economy of the New England Indians," 392. For hunting in native New England, see Bragdon, *Native People of Southern New England,* 117-18; Cronon, *Changes in the Land,* 46-51.

15. Bragdon, *Native People of Southern New England,* 97-98, 187-88; Williams, *Key into the Language of America,* ed. Teunissen and Hinz, 182, 210-14; William Wood, *New England's Prospect,* ed. Alden T. Vaughan (Amherst: University of Massachusetts Press, 1977), 81, 85, 111.

16. Lindholdt, ed., *John Josselyn, Colonial Traveler,* 20; Bragdon, *Native People of Southern New England,* 187-88; White, *Middle Ground,* 507.

17. Williams, *Key into the Language of America*, ed. Teunissen and Hinz, 164; Williams described children stationed in "little watch-houses" to chase birds from cornfields, see 163. On shamans' familiar spirits, see Simmons, *Spirit of the New England Tribes*, 91.

18. Bragdon, *Native People of Southern New England*, 133-34, 195-96.

19. The information in this and the following paragraph is from Lindholdt, ed., *John Josselyn, Colonial Traveler*, 98-99; John Josselyn, *New-Englands Rarities Discovered: In Birds, Beasts, Fishes, Serpents, and Plants of that Country* (London: G. Widdowes, 1672), 20; Robert A. Brightman, *Grateful Prey: Rock Cree Human-Animal Relationships* (Berkeley: University of California Press, 1993), 110-13, 117, 120, 123-32; Adrian Tanner, *Bringing Home Animals: Religious Ideology and Mode of Production of the Mistassini Cree Hunters* (New York: St. Martin's Press, 1979), 155-56.

20. Adriaen Van der Donck, *A Description of the New Netherlands*, ed. Thomas F. O'Donnell (Syracuse,: Syracuse University Press, 1968), 120; Brightman, *Grateful Prey*, 118-19, 132-33.

21. Wood, *New England's Prospect*, ed. Vaughan, 85. For English colonists' fascination with Indian appearances, see Karen Ordahl Kupperman, "Presentment of Civility: English Reading of American Self-Presentation in the Early Years of Colonization," *William and Mary Quarterly*, 3[d] ser., 54 (1997): 193-228.

22. Wood, *New England's Prospect*, ed. Vaughan, 85; Williams, *Key into the Language of America*, ed. Teunissen and Hinz, 127. For archaeological findings, see Charles C. Willoughby, *Antiquities of the New England Indians* (Cambridge: Peabody Museum of American Archaeology and Ethnology, 1935), 106-10, 164, 166, 169-70; Bragdon, *Native People of Southern New England*, 118-19, 187; Patricia E. Rubertone, *Grave Undertakings: An Archaeology of Roger Williams and the Narragansett Indians* (Washington, D.C. and London: Smithsonian Institution Press, 2001), 150-51, 156.

23. William Bradford, *Of Plymouth Plantation 1620–1647*, ed. Samuel Eliot Morison (New York: Alfred A. Knopf, 1952), 84; George R. Hamell, "Mythical Realities and European Contact in the Northeast During the Sixteenth and Seventeenth Centuries," *Man in the Northeast*, 33 (1987): 69; Constance A. Crosby, "The Algonkian Spiritual Landscape," in Peter Benes, ed., *Algonkians of New England: Past and Present*, The Dublin Seminar for New England Folklife, Annual Proceedings 1991 (Boston: Boston University, 1993), 35-41.

24. Williams, *Key into the Language of America*, ed. Teunissen and Hinz, 173-74. James Trumbull translated *ockqutchaun* as woodchuck; see his *Natick Dictionary*, Bureau of American Ethnology, Smithsonian Institution, Bulletin 25 (Washington, D.C., 1903), 277. Other Indian peoples similarly drew on analogies with indigenous creatures in naming Old World animals. The Nahuatl of Mexico initially called a horse *maçatl* (deer), a mare *cihuamaçatl* (female deer), and, interestingly, a sheep *ichcatl* (cotton); see James Lockhart, *The Nahuas After the Conquest: A Social and Cultural History of the Indians of Central Mexico, Sixteenth Through Eighteenth Centuries* (Stanford: Stanford University Press, 1992), 279-80. Mayan Indians at first called a horse a "tapir of Castile"; see Inga Clendinnen, *Ambivalent Conquests: Maya and Spaniard in Yucutan, 1517–1570* (Cambridge: Cambridge University Press, 1987), 137.

25. Williams, *Key into the Language of America*, ed. Teunissen and Hinz, 103, 121, 133, 137, 138, 158, 176, 240.

26. Williams, *Key into the Language of America*, ed. Teunissen and Hinz, 125, 216, 234.

27. White, *Middle Ground*, 25; Richard S. Dunn, James Savage, and Laetitia Yeandle, eds., *The Journal of John Winthrop 1630–1649* (Cambridge and London: Harvard University Press, 1996), 406. For another discussion of Indians' imputing spiritual power to European livestock, see Rebecca Kugel, "Of Missionaries and Their Cattle: Ojibwa Perceptions of a Missionary as Evil Shaman," *Ethnohistory* 41 (1994): 227-44.

28. Christopher L. Miller and George R. Hamell, "A New Perspective on Indian-White Contact: Cultural Symbols and Colonial Trade," *Journal of American History*, 73 (1986–1987): 311-28; White, *Middle Ground*, 25; Constance Crosby, "From Myth to History, or Why King Philip's Ghost Walks Abroad," in Mark P. Leone and Parker B. Potter, eds., *The Recovery of Meaning: Historical Archaeology in the Eastern United States* (Washington, D.C., and London: Smithsonian Institution Press, 1988), 183-209.

29. Williams, *Key into the Language of America*, ed. Teunissen and Hinz, 174. They adopted a similar change in their word for "Englishmen," which became *Englishmánnuck;* see 197.

30. Eliot, *Indian Grammar Begun*, 9; Wood, *New England's Prospect*, ed. Vaughan, 106-7.

31. Cronon, *Changes in the Land*, 64, 130.

32. Dunn, et al., eds., *Journal of John Winthrop*, 52; Virginia DeJohn Anderson, "King Philip's Herds: Indians, Colonists, and the Problem of Livestock in Early New England," *William and Mary Quarterly*, 3[d] ser., 51 (1994): 607-13; Peter Karsten, "Cows in the Corn, Pigs in the Garden, and 'the Problem of Social Costs': 'High' and 'Low' Legal Cultures of the British Diaspora Lands in the 17th, 18th, and 19th Centuries," *Law & Society Review* 32 (1998): 80-83.

33. *Oxford English Dictionary*, s.v. "cattle"; see also Gary L. Francione, *Animals, Property, and the Law* (Philadelphia: Temple University Press, 1995), 34.

34. Allyn B. Forbes, et al., eds., *Winthrop Papers, 1498–1654*, 6 vols. (Boston: Massachusetts Historical Society, 1929–1992), 2:120. On English ideas of empire, see Anthony Pagden, *Lords of All the World: Ideologies of Empire in Spain, Britain and France c. 1500–c. 1800* (New Haven: Yale University Press, 1995), 76-78; Patricia Seed, *Ceremonies of Possession in Europe's*

*Conquest of the New World 1492–1640* (New York: Cambridge University Press, 1995), chap. 1. On free-range livestock husbandry in New England, see Anderson, "King Philip's Herds," 604; Howard S. Russell, *A Long, Deep Furrow: Three Centuries of Farming in New England* (Hanover: University Press of New England, 1976), chap. 4; Cronon, *Changes in the Land*, 141-42; Darrett B. Rutman, *Husbandmen of Plymouth: Farms and Villages in the Old Colony, 1620–1692* (Boston: Beacon Press, 1967), 17-19.

35. Nathaniel Shurtleff and David Pulsifer, eds., *Records of the Colony of New Plymouth in New England*, 12 vols. (Boston: W. White, 1855–1861), 4:190-91. For other examples of Indians being accused of killing livestock without due proof, see Shurtleff and Pulsifer, eds., *Records of the Colony of New Plymouth*, 9:209; Nathaniel B. Shurtleff, ed., *Records of the Governor and Company of the Massachusetts Bay in New England*, 5 vols. (Boston: W. White, 1853–1854), vol. 4, pt. 2, p. 361.

36. Bridenbaugh, ed., *Pynchon Papers*, 1:79-80.

# "A Little I Shall Say":

## Translation and Interculturalism in the John Eliot Tracts

JOSHUA DAVID BELLIN

FROM THE TIME OF THEIR PUBLICATION to the present, the Eliot tracts—the missionary writings by and about John Eliot, Puritan "Apostle" to the Indians of Massachusetts Bay—have been of central importance to students of Puritan-Indian encounter. For early chroniclers such as Cotton Mather, the Eliot texts provided an occasion to reclaim—and redeem—New England's history of contact with the region's native peoples.[1] For antebellum historians tracing the Puritan origins of the nation's manifest destiny, these publications highlighted both the benevolence of colonial policy and the sad inevitability of its failure.[2] Though the exculpatory approach had not entirely lost favor by the mid-twentieth century—as evidenced by Alden Vaughan's *New England Frontier* (1965), which draws on the tracts to prove that "the Puritan never forced his views on the natives, nor did his missionaries ever relent in their efforts to persuade"[3] —recent Eliot scholarship has proceeded along two lines of revision: the first, most strongly identified with Francis Jennings's *The Invasion of America* (1975), assailing the Eliot corpus as a smokescreen for genocidal campaigns mounted under the guise of Christian benevolence;[4] and the second, rooted in the principles of ethnohistory, calling on the texts not as witnesses to exonerate or excoriate the colonists but as occasions to resurrect the voices of Native American converts.[5] For current Eliot scholars, then, the works of the Apostle and his boosters are principally of descriptive and explanatory value: they offer insight into the actions and interactions of Indians and Europeans during an early, critical phase in their mutual experience.

There is no question that the Eliot works represent significant textual markers of intercultural contact. For a number of reasons, however, the assumptions underlying current approaches to these works are problematic. To begin with, Eliot scholarship still takes inadequate account of the refractory nature of the texts—the complexities of their situation, the intricacies of their production, the uncertainties of their reception—or even, in the most extreme instances, of the fact that they *are* texts. This latter tendency has been most pronounced in studies that comb the texts for Indian beliefs and behavior. For instance, in *John Eliot's Mission to the Indians before King Philip's War* (1999), Richard Cogley views the Eliot texts as infallible authorities on Indian convictions and motivations: "There is reason to think . . . that the Nonantum and Neponset Indians blamed Cutshamekin as well as the English for the loss of coastal land. Eliot wrote in *Indian Dialogues* that the Massachusetts had been angry at Cutshamekin. . ."; "The Nonantum Indians were pleased with the location [of their Praying Town]. Eliot explained in 1650 that . . . [the Indians] were 'very willing' to live there. . ."; "The Indians clearly had a predilection for prayer: Eliot noted in 1647 that they 'called all religion . . . praying to God'. . ."[6]

Other writers have admitted that the Eliot texts are not quite the transparent windows Cogley makes them out to be, but, treating the circumstances under which the Indian "voices" embedded in the texts were produced as mere distractions, these scholars have found ways to view the "voices" as autonomous specimens of Indian autobiographical utterance. For instance, though Hilary Wyss's *Writing Indians: Literacy, Christianity, and Native Community in Early America* (2000) grants that writers "had their own purposes" in recording Indian narratives, she nonetheless terms Eliot's Indian narratives "an early form of Native Christian self-expression." What enables Wyss to make this claim is another set of texts: modern ethnohistorical reconstructions of traditional Indian cultures. Accepting *these* texts as transparent and reading the Eliot texts through them, she is able to locate a "Native world view that is distinct from our own Western perspective." The questionable nature of this move should be evident, particularly when one recalls that ethnohistorical interpretations are in large part drawn from the very texts Wyss uses these interpretations to illuminate; but having made this move, Wyss manages to skirt the textual issues she herself has raised, indeed to forget Eliot altogether and characterize the Indians as "writing their own narratives of conversion."[7]

In short, too many studies of the Eliot texts overlook or underestimate the fact that they *are* texts, and highly mediated texts at that. The theoretical issues the Eliot texts raise, however, pertain not solely to *whether* one acknowledges these texts as texts, but to *how* one understands the production of texts under conditions of intercultural contact. For if studies such as Cogley's and Wyss's appear naively trusting of written sources, particularly when placed beside the implacable skepticism of a work such as Jennings's, at the core a common assumption binds these and other writings: the assumption that texts are impervious to the contexts of encounter within which they were born, that texts reveal encounter (or disguise it) but are not affected *by* it. And this conceptual oversight is particularly problematic for at least two reasons: first, because it exempts texts from the ethnohistorical tenet that cultural productions are transformed by encounter; and second, because it ignores the fact that the Eliot texts are themselves manifestly concerned with the ways in which encounter affects the writing of encounter. Throughout the Eliot texts, the unsettling power of encounter is present in a variety of forms, but in none so visibly as in the fact of translation;[8] though premised on translation as the medium for bearing the Christian Word to the Indians (and the Indians' words to Christians), the Eliot texts ultimately figure the acts of translation through which they were forged not as transparent but as tortured and opaque, marring any claim of absolute authority over, or immediate access to, the terms of encounter.[9] What the Eliot writings suggest, then, is that transformation characterizes the texts that speak of encounter as surely as the encounters of which they speak—that, as Barry O'Connell phrases it, in situations of contact there is no "pure medium free from the effects of the other," whether that medium be cultural, material, spiritual, linguistic, or textual.[10]

This paper, accordingly, considers the Eliot texts as both products and productive of the intercultural contexts from which they emerged. It must be emphasized, however, that if the Eliot texts are exceptional in foregrounding encounter, they are representative in being indebted to encounter. In this respect, the Eliot texts challenge the tendency among literary critics to consider texts authored by American Indians as expressions of the intercultural while seeing texts authored by members of the dominant culture as exempt from the intercultural; as an exploration of the Eliot texts will suggest, encounter is the inescapable substratum and environment of *all* American texts. Ultimately, then, this paper illustrates the ways in which our understanding of texts *as* records of encounter is challenged *by* encounter; it thus points toward an ethnohistorical literary criticism, one that considers American texts as inextricably involved in American encounters, mutually shaped by and shaping the situations of contact within which they are generated.

✢  ✢  ✢

Recent scholars of America's colonial encounters have called attention to translation not only as a quotidian necessity—one that enabled the settlers to negotiate treaties, land sales, and political and economic alliances with Indian peoples—but as a symbol of colonial power relations. As Eric Cheyfitz phrases this argument in *The Poetics of Imperialism* (1991), "the very activity of translation, no matter how decorous, . . . is an act of violence. . . . The skilled translator . . . must use force in transporting a word from its proper, or 'natural,' place, but conceals that force, or tries to, under the semblance of the word's willingness to give up its property in itself."[11] Cheyfitz focuses on the correspondences between translation and physical dispossession, but one can apply his argument to the missionary arm of the colonial enterprise: the missionary too uses force to transport the Indians from their "natural" —unregenerate—place, but disguises such force under the semblance of the convert's willingness to relinquish all to God (or God's surrogate). The tendency of colonial translators to camouflage the violence of translation—or even the fact of translation—has been remarked by numerous critics; Stephen Greenblatt argues that colonial translators "either push the Indians toward utter difference—and thus silence—or toward utter likeness–and thus the collapse of [the Indians'] own, unique identity," while David Murray writes of "two absolutely opposed mythical moments of encounter," the "meeting with untouched and unknowable otherness, beyond the reach of language; and the rapport of unproblematic translatability, and of transparency of language."[12] If translation is the inescapable condition of contact, these critics suggest, it is also, or for that reason, the silent term in a colonizing project based on its ability to comprehend all utterance and all meaning within its own symbolic system.

There is, however, another way to view translation, a way hinted at in Cheyfitz's further comment that "in the equivocal play of language . . . no single voice prevails because there is no univocality. Rather, the precarious coherence of each voice can only constitute itself in translation *between* other voices."[13] Translation, in this view, would not only be formative for the texts of encounter but disruptive of those texts' illusion of absolute authority, coherence, or stability. Translation, in this view, would reveal its roots in violence and appropriation, and in that revelation dispel its own assertion of seemliness and seamlessness. Moreover, translation, in this view, would recognize its indebtedness to encounter, its inability to escape the presence of those-it-translates; translation would, finally, admit its inability to exist at all without those-it-translates, and thus admit that encounter entails a network of competing, conflicting, intersecting *translations* across multiple cultural contact points. To view translation in such a way is not to propose some utopian equivalence or equality between languages or acts. It is, rather, to restore texts to the asymmetrical yet joint contexts that translation itself so often seeks to obscure, and thus to consider texts not as fixed terms in an all-encompassing system but as mediums of translation between peoples, negotiations within an intercultural world in which meaning is uncertain, unstable, in flux, and in the process of being forged.

To characterize texts in this way is, actually, to capture both emphases of translation in the Eliot tracts: on the one hand, they design an absolute correspondence between word and meaning; on the other, they confess a radical disjunction between the two. Puritan treatises on hermeneutics or Biblical interpretation, as Ann Kibbey notes, trumpeted the belief that in the transmundane realm, in the Word of God, there existed a perfect relation between word and thing: "In the Christian providential universe, acoustic images are divinely purposeful signs, not arbitrary signs, and however attenuated or oblique their signification as figures might be, there is some intrinsic meaning to be discovered in the relation between the audible figure and the referent. . . . Words as signs are divinely, and therefore significantly, related to their referents." Thus, in addition to the obvious point that translation as a practice made possible the bearing of the Word to the ungospelized nations, translation as an ideal prophesied a capacious and intimate reunion of human languages with the divine Language. One expression of this ideal was the quest in the early modern period for a system of universal language, what Vivian Salmon calls the "almost obsessive desire for . . . the construction of a system of universal symbols which would be comprehensive, unambiguous and entirely free from redundancy"; in such an act of total translation, humanity might return as nearly as possible to the source of all language. Another expression was the Puritan exegetical project, of which providential history and Biblical typology were only the most notable branches, of discovering in the material evidences of the world the underlying truth of God. In Kibbey's view, it was this project that fostered, or dictated, intolerance of alternative forms of belief; elaborating a political and theological system from a hermeneutics of absolutism, the Puritans, she argues, "generate a social imperative" that "persuades them of the fixity and certainty of their own system of reference."[14] If so, then it is plain why any threat to that system, any force that might destabilize the necessary and incorruptible link between word and essence, called forth such disciplinary strategies as are evident in the heresy trial of Ann Hutchinson, one of whose judges—John Eliot—reprehended her "so groce and so dayngerous an opinion" as follows:

> We are not satisfied with what she sayth that she should say now *that she did never deny Inherence of Grace in us, as in a subject,* for she beinge by us pressed soe with it she denyed that thear was *no Graces inherent in Christ himselfe.* . . . She did

playnly expres herselfe to me that thear was *no difference betweene the Graces that are in Hipocrits and those that are in the Saints. . . .* Some will acknowledge the Word Gifts and Frutes but thay deny the word Graces: thay acknowledge actings of the Spirit: and by such Distinctions, I could wipe of[f] all her Repentance in that paper, therfore she shall doe well to express her selfe playnly what her Judgment now is in thease Thinges.

Beyond the doctrinal points Hutchinson's Antinomians contested—points that themselves cut to the heart of Puritan beliefs, inasmuch as they concerned the legitimacy of ministerial interpretation of Scripture and the supposedly manifest opposition of sanctification and sanctimony—what this speech suggests is that Hutchinson unsettled the very referentiality of language: Eliot's address insists on holding her to her word, but her word splinters the "playn" connection between sign and "Thinge."[15] Hutchinson, as she is constructed in Eliot's speech, refuses to translate herself into the divine—or the divines'—ideal and irreproachable Word; she refuses to perform the act of semantic submission captured in one convert's response to missionary pressure in Eliot's *The Indian Dialogues* (1671): "I yield to what you say."[16]

And yet, however Eliot and his brethren might desire—and enforce—such capitulation, the fact that crises such as the one Hutchinson inaugurated were endemic to the Massachusetts Bay colony suggests the authorities' inability to mandate interpretive orthodoxy. That this was so, moreover, was due to their own theoretical division between celestial and mortal languages, a division that relegated human language to a Babel-like state of confusion; as William Scheick sees it, "while the puritans believed in the ultimate denotative definitions of all language from the deity's point of view, they doubted the capacity of fallen human reason to escape the convoluted muddle of connotative meanings in the temporal world."[17] And if, on the one hand, translation could be seen as presaging humanity's ultimate reunion with the numinous language of God, on the other it could be taken to epitomize the falling away from the divine *logos:* the fact that multiple signs could stand for the thing signified indicated how radically postlapsarian language strayed from its divine original. This sense of the instability of human language is preserved in the etymology of the word "translate": to "bear across," to carry from place to place. In addition, along with its current sense of "to turn from one language to another," a seventeenth-century sense of the term was "to change in form, appearance, or substance; to transmute, to transform, alter." Like metaphor, a word to which, Cheyfitz notes, translation was both etymologically and functionally related,[18] translation carried with it more than a hint of duplicity, of willfully severing sound from sense; as one seventeenth-century treatise on the translator's craft put it, "a translator must therefore become like Proteus: he must be able to transform himself into all manner of wondrous things, he must be able to absorb and combine all styles within himself and be more changeable than a chameleon."[19] It is perhaps needless to say that such an image ran counter to the interdictions of Puritan divines; "transforming oneself into all manner of wondrous things" smacked of hypocrisy, stagecraft, even the popish doctrine of transubstantiation: all forms of dissimulation, wrong naming, the sundering of word and thing.

And if translation could cause such disruption in the case of written texts, the contents and lexicons of which the divine knew by heart, it could engender even more disorder in the case of unwritten tongues fundamentally different from the European languages, tongues learned more often than not on the fly, and tongues learned when at all in the teeth of severe prejudices and presuppositions. As

William Leverich, a minister inspired by Eliot to proselytize the Indians, wrote, the nature of the Indian languages was such that incoherence was inevitable:

> though the *Indian* tongue be very difficult, irregular, and
> anomalous, and wherein I cannot meete with a Verbe
> Substantive as yet, nor any such Particles, as
> Conjunctions, &c. which are essentiall to the severall sorts
> of axioms, and consequently to all rationall and perfect
> discourses, and that though their words are generally very
> long, even *sesquipedalia verba,* yet I find God helping, not
> onely my selfe to learne and attaine more of it in a short
> time . . . but also the *Indians* to understand mee fully (as
> they acknowledge) so farre as I have gone, [yet] I am con-
> strained by many ambages and circumlocutions to supply
> the former defect, to express my selfe to them as I may.[20]

"Circum-locutions" are roundabout words, or words going around. They are, in a sense, the words of translation, words unloosed from a fixed locale. "Ambages," too, are words that move (or amble), words unmoored from stable meaning. They are also, according to the *OED,* words of concealment, deceit, equivocation. In Leverich's lament, the Indians' language—like the willful, wandering ways the colonists attributed to the natives—is the language of movement; though he insists, with whatever accuracy or honesty, that he is understood, he grieves that the "plain style," the "rational and perfect discourse" of the meetinghouse, is confounded by this wilderness jargon.

Such carping on the mutability and multiplicity of the Indians' languages forms a recurrent theme in the Eliot tracts. For example, Thomas Shepard, reporting on the "Clear Sunshine of the Gospel" in 1648, writes that "it passeth my skill to tell how the gospel should be generally received by these American natives, considering the variety of languages in small distances of places"; on a visit to the Indians in "remote places about Cape Cod," he testifies, "we first found these Indians (not very far from ours) to understand (but with much difficulty) the usual language of those in our parts. . . . I say therefore, although they did with much difficulty understand [Eliot], yet they did understand him, although by many circumlocutions and variations of speech, and the help of one or two interpreters which were there present." Eliot, too, raises the issue of linguistic diffusion in his remarks on a preliminary translation of the Bible into Wampanoag:

> [the Church elders] moved this doubt whether the Translation I had made was generally understood? to which I answered, that upon my knowledge it was understood as far as *Conecticot:* for there . . . the *Indians* manifested that they did understand what I read, perfectly, in respect of the language, [the elders] further questioned whether I had expressed the Translation in true language? I answered that I feared after times will find many infirmities in it, all humane works are subject to infirmity, yet those pieces that were printed . . . I had sent to such as I thought had best skill in the language, and intreated their animadversions, but I heard not of any faults they found.[21]

Eliot's differentiation of "language"—the words of frail mortals—from "true language"—the eternal Word of God—evokes the problem of translation, as does the fact that to vindicate his work, he must call on the very figure of *place*—the Indians understand him here, and there (but maybe not elsewhere)—which points up the inherent instability of the translated word.

And in turn, what these recurrences to the difficulty of the Indian tongues suggest is not merely the dismissive attitude Europeans held—though that attitude is on display too, as in Cotton Mather's

derisive remark that "one would think [Indian words] had been growing ever since Babel unto the dimensions to which they are now
extended"—but the heightened stakes of intercultural translation.[22]
The fearful consequences of a linguistic misstep are intimated in
Eliot's *Late and Further Manifestation of the Progress of the Gospel* (1655), which
details an examination of Indian novitiates as a preliminary test in
their advancement toward church-estate:

> Seeing all these things are to be transacted in a strange
> language, and by Interpreters, and with such people as
> they be in these their first beginnings . . . I requested the
> Assembly, That if any one doubted of the Interpretations
> that should be given of [the Indians'] Answers, that they
> would Propound their doubt, and they should have the
> words scanned and tryed by the Interpreters, that so all
> things may be done most clearly. For my desire was to be
> true to Christ, to their soules, and to the Churches. . . . It
> is a great matter to betrust those with the holy priviledges
> of Gods house, upon which the name of Christ is so
> much called, who have so little knowledge and experience
> in the wayes of Christ, so newly come out of that great
> depth of darknesse, and wild course of life; in such dan-
> ger of polluting and defiling the name of Christ. . . .
> Hence it is very needfull that this proceeding of ours at
> first, be with all care and warinesse guided.[23]

In this passage, the repeated references to the loss of truth and
clarity betoken the threat of semantic and interpretive irregularities
that, according to Puritan theory, lurked within the Word in the
hands of all people, and much more so in the hands of "such people
as they be." Henry Whitfield, in his prefatory comments to the Eliot
tract *Strength out of Weaknesse* (1652), approaches the dilemma of the mis-

sionary translator from a related angle when he exhorts the reader to "consider . . . by how many the Gospel is perverted, being made *another gospel*, by strange Interpretations; one of the great acts of *Sacriledge* of our times, stealing the sense of the Scripture from the words of the Scripture."[24] By "perverters," Whitfield would seem to conceive such monsters as the Antinomians; as such his warning serves rhetorically to contrast the acts of these sacrilegious adversaries with the faithful works of Eliot himself. Yet, oddly, his reproving terms are ideally suited to Eliot, who was literally engaged in making the gospel "another gospel" by translating it into a supposedly barbarous tongue—thereby risking the severance of "sense" from "words" —and who threatened, by disseminating this amphibious gospel to supposed barbarians, to set loose any number of "strange interpretations." Eliot himself had implied at least a figurative likeness between the Antinomians and the Indians when, urging Hutchinson's banishment at the conclusion of her trial, he cited Revelations 22:15: "For without *shalbe* dogges & encha[n]ters, & whoremongers, & murtherers, & idolaters, & whosoeuer loueth or maketh lyes."[25] In 1637, Eliot had not begun preaching to the Indians, or even learning their tongues; but it is nonetheless intriguing that the text he chose as a means of justifying Hutchinson's exile was one proverbially applied to the Indians. In common with his fellows, Eliot represented the realm of the Indians as the realm of fallen, translated language.

And by the terms of this representation, to translate *"this perfect Word of God"* into the babble of the New World was fraught with peril: not only might the preacher be led astray or the Word polluted and defiled, but the fate of immortal souls hung upon the proper construction of a text, a phrase, a word.[26] Given these hazards, it is unsurprising that Eliot's announced goals involved eliminating translation as swiftly and as far as possible. On the one hand, in the words of his successor as overseer of the missionary program, the Apostle hoped for "the Indians, especially the children and youth, [to] be taught to speak, read, and write, the English tongue"; on the other, in Eliot's own words, he longed for a time when he might relinquish local control to native speakers: "An *English* young man raw in that language," he wrote in 1670, "coming to teach among our Christian *Indians,* would be much to their loss; there be of themselves such as be more able, especially being advantaged that he speaketh his own language."[27] (Eliot's final work in the period before King Philip's War, the fictionalized *Indian Dialogues* of 1671, has customarily been seen as a training manual for the legions of Indian missionaries he seems to have fancied sending into the field.) Nor, along the same lines, is it surprising that Eliot promoted catechetical methods of instructing his converts; for the catechism, favored by Puritans as a teaching tool perhaps because its rigid format and emphasis on repetition seemed the aptest way to bridle interpretive freedom, might have seemed even more suited to curb the wayward energies of intercultural translation.[28]

Eliot's first publication in an Algonquian language was a catechism, and according to Whitfield he put it to good use: "all the Copies [Eliot] setteth his Schollers when he teacheth them to write, are the Questions and Answers of the Catechisme, that so the Children may be the more prompt and ready therein." Eliot likewise emphasized the catechism's value as a vehicle of memorization: "I catechize the children and youth, wherein some are very ready and expert; they can readily say all the commandments, so far as I have communicated them, and all other principles about the creation, the fall, the redemption by Christ, etc., wherein also the aged people are pretty expert, by the frequent repetition thereof to the children, and are able to teach to their children at home, and do so."[29] Indeed, the catechism informed Eliot's writings as a whole: his *Late and Further Manifestation* contains the (translated) transcript of a public catechism, while his *Indian Dialogues* more subtly reinvents the catechism in the form of imagined theological skirmishes between converts and their unconverted kin. That the catechism's strength lies in its ability to regulate potentially heretical utterances is suggested by the following exchange from *A Late and Further Manifestation:*

> Q. *Have not some Indians many Gods?*
> A. They have many Gods.
> Q. *How doe you know these Gods are no Gods?*
> A. Before the English came we knew not but that they
> were Gods, but since they came we know they are
> no Gods.[30]

Similarly, throughout the *Indian Dialogues,* the objections of the unregenerate are raised precisely so that they may be negated:

> Powwow: You tell us of the Englishman's God, and of his laws. We have Gods also . . . and laws also by which our forefathers did walk. . . . Let us alone, that we may be quiet in the ways which we like and love, as we let you alone in your changes and new ways.

> Piumbukhon: You have spoken many things, which do minister to me of much discourse.[31]

Here the Indians' translated speech, rather than challenging Christian idiom or ideology, becomes matter for ministerial "discourse." In the regimentation of the catechism, the fictions of the *Indian Dialogues,* and the ethereal truisms of primers like his *Indian Grammar Begun* (1666), Eliot achieves an image of translation akin to that of the *Grammar's* title page, an image of transcendent, unvarying "Rules" (by far the largest word on the page) and of the millennial restoration of divine utterance promised by the Biblical epigraph: "It shall come that I will gather all Nations and Tongues, and they shall come and see my Glory."[32]

But in the words of M. M. Bakhtin, whose theories of discourse are integral to current formulations of literary dialogism or multi-vocalism, language is "unitary only as an abstract grammatical system of normative forms, taken in isolation from the concrete, ideological conceptualizations that fill it, and in isolation from the uninterrupted process of historical becoming that is a characteristic of all living language." So it is with the Eliot texts: if in the abstract they seem to master all speech, in practice they call repeated, insistent attention to issues of translation. On the one hand, the texts routinely—and strikingly, considering the systematic erasure of Indian speakers in comparable texts well into the twentieth century—give credit to the missionary's Native American assistants, as in the following acknowledgment: "I having yet but little skill in their language . . . I must have some Indians, and it may be other help continually about me to try and examine Translations." Similarly, Eliot writes in another place, "it hath pleased God this winter much to inlarge the abilitie of him whose helpe I use in translating the Scripture, which I account a great furtherance of that which I most desire, namely, to communicate unto them as much of the Scriptures in their own language as I am able. . . . I trust in the Lord that we shall have sundry of them able to reade and write, who shall write every man for himselfe so much of the Bible as the Lord shall please to enable me to translate."[33] Eliot, notably, phrases these and other statements so as to minimize the Indians' role, suggesting that it is he alone who handles the translating while the Indians serve solely as scriveners or proofreaders.[34]

Yet when one places such statements within the context of the Eliot tracts as a whole, they not only draw attention to the Indian presence but become part of a larger discourse of translation as a highly visible, highly charged act, at once essential and unattainable. In a typical statement, Eliot beseeches that "utterance may be given mee, and further knowledge of their language, wherein for want of converse, I can make but slow progresse"; he regrets the limitations on his "liberty of speech, . . . being very unskillful in their Language." Elsewhere, he confesses that "as for my preaching, though such whose hearts God hath bowed to attend, can picke up some knowledge by my broken expressions, yet I see that it is not so taking, and effectu-all to strangers, as their owne expressions be, who naturally speake unto them in their owne tongue."[35] Eliot's reference to "broken" expressions is not merely a figure of speech (though *as* a figure of speech, a metaphor, it partakes of the imprecision it bewails); in translation, this reference suggests, the word is broken, maimed, its essence lost. Eliot's peers second his doubts; Shepard, for instance, rues in an early tract that "my brother Eliot, who is preacher to them . . . can as yet but stammer out some pieces of the word of God unto them in their own tongue," while Cotton Mather, retrospectively eval-uating the Apostle's labors, concludes, "There are many words of Mr. Eliot's forming which [the Indians] never understood. This they say is a grief to them. Such a knowledge in their Bibles as our English ordinarily have in ours, they seldom any of them have." Even when Eliot's fellows vouch for his probity and precision, their testimonials are couched in self-defeating terms, as in the following certificate from *A Late and Further Manifestation:* "In the conclusion, the Elders saw good to call upon the Interpreters to give a publick testimony to the truth of Mr *Eliots* Interpretations of the *Indians* Answers, which Mr *Mahu,* and the two Interpreters by him, did, all speaking one after another, to this purpose, *That the Interpretations which Mr Eliot gave of their Answers, was for the substance the same which the* Indians *answered, many times the very words which they spake, and always the sense.*"[36] Inasmuch as the issue at stake was precisely the separation of "words" from "sense," to reit-erate the breach could hardly be said to heal it. Similarly, Richard Mather's endorsement prefixed to *Tears of Repentance* (1653), Eliot's collection of Indian conversion narratives co-edited with Thomas Mayhew, founders on the rock of translation:

> But how shall we know that the Confessions here related, being spoken in [the Indians'] Tongue, were indeed uttered by them in such words, as have the same significa-tion and meaning with these that are here expressed, for we have only the testimony of one man to assure us of it? It is true, we have only the testimony of one man for it; but yet it is such an one . . . whose integrity and faithful-ness is so well known in these Parts, as giveth sufficient satisfaction to beleev that he would not wittingly utter a falshood in any matter whatever, and much less so many falshoods, & that in such a publick manner, in the view of God & the World, as he must needs have done if he have coyned these Confessions of his own head, and have not to his best understanding truly related them in our Tongue, according as they were uttered by them in theirs.

Even if, as Mather insists, Eliot has "not wittingly" borne false witness, such proofs appear less than conclusive in light of what Eliot implies of his "best understanding":

> oft I was forced to inquire of my interpreter (who sat by me) because I did not perfectly understand some sentences. . . . I have been true & faithful unto their souls, and in writing and reading their Confessions, I have not knowingly, or willingly made them better, than the Lord helped themselves to make them, but am verily perswaded on good grounds, that I have rather rendered them weaker (for the most part) than they delivered them; partly by missing some words of

69

weight in some Sentences, partly by my short and
curt touches of what they more fully spake, and partly by reason of the different Idioms of their
Language and ours.[37]

In such evaluations, Eliot casts himself not as the eloquent
Apostle but as the lowly functionary, appalled by an assignment to
which he is dedicated in the spirit but unequal not so much in the
flesh as in the tongue.

There are, of course, any number of ways to explain such representations. The simplest is that Eliot, whatever his comfort with the
printed page, is as stymied as he says by the intricacies of the spoken
word; unequipped by schooling and uninclined by faith to confront
the special linguistic difficulties that oral performance institutes,
Eliot vainly tries to fix the ephemeral instrument of speech: "I doe
know assuredly that many Godly and savory matters, and passages
have slipped from me, and these [published] expressions are but a little of a great deale. I know not that I have added any matter, which
they spake not, but have let slip, much which they spake."[38] Following
this lead, one could conclude that Eliot's classical language training
and slapdash fieldwork were wholly inadequate to the task he had
essayed: "The language that John Eliot constructed and used," one
critic writes, "has no value for students of the American aborigines.
His compositions in it are 'a tragic monument of missionary zeal and
of the pre-scientific study of the Indian tongue.'"[39] Taking such a critique down another path, one could conclude with Eliot's harshest
judges that the belaboring of language difficulties is a self-fulfilling
prophecy, permitting Eliot a safe—because seemingly unfeigned—
excuse for the mission's dereliction of its professed duty. More char-
itably, one could say that a commitment to unburdening oneself in
public demanded Eliot's self-flagellation; that, for the greater glory of

the Father, the weakness of the human vessel must be acknowledged; or even that Eliot's ritualistic apologies serve as apologia. Nor do Eliot's recriminations lack an overtly calculating ingredient: to insist that the published works contain but pale traces of the Indians' actual expressions is to suggest to the colony's overseers and to potential sponsors that the Indians are advancing more rapidly in the course of godliness than may genuinely have been the case.

Any of these interpretations is plausible; all may be part of the larger picture. To approach the matter in another way, however—one that insists not on unearthing extra-textual motivations but on seeing the texts as "motivated" by the textual dynamics they themselves express—one might propose that the magnifying of interlinguistic issues signals the fact that interlinguistic issues *are* magnified in situations of contact; that within contexts of encounter, there is no issue that does not become involved in, or better that does not originate in, negotiations among languages. For Puritan writers, missionaries, and divines, interlinguistic issues may have possessed special ideological and practical valences. But beyond those considerations, or more precisely channeled through those considerations, was the fact of multiple languages, and hence of translation, as the very environment of encounter: the agency of communication and miscomprehension, the subject of agreement and dispute, the instrument through which meaning, in the Eliot texts as in all texts of encounter, is forged. As such, if the critic finds herself or himself, like the Puritans, unable to read through these texts to a single or stable reality, this is because the critic must work with texts composed under conditions of multiplicity and indeterminacy; if what emerges from the Eliot texts is less a coherent narrative than a series of fractured tales or takes, each offering a glimpse of some proposed whole before resolving into uncertainty, this is because each has passed through, each exists within, processes of translation that are beyond any text's, or series of texts', purview.

In this light, it is intriguing that the recorded words of Eliot's converts express a similar preoccupation and bafflement with the linguistic territory that Eliot and his brethren were traversing, and hence with the same sorts of concerns communicated in Eliot's and his peers' commentaries on the converts' words. For instance, in the earliest encounters between Eliot and the Indians, those recorded in John Wilson's *The Day-Breaking, if Not the Sun-Rising, of the Gospel with the Indians in New England* (1647), the questions that the Indians are presented as having raised regard the very issues of verbal definition and differentiation that Eliot, still young in his language studies, might have raised himself: "1. Because some Indians say that we must pray to the Devill for all good, and some to God; they would know whether they might pray to the Devill or no. 2. They said they heard the word humiliation oft used in our Churches, and they would know what that meant? 3. Why the English call them Indians, because before they came they had another name? 4. What a Spirit is?" (This final question is particularly tantalizing, given the importance laid on "spirit" not only in Puritan theological texts but in Puritan translation theory.) Later reported questions broach the potential for subterfuge and confusion in language: *"If a man know Gods Word, but beleeve it not; and he teach others, is that good teaching? and if others beleeve that which he teacheth, is that good beleeving, or faith?";* "May a man have good words and deeds and a bad heart, and another have bad words and deeds, and yet a good heart?"; *"What is the reason, that seeing those English people, where he had been, had the same Bible that we have, yet do not speake the same things?"*[40]

Similarly, it is notable that the Indians' documented thoughts about prayer—the verbal, and visible, component of devotional practice—speak to some of translation's central issues. On the one hand, the paradox that human linguistic diversity folds into divine linguistic unity arises when one Indian is quoted as asking "whether Jesus Christ did understand, or God did understand *Indian* prayers," or when another's confession reads, "then I thought, if I prayed to God in our Language, whether could God understand my prayers in our Language; therefore I did ask Mr. *Jackson,* and Mr. *Mahu,* If God understood prayers in our Language? They answered me God doth understand all Languages in the World." On the other hand, the repeated threat of disjunction between word and spirit takes the form of multiple confessions of religious formalism or pretense: "I do not truly pray to God in my heart: no matter for good words, all is the true heart"; "a great part of the Word stayeth not in my heart strongly"; "I pray but outwardly with my mouth, not with my heart"; "God have given unto me instruction, and causeth me to pray unto God, but I only pray words. . . . Sometimes I say the great and mighty God is in Heaven, but these are but words, because I do not fear this great and mighty God; . . . sometimes I say I know Christ, because I know he died for us, and hath redeemed us, and procured pardon for us: yet again I say I sin, because I beleeve not Christ."[41] It is perhaps because such expressions seem so obviously to pertain to spiritual matters that critics have overlooked the fact that they pertain to linguistic matters as well. Or, to put this another way, such expressions illustrate that in the textual records that form our principal surviving evidence of Puritan and Indian encounter, the spiritual and the linguistic are necessarily intertwined and interdependent.

As with the Puritan writers' reflections on translation, there are many ways to deal with the Indians' recorded expressions. The simplest, and the one to which most scholars have been attracted, is to take them at face value as the strivings and misgivings of people seeking to come to terms with radically new linguistic, religious, and cultural demands. For like Eliot—though with additional burdens and urgencies of which he had little experience and perhaps no knowledge—the Praying Indians were living within contexts of translation; like him, they were struggling with language on the border between cultures, with words, thoughts, and beliefs unsettled from a fixed and familiar place and carried into new territory. But if this is the case, then one should not insist that the Indians' words belong entirely to them, and thus accept these words as, for instance, unambiguously indicating the Indians' penchant for prayer. Neither, however—and for the same reason—should one insist that these words belong entirely to Eliot. And this is so not simply because of the difficulty, or impossibility, of reading through these printed words to the utterances and identities of their original speakers; more importantly, the lack of transparency in the printed words—the barriers to assigning a perfect correspondence between word and thing, speech and speaker—exists, once again, because the words were forged through acts of translation, through encounters that trouble pristine categories of linguistic or cultural ownership, authority, immediacy. Thus to say that it is uncertain whether the words in the Eliot texts belong to Eliot or to the Indians is to say that they belong to both—which is to say that they belong to neither. It is to say, in Cheyfitz's words, that in situations of encounter "each language is incomplete and thus dependent on its translation by all the others for its completeness"; or to say, in the words that with some slight variations begin each convert's address in Eliot's *Further Accompt*—the words that have provided the title to this paper—"A little I shall say, according to that little I know."[42] What these words suggest is that the Eliot tracts, for all their insistence on translation as their sole prerogative, were themselves translated through the forces of encounter; that the texts were jointly authored by multiple parties— Eliot, his converts, his interpreters—each of whom relied on all the others to achieve expression. In situations of encounter, these words suggest, no one can say it all—no one's words can contain or control all meaning, for no *one's* words exist outside the presence of others.

To say this, it must be repeated, is not to deny the power over Indian languages and lives that Eliot's people possessed; any number of factors—not least the uncertainty of what theories of translation seventeenth-century northeastern Indians embraced—makes it difficult to pinpoint the effect the Indians under Eliot's employ and tutelage, or more broadly the Indian presence, had in translating *his* language.[43] To be sure, the formula "a little I shall say," a phrase that is not characteristic of any of the public speech acts—such as sermons or conversion accounts—recorded of English speakers of the period, might be taken as indicative of such a theory; not only would this expression suggest a more fundamentally performative conceptualization of language than the text-based model touted by Eliot's people, but it would accord with current formulations of Indian self-representation as dialogic or, to borrow Arnold Krupat's term, "synecdochic," "marked by the individual's sense of himself in relation to collective social units or groupings."[44] To view the Eliot texts as arising from an environment of communal utterance would open up a range of intriguing possibilities: that the texts' semantic difficulties may indicate the resistance a unitary theory of language met from an indigenous one; that the moments in which the words of *"sundry"* speakers appear as the words of *"one man"* may signal Eliot's efforts to corral a polyvocal model of speech;[45] that, conversely, the moments in the texts in which the Indians are represented as complementing, supplementing, or revising each other's orations may represent the failure of the texts to countermand this model;[46] even that, as in one instance in which a member of Eliot's party offers a lively record of a convert's performative, participatory sermon, Indian discourse may have challenged not only Euro-American texts but the orthodox forms of worship within which the converts, like their teachers, were expected to confine themselves.[47]

But whatever the merits of such suggestions—and these are considerable, for at the very least, theorizing the reciprocal foundations of translation in the Eliot texts further marks these texts as dynamic sites of encounter rather than as repositories for unmediated Indian or Euro-American voices—it is important to balance a recognition of encounter as formative for American texts with a skepticism as to what, precisely, were the roles of any one party in that encounter; it is important to view the Eliot texts as products of communal utterance without reducing the communal to the distinctive product of any one culture. And translation both encourages and makes possible such a border position; translation enables us to see, among other things, how unrevealing texts are of the circumstances of their production, and in that impenetrability how revealing they are as well. Translation enables us to see that it is not solely texts authored by American Indians that register the presence of Indian peoples (and the Eliot texts, it should be said, could as easily be seen as having been authored by American Indians as by their Christian mentor); translation enables us to see that *all* American texts bear the imprint of the conflicts, transactions, and interchanges between peoples that gave them birth. Translation enables us to see that the Indian presence is at once more elusive and more decisive than scholars of colonial texts typically allow; translation enables us to see that the Indian presence is not obviously or straightforwardly evident in colonial texts in large part *because* that presence has played a role in shaping texts such that they defy the obvious or the straightforward. Translation, finally, enables us to see that if no American text can be read as the utopian school of Puritan theory represented language—as a pattern of lucent signs, each ligatured to its one only and consummate object— this is because all American texts are contested and contrived *between* cultures, and thus infused with multiple, contending, interpenetrating utterances and objectives. For even the immaculate Word Eliot carried into the wilderness came back in a new, translated form.

# Notes

1. See Cotton Mather, "The Triumphs of the Reformed Religion in America: Or, the Life of the Renowned John Eliot," in his *Magnalia Christi Americana,* ed. Samuel G. Drake (Hartford: Silas Andrus, 1855), 1:526-83.

2. On the antebellum revival of Eliot, see Joshua David Bellin, "Apostle of Removal: John Eliot in the Nineteenth Century," *New England Quarterly* 69 (1996): 3-32.

3. Alden T. Vaughan, *New England Frontier: Puritans and Indians, 1620–1675* (Boston: Little, Brown, 1965), 333. For a more recent exculpatory study, see Philip Ranlet, "Another Look at the Causes of King Philip's War," *New England Quarterly* 61 (1988): 79-100.

4. See Francis Jennings, *The Invasion of America: Indians, Colonialism, and the Cant of Conquest* (New York: Norton, 1975), 228-53; Kenneth M. Morrison, "'That Art of Coyning Christians': John Eliot and the Praying Indians of Massachusetts," *Ethnohistory* 21 (1974): 77-92; Neal Salisbury, "Red Puritans: The 'Praying Indians' of Massachusetts Bay and John Eliot," *William and Mary Quarterly* 31 (1974): 27-54; and George Tinker, *Missionary Conquest: The Gospel and Native American Cultural Genocide* (Minneapolis: Fortress, 1993), 21-41.

5. See Elise M. Brenner, "To Pray or to Be Prey: That is the Question. Strategies for Cultural Autonomy of Massachusetts Praying Town Indians," *Ethnohistory* 27 (1980): 135-52; Robert James Naeher, "Dialogue in the Wilderness: John Eliot and the Indian Exploration of Puritanism as a Source of Meaning, Comfort, and Ethnic

Survival," *New England Quarterly* 62 (1989): 346-68; James P. Ronda, "'We Are Well As We Are': An Indian Critique of Seventeenth-Century Christian Missions," *William and Mary Quarterly* 34 (1977): 66-82; and Harold W. Van Lonkhuyzen, "A Reappraisal of the Praying Indians: Acculturation, Conversion, and Identity at Natick, Massachusetts, 1646–1730," *New England Quarterly* 63 (1990): 396-428.

6. Richard W. Cogley, *John Eliot's Mission to the Indians before King Philip's War* (Cambridge, Mass.: Harvard University Press, 1999), 57, 105, 125. Even scholars critical of Eliot's mission have accepted the tracts' authority; Dane Morrison writes that he has attempted to "look beyond the ethnocentrism of the missionaries and the propaganda of their 'Indian tracts,'" yet he draws heavily on the tracts to reconstruct Indian beliefs (*A Praying People: Massachusett Acculturation and the Failure of the Puritan Mission, 1600–1690* [New York: Peter Lang, 1995], xvii, 1-36).

7. Hilary E. Wyss, *Writing Indians: Literacy, Christianity, and Native Community in Early America* (Amherst: University of Massachusetts Press, 2000), 9, 25, 27, 5. For the use of ethnohistories to bypass textual issues in primary sources, see also Henry Warner Bowden and James P. Ronda, eds., *John Eliot's Indian Dialogues: A Study in Cultural Interaction* (Westport, Conn.: Greenwood, 1980), 5-21, 28-32; and Jean M. O'Brien, *Dispossession by Degrees: Indian Land and Identity in Natick, Massachusetts, 1650–1790* (Cambridge: Cambridge University Press, 1997), 14-22, 52-60. Even more astonishing is an essay by Charles L. Cohen that, having reconstructed Indian religious beliefs almost entirely from the Eliot tracts, concludes that "Massachusett culture had failed" to equip Indians with the skills necessary to succeed as Christian converts ("Conversion among Puritans and Amerindians: A Theological and Cultural Perspective," in *Puritanism: Transatlantic Perspectives on a Seventeenth-Century Anglo-American Faith,* ed. Francis J. Bremer [Boston: Massachusetts Historical Society, 1993], 244).

8. Though "interpretation" is the more accurate term for much of what I discuss, I use "translation" both for simplicity's sake and because I see it as the more embracing term.

9.  For a quite different reading of Eliot's translations, see Edward G. Gray, *New World Babel: Languages and Nations in Early America* (Princeton: Princeton University Press, 1999), 56-84.

10. Barry O'Connell, introduction to *On Our Own Ground: The Complete Writings of William Apess, a Pequot*, ed. O'Connell (Amherst: University of Massachusetts Press, 1992), lv.

11. Eric Cheyfitz, *The Poetics of Imperialism: Translation and Colonization from "The Tempest" to "Tarzan"* (New York: Oxford University Press, 1991), 37. See also Vicente L. Rafael, "Gods and Grammar: The Politics of Translation in the Spanish Colonization of the Tagalogs of the Philippines," in *Notebooks in Cultural Analysis*, vol. 3, ed. Norman E. Cantor (Durham, N. C.: Duke University Press, 1986), 97-133.

12. Stephen J. Greenblatt, "Learning to Curse: Aspects of Linguistic Colonialism in the Sixteenth Century," in *First Images of America: The Impact of the New World on the Old*, ed. Fredi Chiappeli (Berkeley: University of California Press, 1976), 2:575; David Murray, *Forked Tongues: Speech, Writing and Representation in North American Indian Texts* (Bloomington: Indiana University Press, 1991), 2.

13. Cheyfitz, *Poetics of Imperialism*, 38-39.

14. Ann Kibbey, *The Interpretation of Material Shapes in Puritanism: A Study of Rhetoric, Prejudice, and Violence* (Cambridge: Cambridge University Press, 1986), 18-19; Vivian Salmon, *The Study of Language in 17th-Century England*, ed. E. F. K. Koerner (Amsterdam: John Benjamins, 1979), 129; Kibbey, *Material Shapes*, 41.

15. John Eliot, quoted in "Report of the Trial of Mrs. Anne Hutchinson," in *The Antinomian Controversy, 1636–1638: A Documentary History*, ed. David D. Hall (Middletown, Conn.: Wesleyan University Press, 1968), 363, 378, 381. I am indebted here to Patricia Caldwell, "The Antinomian Language Controversy," *Harvard Theological Review* 69 (1976): 345-67.

16. John Eliot, *Indian Dialogues*, ed. Bowden and Ronda, 103.

17. William J. Scheick, *Design in Puritan American Literature* (Lexington: University of Kentucky Press, 1992), 19.

18. Cheyfitz, *Poetics of Imperialism*, 35.

19. Petrus Danielus Huetius, *De Interpetatione Libri Duo* (1683), in *Translation/History/Culture: A Sourcebook*, ed. André Lefevere (London: Routledge, 1992), 89.

20. William Leverich, in Henry Whitfield, *Strength out of Weaknesse: Or a Glorious Manifestation of the Further Progresse of the Gospel Among the Indians in New-England* (London: M. Simmons, 1652), 22.

21. Thomas Shepard, *The Clear Sunshine of the Gospel Breaking forth upon the Indians in New England* (1648), in *The Works of Thomas Shepard* (Boston: Doctrinal Tract and Book Society, 1853; repr. New York: AMS, 1967), 3:489, 463; John Eliot, *A Further Accompt of the Progresse of the Gospel amongst the Indians in New-England* (London: M. Simmons, 1659), 2.

22. Mather, *Magnalia*, 561.

23. John Eliot, *A Late and Further Manifestation of the Progress of the Gospel Amongst the Indians in New-England* (London: M. Simmons, 1655), 5, 9, 21.

24. Whitfield, "To the Christian Reader," in *Strength out of Weaknesse*, n. p.

25. Rev. 22:15, *The Geneva Bible* (1560; repr. Madison: University of Wisconsin Press, 1969). For Eliot's quotation of this verse, see Hall, ed., *Antinomian Controversy*, 385.

26. Eliot, in Henry Whitfield, *The Light Appearing More and More towards the Perfect Day* (1651), in *Collections of the Massachusetts Historical Society*, 3d ser., vol. 4 (1833), 120.

27. Daniel Gookin, *Historical Collections of the Indians in New England*, in *Collections of the Massachusetts Historical Society*, 1<sup>st</sup> ser., vol. 1 (1792; repr. New York: Arno, 1972), 79; John Eliot, *A Brief Narrative of the Progress of the Gospel* (London: John Allen, 1670), 5.

28. See John Morgan, *Godly Learning: Puritan Attitudes towards Reason, Learning, and Education, 1560–1640* (Cambridge: Cambridge University Press, 1986), 152-55.

29. Whitfield, *Strength out of Weaknesse*, 7; Eliot, in Shepard, *Clear Sunshine*, 474.

30. Eliot, *Late and Further Manifestation*, 12.

31. Eliot, *Indian Dialogues*, ed. Bowden and Ronda, 87-88.

32. John Eliot, *The Indian Grammar Begun* (Cambridge: Marmaduke Johnson, 1666), title page.

33. M. M. Bakhtin, "Discourse in the Novel," in his *The Dialogic Imagination: Four Essays*, ed. Michael Holquist, trans. Caryl Emerson (Austin: University of Texas Press, 1981), 288; Eliot, in Whitfield, *Light Appearing*, 121; Eliot, in Whitfield, *Strength out of Weaknesse*, 4-5.

34. For a reconstruction of the role of Eliot's interpreters, see Jill Lepore, *The Name of War: King Philip's War and the Origins of American Identity* (New York: Vintage, 1998), 29-47.

35. Eliot, in Edward Winslow, *The Glorious Progress of the Gospel Amongst the Indians in New England* (London, 1649), 14; Eliot, in Whitfield, *Strength out of Weaknesse*, 15, 7.

36. Shepard, *Clear Sunshine*, 486; Cotton Mather, quoted in George Parker Winship, *The New England Company of 1649 and John Eliot* (New York: Burt Franklin, 1968), xlviii; William Walton, in Eliot, *Late and Further Manifestation*, 20.

37. Richard Mather, in John Eliot and Thomas Mayhew, *Tears of Repentance: Or, A Further Narrative of the Progress of the Gospel amongst the Indians in New-England* (1653), in *Collections of the Massachusetts Historical Society*, 3<sup>d</sup> ser., vol. 4 (1833), 220-21; Eliot, *Tears of Repentance*, 243, 245.

38. Eliot, *Further Accompt*, 20.

39. Winship, *New England Company*, xlviii-xlix. For a reassessment of Eliot as linguist, see Stephen Guice, "The Linguistic Work of John Eliot" (Ph.D. diss., Michigan State University, 1990).

40. John Wilson, *The Day-Breaking, if Not the Sun-Rising, of the Gospel with the Indians in New-England* (1647), in *Old South Leaflets* vol. 6 (New York: Burt Franklin, 197-?), 17; Whitfield, *Light Appearing*, 128, 130, 136.

41. Wilson, *Day-Breaking*, 4; Waban, in Eliot and Mayhew, *Tears of Repentance*, 231, 232; Robin Speene, in *Tears of Repentance*, 248; Ephraim, in *Tears of Repentance*, 259; Nishohkou, in *Tears of Repentance*, 250, 251.

42. Cheyfitz, *Poetics of Imperialism*, 135; Nishohkou, in Eliot, *Further Accompt*, 10.

43. On mutual translation, see Kristina Bross, "Dying Saints, Vanishing Savages: 'Dying Indian Speeches' in Colonial New England Literature," *Early American Literature* 36 (2001): 325-52; Louise Burkhart, "The Amanuenses Have Appropriated the Text: Interpreting a Nahuatl Song of Santiago," in *On the Translation of Native American Literatures*, ed. Brian Swann (Washington, D.C.: Smithsonian, 1992), 339-55; and Vicente Rafael, "Confession, Conversion, and Reciprocity in Early Tagalog Colonial Society," in *Colonialism and Culture*, ed. Nicholas B. Dirks (Ann Arbor: University of Michigan Press, 1992), 65-88. Tracy Leavelle's unpublished essay on Jesuit translations of sacred texts into the Illinois language, "The Language of Illinois Christianity: Translation and Reception, Mediation and Meaning in the French-Illinois Religious and Linguistic Encounter," offers concrete evidence of the linguistic, cultural, and religious negotiations that take place within the borderland of translation.

44. Arnold Krupat, *Ethnocriticism: Ethnography, History, Literature* (Berkeley: University of California Press, 1992), 212.

45. Eliot, *Late and Further Manifestation*, 10.

46. See Eliot, *Late and Further Manifestation*, 13-15; and Eliot, *Further Accompt*, 8-19.

47. See John Wilson, in Whitfield, *Strength out of Weaknesse*, 18-19.

# Falling "Into a Dreame"

## Native Americans, Colonization, and Consciousness in Early New England

ANN MARIE PLANE

N EARLY THREE CENTURIES AGO, in a remote Wampanoag Indian community on the island of Martha's Vineyard, a woman lay on her sickbed, in the grips of a final illness. Abigail Kesoehtaut knew that she was likely to die. After several days of anxious struggle, she found a lasting peace when "The Spirit of God did bear witness with her Spirit, that she was a Child of God, and had a Right to the Inheritance laid up in store for his Children."[1] Abigail's sister (unnamed in the sources), who was caring for her in her last days, was very troubled by Abigail's impending death. She "long'd for a more full Assurance in her Sister's Well-being," and, in particular, she wondered whether Abigail would go "out of this World in a State of Grace."[2] One night, during the sick woman's last hours, this caretaker fell asleep and began to dream:

> as she thought, she [Abigail's sister] plainly heard a Voice
> in the Air over the top of the House, saying in her own
> Language, *Wunnantinnea Kanaanut*, the same being diverse

84

times repeated, which Words may be thus rendered in English, tho they are much more emphatical in Indian, There is Favour now extended in Canaan; there is Favour, &c. The person that in her Sleep thought she heard such a Voice, supposed it to be a Voice from Heaven by the Ministry of Angels, sent to give her Satisfaction in the Case that did distress her: and [still dreaming] she was exceeding refreshed with the good Tidings which she thought she had in this wonderful way received; but while she was transported with the Thoughts of God's conde-scending Goodness thus manifested to her, and her Heart filled with unspeakable Delight, to her great Grief, some Person, as she thought, awaked her, and wake she did, but she could not find that any Person called her.3

Newly troubled by her thoughts, the woman appears to have con-sulted the Reverend Experience Mayhew, missionary to Martha's Vineyard, for guidance in interpreting this remarkable occurrence. The dream report appears in his 1727 book of native biographies, *Indian Converts*. Mayhew appended a "Query" to the story, asking "Whether the Person that dreamed the dream now related, ought to take any other notice of it, than she should of any common Dream; or what she should think concerning it?" And he attached a further plea to his readers, that "A Solution of this Problem would greatly satisfy both the Person that had the Dream, and him that has relat-ed it."4

This essay explores the exchange that took place between Abigail Kesoehtaut's sister and Experience Mayhew on Martha's Vineyard so long ago. It employs a variety of approaches drawn from cultural his-tory, based on my interest in the interactions between colonists and natives in colonial New England. At the same time, it is rooted in literature about dreaming, which facilitates a more nuanced understanding of the interaction of psyche and culture in colonial society. Colonial New England society, of course, comprised at least two distinct cultural groups, each with its own understandings of dreams, dreaming, and dream interpretation. On the one hand were various groups of colonists—most of them radical reformed Protestants—who had arrived in the region in the 1620s and 1630s in a rapid and successful migration of families. Sharing common religio-political goals to a large extent, these immigrants/invaders aimed to reproduce much of early modern English agrarian society, although they also hoped to integrate secular governance with radical Protestant social reforms. Religious beliefs gave rise to congregationalism, a rejection of traditional church institutions that also emphasized a legal and social order grounded in scriptural literalism. New England lands also remained home to Algonquian-speaking villagers, who, although devastated by successive waves of epidemic disease, nevertheless sought to continue longstanding cultural and subsistence practices, which they sometimes now enhanced through new exchanges, both for European material goods and for spiritual contact with the powerful Christian God.[5]

The colonists had many theories about dreams as a source of divine revelation. Seventeenth-century colonists reported dreams for several reasons; in particular, they were considered to have the potential to be of great religious or even predictive significance. The prominent Boston merchant Samuel Sewall always made careful notes of his dreams in his diary. In one instance, he dreamt that a small boy had made away with a special gold watch, which Sewall regained only with great effort. In his diary, Sewall noted—as would any good Puritan—"When I awaked I was much startled at it. The Lord help me to watch and pray that I may not enter into Temptation."[6] Such startling dreams warranted reflection as a part of the continuous "watchful" self-scrutiny that was in keeping with every pious person's devotional duties. As Alan Macfarlane noted in his famous account of the seventeenth-century English Puritan minister Ralph Josselin, nothing occurred at random. Instead, the clergyman's diary reveals that he, like Sewall, lived in "a constant state of watchfulness and worry" because "the world of phenomena [like dreams] was seen as purposeful and comprehensible; a long enough search would discern the source of almost every event."7 Even a dream—or especially a dream—warranted scrutiny.

Of course, in addition to occasioning the "private" reflections and watchfulness of diarists like Sewall, the dreams of early-modern European colonists drew public notice as well. Reports of dream-like "apparitions" were sometimes entered as evidence in court cases as part of the "spectral testimony" presented in trials for witchcraft or murder.8 Reports of predictive dreams regularly made the rounds in neighborhood gossip and in regional popular culture. Thus, in 1728 the Reverend John Comer recorded in his diary the remarkable fact that Deborah Greenman, struck dead by lightning, had dreamed of the accident two days before and had shared the dream with her sister.9

English newcomers quickly turned their attention to remarkable Indian dreams, and dreaming sometimes provoked conversation among members of the two groups about the colonial encounter, as was the case when Abigail Kesoehtaut's sister disclosed her worries to Experience Mayhew. John Eliot's writings about a trip to Cape Cod include an example from the 1640s. On this trip, an Indian man (perhaps a shaman?) told the English missionaries that he had long ago dreamt of a man, dressed "all in black" like a preacher. This figure had reassured the dreamer that "he and his Papooses should be safe, and that God would give unto them *Mitchen*, [that is,] victualls and other good things."10

Sigmund Freud, of course, theorized that all dreams are disguised expressions of repressed wishes. In his view, the true meaning of the dream (the latent dream thoughts) undergoes an elaborate process of distortion that results in the dream as experienced (the manifest content of the dream). Various processes are employed in the "dream work." Three fundamental transformations occur. The first is condensation (the merging of several ideas, people, locations, time frames, and so forth into one figure or element). The second is displacement (the shifting of strong feeling from the pertinent arena or individual to another person, place, or set of events apparently chosen at random). And the third is symbolization (the incorporation of personally, culturally, or, as Freud posited, universally meaningful elements). These processes are all employed to transform unacceptable or unbearable latent dream thoughts into acceptable, though often puzzling and disconnected, images. These images are then strung together into a story, a final process that Freud termed "secondary revision." Clearly, the dream of Abigail's sister, though its wish is relatively undisguised, is highly narrativized. It passed through several stages of revision, not only in the creation of the dream and during the dreamer's awakening, but also again when it was related to Mayhew and later retold by him.

By gathering the dreamer's associations (in the form of memories, thoughts, images and feelings) with different elements of the dream, Freud developed a way to trace a path "from the disguised surface to the hidden secrets [wishes] lying underneath."[11] Psychoanalysts since Freud have made many modifications to this basic theory. Most now accord great significance to the context in which the dream is reported, and especially to what the dream communicates about the dreamer's relationship to the listener/analyst.[12]

Cultural anthropologists have also made important advances on early psychoanalytic theory, especially by emphasizing the ways in which culturally specific narrative forms influence the process of "secondary revision." As Waud Kracke stresses, the sensory and visual experience of dreaming is always reshaped through language. Our understanding of dream productions is inevitably filtered "through our language-centered thought processes," and thus, "a dream recounted ends as a narrative."[13] Hence, dream reports are embedded in cultural context in terms of imagery, in terms of emotional style, and in terms of the protocols for narration and interpretation.[14] Dream images have highly specific, rather than transparent or universal, meanings. Barbara Tedlock suggests that the concept of manifest content be expanded to include indigenous "dream theory" and "[culturally prescribed] ways of sharing, including [an exploration of] the relevant discourse frames and the cultural code for interpretation."[15]

With a grasp of these perspectives, one may return to the dream that troubled Abigail's sister. Written in English, by a missionary rather than the dreamer herself, the dream report is thus revealed to be a highly compromised piece of historical evidence, at least in terms of its ability to provide direct access to the dreamer's experience. In the 1970s, historians such as Alan Macfarlane and Peter Burke observed that the historical dream narrative is "doubly censored." It is filtered not only through the normal process of secondary revision, but also through its conversion into a fixed, written form.[16] But even such a highly mediated text is useful. Sadly, historians have often failed to explore dreams in early America. A dream text like this one, however, is crucial evidence of a rich and meaning-filled cultural encounter.[17]

\* \* \*

The remainder of this essay explores what I see as the communications embedded in the dream report of Abigail Kesoehtaut's sister. First, this woman's dream speaks clearly of great losses, those of the past and those yet to come. In this regard, it reflects the immediate concerns of Native Americans of the seventeenth and eighteenth centuries. Even before Europeans took up residence in southern New England, contacts with fishermen, traders, and explorers had taken their toll on native communities. With no resistance to microbes common on the Eurasian landmass, American Indians suffered and died of diseases in immense numbers. Mortality rates of seventy-five to ninety percent were not uncommon. One author, Thomas Morton, described post-epidemic villages as a sort of "New-Found Golgotha," filled with the bodies and bones of natives who died without help or hope.[18] Such epidemics continued throughout the first generations of English colonization, while native vulnerability to disease was exacerbated by warfare and growing poverty.

In this context, Abigail's impending death filled her sister with considerable anxiety about the state of their eternal souls. Prior to the dream itself, Mayhew reported that Abigail found peace only when "The Spirit of God" bore "witness with her Spirit, that she was a Child of God and had a Right to the Inheritance laid up in store for his Children." As Abigail's sister nodded off, ostensibly worrying for Abigail's soul, she also anticipated a painful loss and, perhaps, discovered other complex feelings associated with the death of a sibling.

While there were "real" reasons for these women to be consumed with anxiety, their stance also accorded completely with the demands of Puritan Calvinist teachings. As Samuel Sewall's dream report demonstrated, Puritans encouraged devout men and women to cultivate a constant anxiety about both the state of their souls and the fragility of life. Puritan New Englanders exhibited a sense of God's fearsome judgment, particularly in their scrupulous attention to various "wonders," including storms, unusual events, remarkable providences, and startling dreams, all of which carried important messages.[19] In Mayhew's text, then, both the ardor of the missionary's message and the power of his orthodox teachings are at work. This makes sense, since the book—-which fits squarely within the well-established literary genre of "exemplary deaths" of pious men, women, and children—-was intended to convey the progress of sincere Christian conversion among the Indians.[20]

This concern with salvation bespeaks a still larger internal struggle between anxiety and reassurance. Consider, for example, the "Voice in the Air over the Top of the House," which reassured Abigail's sister. Viewed metaphorically, this voice represents a part of the dreamer's psyche, in which a sense of safety and confidence resided. As Mayhew made clear, the woman's longing "for a more full Assurance" —her great anxiety "in the Case that did distress her" — was, by this voice, much relieved. He reported, "she was exceeding refreshed," and "Her Heart filled with unspeakable Delight" at this "Ministry of Angels, sent to give her Satisfaction." In opposition to the reassuring voice (and thus the reservoir of reassurance she harbored within her), stood her fears as revealed in the latter part of the dream, when Abigail's sister was awakened "to her great Grief" by some invisible person. This awakening plunged her back into the state of worry, anxiety, grieving, and anticipation of loss in which she had begun the night, and which she had, through the dream (Freud's "wish fulfilled"), temporarily relieved.

The story change in the scene—a shift from the reassurance of angelic voices to the sudden urging by an unknown person to "awake"—replicated the central tension in Abigail's sister's life. How could she find safety in a world of tormenting worries and afflictions? The fact that the voice urged her to "awake" was no accident, of course. Just as Samuel Sewall was prodded by his dream to keep a closer "watch" on himself, Abigail's sister appears, as would any good Puritan, to have "awakened" to the uncertain state of her soul. The dream even used exactly the same language as that of a good Puritan preacher speaking to his parishioners. The anxiety of the dream then, in its intensity and mode of expression, represents not only the psychic fruits of Puritanism, but also the precarious situation of Native Americans in the colonized society of eighteenth-century New England.

There is a second key communication buried in this dream narrative. It is significant that this dream offered an opportunity for communication and collaboration between the dreamer and Mayhew himself. In this sense, Abigail's sister may have been continuing a practice common among Native Americans of this region, a sort of "performative" dreaming.[21] In seeking out someone to listen to her dream, she was acting upon the dream experience to fulfill or complete the dream's message, a widespread approach to dreaming that, in many cultures, can require the performance of particular rituals. The connection of dreams to ritual practice is well documented among the seventeenth-century Iroquois to the west of New England, and similar observances took place among southern New England Algonquians as well, though here the evidence is considerably more sketchy.[22] Dreams were clearly seen as meaning-filled, and New England natives assiduously sought to read those meanings. Thus Roger Williams noted in 1643, "When they have a bad Dreame, which they conceive to be a threatning from God, they fall to prayer at all times of the night, especially early before day."[23]

Shamans paid particular heed; dreaming enabled them to make contact with powerful forces, or "manitous," which allied with them to effect healing or harm. Individuals seem to have acquired shamanic status through important dream experiences, and many healing ceremonies depended upon a shaman's success in battling malignant forces in supernatural contests that sometimes took place during sleep-like trances or periods of unconsciousness.[24] Thus, in 1647, two Christian Indian youths reported that "if any of the Indians fall into any strange dreame wherein *Chepian* ["the devil"] appears unto them as a serpent, then the next day they tell the other Indians of it, and for two dayes after[ward] the rest of the Indians dance and rejoyce for what they tell them about this Serpent, and so they become their Pawwaws."[25]

Insofar as it has been possible to reconstruct indigenous dream theories, scholars have posited that southern New England Algonquians conceptualized the self as containing a "dream soul" that traveled outside the sleeping body during dreams.[26] As such, neither thought (whether waking or sleeping) nor the self were necessarily conceptualized as being contained within the body.[27] Because of these beliefs, early Christian missionaries fielded questions from Indians puzzled about the status of dreams and, more particularly, from those concerned about their personal accountability for thoughts and actions that had occurred during dreams. Thomas Shepard reported that during an early meeting between English missionaries and potential converts, "the Indians were serious" and asked many questions, including "Whether they should beleeve Dreames?"[28] On another occasion, the Indians seemed in their questions to be much concerned about "the evill of thoughts and dreames."[29]

But if Puritans and natives shared a belief in dreams as filled with meaning, New England Algonquians chose to act upon those meanings in ways that seemed strange to English observers. Once again, it was that careful observer, Roger Williams, who recorded the details of a ceremony that followed one particularly powerful dream event. In his famous account of the Narragansett people of Rhode Island, Williams described his visit "to an Iland of the wildest [people or places] in our parts." Here "in the night an Indian (as he said) had a vision or dream of the Sun (whom they worship for a God) darting a Beame into his Breast." The man "conceived [this dream] to be the Messenger of his Death: this poore Native call'd his Friends and neighbours, and prepared some little refreshing for them, but himselfe was kept waking and fasting in great Humiliations and Invocations for 10. dayes and nights."[30] Williams had trouble communicating with these people: "little could I speake to them to their understandings, especially because of the change of their Dialect, or manner of Speech from our neighbours."[31] Yet he did try to convey the basics of Christian belief to them, and "at parting many burst forth, Oh when will you come againe, to bring us some more newes of this God?"[32] Clearly, although Williams may have shared the natives' notions about the predictive power of dreams, especially as portents of death, he worked to disabuse them of their faith in the efficacy of such rituals as "waking and Fasting" and "Humiliations and Invocations," at least as associated with particular dream events.[33]

Thus, when Abigail Kesoehtaut's sister sat down with Experience Mayhew to discuss her unusual dream, she brought to the table a repertoire of imagery, interpretation, and ritual through which to make sense of this meaning-filled event. For his part, the missionary brought a long tradition of wonder-lore, of anxious Puritan self-scrutiny, and of deathbed observation with which to interpret the message of this Indian woman's dream. By the eighteenth century, Wampanoags would have been thoroughly exposed to such Puritan and English ideas. Mayhew, as a fully bilingual and fairly bi-cultural individual, would have had some understanding of traditional Wampanoag dream sharing and dream interpretation. To what extent each of these cultural traditions contributed to the conversation that emerged must remain anyone's guess, although clearly these different understandings had become fully entangled over the previous two generations of intimate colonial contact. Perhaps the conversation between this Wampanoag woman and the English missionary consti-tuted a sort of "middle ground," a cultural terrain of dream inter-pretation that neither individual fully owned or understood.[34]

Of course, Mayhew himself did not dare to represent the full syncretism of this encounter. Instead, he recast the conversation as an orthodox Christian examination of a powerful dream event—a sign of his exemplary efforts on behalf of Indian Christians, and further evidence of the successful conversion of a pious Indian family. Significantly, he shied away from venturing an opinion about the dream's worth, and instead invited his more learned readers to posit their views of whether this dream was to be believed, or even deserved "any other notice" than "any common Dream." Thus, in his report, the dangers of the middle ground were covered over, and the potential exposure of syncretic deviation was again recast as evidence of orthodox, modest, and exemplary piety.

But there is a third message in this dream, one that pushes the modern reader well beyond the territory Mayhew chose to map. For while clearly his discussion of this dream suggests the growing dominance of English culture, it also contains hints of the Wampanoags' distinctive experiences as a colonized people. Dreaming and dream sharing may have provided important avenues of release for aggressive resistance to English colonization. Just as dreams can provide a modern analysand with the means to explore difficult, embarrassing, or potentially dangerous materials, dreams could have enabled Wampanoags to explore, both internally and in conversation with colonizers like Mayhew, an assertion of native presence and native self-worth despite Christian teachings and English dominance.

Consider once again the Voice in the Air. In this respect, the dream and its context speak to the much larger question of the Indians' place in eighteenth-century social hierarchies and assert the value, worth, and equality of all souls before God. The Voice offered its words of comfort not in English but in Massachusett. Its message was translated only through Mayhew's intervention. The Voice said, "Wunnantinnea Kanaanut," repeating these words several times. As

Mayhew admitted, he toned down their meaning, rendering them "in English, tho they are much more emphatical in Indian," as "'There is Favour now extended in Canaan.'" Canaan, in this sense, is God's Promised Land, God's reward for the saved (i.e., heaven). Abigail's sister dreamt of this Christian redemption in the Massachusett language. This by itself was not so remarkable—quite likely the entire dream report represented Mayhew's translation of an experience told to him in Massachusett. Yet it is significant in that he left this one phrase in the original words: God apparently spoke the language of the Wampanoags with considerable fluency.

Abigail herself had found deathbed assurance that she, an Indian and (like every human) a sinner, would, at death, still be "a Child of God." God's Massachusett utterances in Abigail's sister's dream now hammered home to an English audience that the assurance of a place in heaven—communicated via a wondrous angelic "Voice"—could be achieved by Indians as well as by Englishmen. The political power of this Christian egalitarianism would have fairly leapt off the page for Mayhew's contemporaries. Yet how could they have denied a communication that seemed to have come from God's own messenger?

Though Abigail's sister reported a dream that, in every way, seemed to echo orthodox Puritan practices, the strange Voice, as reported, taught Mayhew and his readers that natives might be both fully Christian and fully native. Moreover, unlike earlier seventeenth-century missionaries, who had focused on translating Christian texts into Massachusett, eighteenth-century missionaries had focused on getting Indians to use English instead of Massachusett, thus obviating the need for costly and time-consuming translations. The Voice spoke, however, in a defiant embrace of Massachusett, speaking its Christian message with more vigor than could be found in English translation. In this way, the narration of Abigail's sister's dream expressed resistance to colonial hegemony. The use of dream reports to counter European cultural dominance is found in other colonial contexts as well. For example, in studies of colonial South Africa, anthropologists John and Jean Comaroff have argued that dreams, dream narration, and various forms of ritual action constitute truly counter-hegemonic communications even when the dominance of the colonizer is apparently seamless. The puzzling nature of such communications indicates a refusal "to answer to the voice of the dominant, or in the spoken voice at all," suggesting that such rare counter-hegemonic communications "frequently seek out alternate modes of expression."[35] Taking a slightly different approach and emphasizing the psychodynamics of racism, Méchal Sobel has argued that dreams can provide individuals with "a protected place for negotiations with the other," including parts of themselves constellated as "other" and frequently (as she demonstrates) symbolized through racially "other" figures.[36]

Moreover, when Abigail's sister hurried to Mayhew to explore this wondrous voice, she "performed" her dream and carried this explicit (and defiant) message to his very chamber. God has laid up a store in heaven for those who have bravely endured the grossest earthly inequities. God's Massachusett fluency opens, in metaphor, a place in heaven for all natives who seriously seek "*Kanaanut.*"

Did her message get through? Apparently enough of it did to leave Mayhew himself worried by this curious dream. His final queries to the reader made this puzzlement quite clear. When he asked for guidance from his fellow ministers and other men of experience who might judge the significance of God's speech, he made it plain that the dreamer would not be the only person relieved to find an answer. As Mayhew noted, "A Solution of this Problem would greatly satisfy" he "that has related" her dream in writing, that is to say, Mayhew himself.

Of course, the report we have before us is Mayhew's text, not that of the dreamer herself. And, as such, it is perhaps not surprising that it reveals at least as much about the anxious position of English missionaries in relation to exemplary Indian converts as it does about the cultural syncretism of eighteenth-century Wampanoag Christianity. Experience Mayhew long hoped to obtain his own sort of "Favour" in "Canaan"—a settled ministry. But neither Indians nor Englishmen would ever call him to a congregation, and he would instead content himself with peripatetic preaching to the Indians and administration of charity among the Wampanoags of Martha's Vineyard.[37] There is also profound cultural insecurity mingled with Mayhew's personal concerns. As I have argued in the second chapter of my recent book, missionary literature quite predictably lauded notable successes among the so-called "praying Indians." But missionary authors were also surprisingly vociferous in expressing their insecurities—including their fear that corrupt Englishmen had forever lost God's favor, and that they performed only the final errand of bringing Christianity into the wilderness. Perhaps, they feared, they were just the vessels by which the true Israelites—the Indians—would be delivered from a spiritual enslavement in sin and ignorance unto a new Canaan.[38]

Surely one can now understand why Abigail Kesoehtaut's sister experienced a restless night. Her dream report reveals the complex, painful, and anxious situation of Native Americans and English colonizers in this eighteenth-century colonial society. By reading attentively in both a psychologically and a culturally sensitive manner, one can recapture to at least some degree how dreams might have changed dreamers, hearers, and the colonial conversations of eighteenth-century New England. English colonists and Native Americans each brought their own assumptions about the meaningful nature of dreams to their encounters. Moments of collaborative interpretation and public narration as recorded by Mayhew and others allow us to eavesdrop on an unusual conversation between Englishmen and Native Americans about the meanings of their dreams. Such careful attention makes it possible to explore some of the connections between consciousness and colonization. The unconscious productions of a particular dreamer conveyed religious, cultural, and personal preoccupations, but they also betrayed continuing simmering resentment and resistance. The resulting dream narrative was shaped both by pre-existing cultural/linguistic models and by anxious conversation with the other before it entered into cultural discourse as a new narrative. Such dream narratives expressed both acquiescence and resistance to English colonization, and, at the same time, they allowed a mutual exploration of the growing English dominance over New England's Native American peoples.

# Notes

I am grateful for the assistance of the Stoller Foundation for Research in Psychoanalysis and Culture and for the support of many individuals, especially the psychoanalysts who have so generously given their time to answer my questions and to comment upon this work in progress. Any errors or misreadings remain mine alone. I acknowledge Gerry Aronson, David James Fisher, Jill Anne Kowalik, Peter Loewenberg, Joseph Natterson, and Richard Weiss, with special thanks to James E. Bews, Allen E. Bishop, Edward English, Carol Lansing, Maggie Magee, Ursula Mahlendorf, and Diana C. Miller.

1.  Experience Mayhew, *Indian Converts, or, some Accounts of the Lives and Dying Speeches of a considerable number of the Christianized Indians of Martha's Vineyard, in New England* (London: Samuel Gerrish, 1727), 146.

2.  Mayhew, *Indian Converts*, 147.

3.  Mayhew, *Indian Converts*, 147-48.

4.  Mayhew, *Indian Converts*, 148.

5.  Some important recent works on Indian persistence in New England include: Colin G. Calloway, ed., *After King Philip's War: Presence and Persistence in Indian New England* (Hanover: University Press of New England, 1997); Daniel R. Mandell, *Behind the Frontier: Indians in Eighteenth-Century Eastern Massachusetts* (Lincoln: University of Nebraska Press, 1996); Jean M. O'Brien, *Dispossession by Degrees: Indian Land Holding and Identity in Natick, Massachusetts, 1650–1790* (New York: Cambridge

University Press, 1997); William S. Simmons, *Spirit of the New England Tribes: Indian History and Folklore, 1620–1984* (Hanover: University Press of New England, 1986).

6.   Samuel Sewall, *The Diary of Samuel Sewall, 1674–1729*, 2 vols., ed. M. Halsey Thomas (New York: Farrar, Straus and Giroux, 1973), 2: 1062-63.

7.   Alan Macfarlane, *The Family Life of Ralph Josselin, a Seventeenth-Century Clergyman* (1970; repr. New York: W. W. Norton and Co., 1977), 193.

8.   Cf. Paul Boyer and Stephen Nissenbaum, eds., *Salem Village Witchcraft: A Documentary Record of Local Conflict in Colonial New England* (Belmont, Calif.: Wadsworth Publishing Co. [1972]). John Putnam Demos, *Entertaining Satan: Witchcraft and the Culture of Early New England* (New York: Oxford University Press, 1982), 192; on dreams of witches (as distinct from actual "spectral appearances," see p. 186. See also sources on dreams and religious controversy in medieval and early modern European contexts, esp. Carlo Ginsberg, *Night Battles: Witchcraft and Agrarian Cults in the Sixteenth and Seventeenth Centuries*, trans. John and Anne Tedeschi ([1966 Ital. ed.] New York: Penguin Books, 1986). One example involved a Rhode Island murder case in which John Brigs testified that his slain sister visited him as a nighttime apparition: See Deposition of John Brigs, May 12, 1673, in *R. v. Thomas Cornell*, Superior Court of Judicature, Book A, p. 13, Supreme Court Judicial Records Center, Pawtucket, R.I.

9.   John Comer, May 31, 1728, "The Diary of John Comer [1704– 1734]," ed. C. Edwin Barrows with James W. Willmarth, *Collections of the Rhode Island Historical Society* 8 (1893): 54. The English minister Ralph Josselin hoped that he "'might even forseeingly dream,'" and quoted a woman "who was warned of her death in a dream." Macfarlane, *Family Life*, 183.

10.   For a full discussion, see my *Colonial Intimacies: Indian Marriage in Early New England* (Ithaca: Cornell University Press, 2000), 45-47.

11. Stephen A. Mitchell and Margaret A. Black, *Freud and Beyond: A History of Modern Psychoanalytic Thought* (New York: Basic Books, 1995), 8-9.

12. Mitchell and Black, *Freud and Beyond*, 261, n. 5.

13. Waud Kracke, "Myths in Dreams, Thoughts in Images," in Barbara Tedlock, ed., *Dreaming: Anthropological and Psychological Interpretations*, A School of American Research Book (New York: Cambridge University Press, 1987), 34-37, quotation p. 36.

14. Gilbert Herdt, "Selfhood and Discourse in Sambia Dream Sharing," in Tedlock, ed., *Dreaming: Anthropological and Psychological Interpretations*, 59-64.

15. Barbara Tedlock, "Dreaming and Dream Research," in Tedlock, ed., *Dreaming: Anthropological and Psychological Interpretations*, 25.

16. See Macfarlane, *Family Life*, 183; Peter Burke, "L'histoire Sociale des Rêves," *Annales: Économie, Sociétés, Civilisations* 28 (1973): 333.

17. The best recent psychoanalytically-informed study of dreaming in early America is Méchal Sobel, *Teach Me Dreams: The Search for Self in the Revolutionary Era* (Princeton: Princeton University Press, 1999). Earlier studies mostly reject or ignore psychoanalytic explanations. See, for example, Susan Sleeper-Smith, "The Dream as a Tool for Historical Research: Reexamining Life in Eighteenth-Century Virginia Through the Dreams of a Gentleman: William Byrd, II, 1674–1744," *Dreaming* 3 (1993): 49-68; William H. McGowan, "The Dream of Ezra Stiles: Bishop Berkeley's Haunting of New England," *Studies in Eighteenth-Century Culture*, vol. 11, ed. Harry C. Payne (Madison: University of Wisconsin Press, 1982), 181-98. As Peter Gay has noted, "It is interesting, though a little disheartening, to see how little some historians have done with Freud." Peter Gay, *Freud for Historians* (New York: Oxford University Press, 1985), 33.

18. Thomas Morton, *New English Canaan, or New Canaan. Containing an Abstract of New England* (Amsterdam: Jacob Frederick Stam, 1637), 132-33.

On epidemics, see Neal Salisbury, *Manitou and Providence: Indians, Europeans, and the Making of New England, 1500–1643* (New York: Oxford University Press, 1982), 101-5.

19. See David D. Hall, *World of Wonders, Days of Judgment: Popular Religious Belief in Early New England* (New York: Alfred A. Knopf, 1989), chap. 2, esp. 71-75.

20. Hall, *World of Wonders, Days of Judgment*, 56-57.

21. Barbara Tedlock, "Zuni and Quiche Dream Sharing and Interpreting," in Tedlock, ed., *Dreaming: Anthropological and Psychological Interpretations*, 116-123.

22. During the *Ononharoia*, or "Feast of Fools," "men and women ran madly from cabin to cabin, acting out their dreams in charades and demanding the dream be guessed and satisfied." Anthony F. C. Wallace, "Dreams and Wishes of the Soul: A Type of Psychoanalytic Theory among the Seventeenth Century Iroquois," *American Anthropologist* 60 (1958): 240. Iroquoian theory posited that each dream expressed a wish or *Ondinnonk* ("secret desire of the soul") and held that the best thing to do with these wishes was to satisfy them, either literally or through symbolic actions; see "Relations of Father Ragueneau, 1647–1648," cited in Wallace, "Dreams and Wishes," 237-38.

23. Roger Williams, *A Key into the Language of America*, ed. John J. Teunissen and Evelyn J. Hinz (Detroit: Wayne State University Press, 1973), 107-8.

24. Kathleen Bragdon, *Native People of Southern New England, 1500–1650* (Norman: University of Oklahoma Press, 1996), 20 1-5.

25. The Pawwaws "cure the sick by certaine odd gestures and beatings of themselves, and then they pull out the sicknesse by applying their hands to the sick person and so blow it away: so that their Pawwaws are great witches, having fellowship with the old Serpent, to whom they preay, and by whose meanes they heale sicke persons, and (as they said also)

will dew [?] many strange juglings to the wonderment of the Indins. They affirmed also that if they did not cure the sick party (as very often they did not) that then they were reviled, and sometime killed by some of the dead mans friends, especially if they could not get their mony againe out of their hands, which they receive afterhand for their care." [Thomas Shepard], *The Day-Breaking if Not the Sun-Rising of the Gospell with the Indians in New-England* (London: Richard Cotes for Fulk Clifton, 1647), 21-22.

26.  Bragdon, *Native People*, 190-91; Simmons, *Spirit of the New England Tribes*, 44-45.

27.  Peter Nabokov, "Native Views of History," in *The Cambridge History of the Native Peoples of the Americas*, vol. 1: North America, ed. Bruce G. Trigger and Wilcomb E. Washburn (New York: Cambridge University Press, 1996), pt. 1, 1-59.

28.  [Shepard], *Day-Breaking*, 18.

29.  Edward Winslow, *The Glorious Progress of the Gospel amongst the Indians in New England* (London: for Hannah Allen, 1649), 25.

30.  Williams, *Key into the Language*, 108.

31.  Williams, *Key into the Language*, 108.

32.  Williams, *Key into the Language*, 108.

33.  Williams, *Key into the Language*, 108.

34.  See Richard White, *The Middle Ground: Indians, Empires, and Republics in the Great Lakes Region, 1650–1815* (New York: Cambridge University Press, 1991).

35.  See John Comaroff and Jean Comaroff, *Ethnography and the Historical Imagination, Studies in the Ethnographic Imagination*, ser. eds. John Comaroff, Pierre Bourdieu, and Maurice Bloch (Boulder: Westview Press, 1992), 257.

36. Méchal Sobel, "The Revolution in Inner Selves: Black and White Inner Aliens," in *Through a Glass Darkly: Reflections on Personal Identity in Early America*, ed. Ronald Hoffman, Méchal Sobel and Fredrika J. Teute, (Chapel Hill: University of North Carolina Press, for the Omohundro Institute in Early American History and Culture, 1997), 166, 170-77, quotation p. 188. See also her more recent book, *Teach Me Dreams*, cited above.

37. Bragdon, *Native People*, 10, 11-12. See also William Kellaway, *The New England Company: 1649–1776, Missionary Society to the American Indians* (New York: Barnes and Noble, 1961), 240-41.

38. Plane, *Colonial Intimacies*, chap. 2, *passim*.

# The Changing Nature of Indian Slavery in New England, 1670–1720

MARGARET ELLEN NEWELL

ISTORIES OF SLAVERY AND THE "CONSTRUCTION OF RACE" in early America—the emergence of theories of racial inferiority and superiority and the translation of these rigid racialized categories into law and other institutions—generally focus on the encounter between Europeans and Africans.[1] Yet, Native Americans constituted the vast majority of those enslaved by European regimes in the Americas prior to 1700. Recent scholarship points to the prevalence of Indian slaves and slave-trading throughout North America. In colonial regions as diverse as Louisiana, Canada, New Mexico, and South Carolina, captive Indians represented anywhere from a substantial portion to the sole source of slave labor exploited by European colonists through the early eighteenth century.[2]

Colonial New England was no exception to this rule. Although travelers' accounts, court records, newspapers, and diaries attest to the presence of Indian slaves and servants in New England during the colonial era, the subject has received little scholarly attention.[3] Standard histories of the region stress the primacy of the household unit (as opposed to plantation or large-scale enterprise) and the colonists' tendency to rely on family labor. In other words, the supposition is that the New England colonists simply did not need slave labor—that Indian servitude was peripheral and incidental. The reality is that New England armies, courts, and magistrates enslaved more than 1200 Indian men, women, and children in the seventeenth century alone, and bound many others into finite terms of servitude.

The ongoing enslavement of Indians did raise some distinct legal, ethical and practical problems for European colonizers, however, and the legal framework for Indian slavery in New England changed dramatically between 1670 and 1720. Prior to 1700, the vast majority of Indian slaves in New England were war captives and non-combatant refugees who found themselves "sold and devoted unto servitude" among the English settlers in the wake of the Pequot War of 1637, King Philip's War of 1675–76, and the wars with the Eastern Indians that followed into the 1680s and 1690s. Provincial governments and courts periodically condemned native peoples within their jurisdictions to "perpetuall slavery" or servitude for a variety of infractions during peacetime, but such cases were rare before 1670. In the decades following King Philip's War, however, a shift took place. A combination of influences, including pressure from British officialdom, security concerns, the cessation of war in southern New England, and the colonists' successful assertion of authority over the tribes that lived there, caused changes in colonial policy towards Indian slavery. In a sense, free Native Americans in southern New England became legal "insiders" through subjection to the authority of the colonial governments. Outright enslavement of war captives declined, as did exports of New England Indians to other plantations. Connecticut, Massachusetts, and Rhode Island created new laws and institutions designed to protect and to regulate the New England Indians.

Yet, despite (and to a certain extent because of) these changes,

Native American slavery and involuntary servitude persisted after 1700, albeit in different forms. Some would-be owners purchased Indians imported from outside the region in order to evade the laws against enslaving local Indians. Most notably, however, the practice of judicial enslavement—the sentencing of Native Americans to long periods of involuntary service to settle debts, as well as civil and criminal penalties—increased dramatically. At the same time, even as they formally recognized the collective rights of free Indians, the New England governments crafted new racially-based tax and legal codes that further eroded the status of Indian servants. In effect, the colonial assemblies created a "race frontier" that stripped unfree people of color—Indian, African, and mixed-race slaves and servants—of certain rights enjoyed by their white counterparts. Thus the experiences of these Indian servants and slaves, and the attitudes of the New Englanders who enslaved them, shed light on both the legal evolution of New World chattel slavery and the emerging definitions of race in early America.

* * *

New England armies, courts, and magistrates turned to Indian slavery from the first decade of settlement. Binding Indians simultaneously offered a solution to labor shortages and a means of punishing and controlling local native populations. During the Pequot War, the United Colonies and their Niantic, Narragansett, and Mohegan Indian allies all shared in the war's human spoils. Victorious generals Israel Stoughton and Samuel Davenport remitted approximately 250 native captives to Connecticut and Massachusetts authorities in June and July of 1637 to "be disposed aboute in the townes" as household servants.[4] Not all of the captives remained in New England, however; of the prisoners brought to Boston, Governor John Winthrop noted that seventeen women and children composed part of the cargo on the trading ship that initiated the colony's much-desired trade with the Atlantic and Caribbean islands.[5] By the 1640s, Winthrop was fielding requests from the governor of Bermuda for Indian slaves, and other New Englanders were urging a war against the Narragansetts for the "gaynefull pilladge" of securing Indian workers.[6] Already by 1676, then, sales like these had placed Native American workers in households throughout southern New England. Women worked as household servants; children tended livestock and worked in the fields; men did fieldwork as well as skilled labor, entered the maritime trades, and later served in the provincial forces on their masters' behalf.

Enslavement of Native Americans elicited few protests from anyone besides the Indians themselves, at least initially. This absence of discussion is itself interesting. Whereas the establishment of Indian labor drafts and de facto enslavement in New Spain prompted lengthy public debates over whether indigenous peoples represented a lower order of life in the Aristotelian schema, most ministers and officials in New England affirmed the Indians' essential humanity. Massachusetts Bay's 1641 legal code, the Body of Liberties, and its 1647 revision defined "man stealing" as a capital crime, and authorities did intervene on several occasions to free both Africans and Indians whom they adjudged to have been kidnapped and wrongfully enslaved.

To justify the taking of Indian slaves in warfare, though, New England authorities turned to Grotius as well as Mosaic and common law sources. English precedents existed for condemning criminals convicted of capital crimes and non-Christian prisoners captured in a "just war" to a set term of enforced service sometimes referred to as "slavery." Scots prisoners of war served as indentured servants in Barbados and New England in the 1640s and 1650s, and a few unruly English settlers accused of treason found themselves "enslaved" in early Bermuda.[7] For whites, slavery in these circumstances was neither a permanent nor a heritable status; after serving their terms, the condemned could expect to regain their former rights and privileges as freeborn English citizens. Native captives faced a vastly different situation.

The precise status of these Indians is difficult to determine. "Slavery" and "servitude" were slippery terms in seventeenth-century America; contracts, writs, and bills of sale often used them interchangeably. A "slave" might be freed after a set term, just like an indentured servant. Chattel slavery as a legal system evolved slowly, the product of piecemeal construction. In the case of the Pequot captives, some had set terms of service, but others apparently served for life. Runaway Pequots appeared in court records more than ten years after the war's end, and the citizens of Hingham, Massachusetts, testified in 1676 to the long presence in their community of "Indian Servants part of them being Captives and part of them apprentices for years: some of which were bought with money and some given to ye Petitioners."[8] Certainly, those New England Indians who were exported to Bermuda, Providence Island, or other plantations became chattel slaves.

Moreover, English "slaves" were men, while the vast majority of the natives enslaved by the United Colonies were non-combatant women and children. This departure from precedent disturbed a few colonists. Roger Williams of Rhode Island privately wondered whether the colonists had the legal or moral right to enslave innocent women and children. In the end, Williams concluded that such slavery was a legitimate tool of war, since "the Enemie may lawfully be weakned and despoild of all Comfort of Wife, Children, etc."[9] But, he counseled Governor Winthrop that a tributary system or a finite period of servitude followed by freedom for Indian captives would be more politic than enslavement. Some confusion also existed over whether the "just war" rationale made it appropriate for a third party to purchase war captives from the nations at war, but such objections faded by the 1670s.

In addition to enslavement during warfare, colonial governments and courts condemned individual Indians to terms of service or "perpetuall slaverie" for a variety of infractions, ranging from sheltering enemy Indians, debt, and theft to "insolent carryage." By the 1650s, Indians began to appear before English courts with greater frequency, as the colonial governments asserted their legal jurisdiction over larger territories and the native groups and individuals who inhabited them. In 1659, the General Assembly of Rhode Island decreed that any Indian convicted of theft or property damage who failed to "pay and discharge all the damages, costs, and restitutions by law due" could "be sould as a slave to any forraigne country of the English subjects."[10] The Assembly viewed sale as a particularly appropriate penalty in cases where the defendants showed "insolency." In 1673, Plymouth officials passed a similar law, which permitted creditors to bind debtor Indians into terms of service. Criminal sentences occasionally involved servitude as well. Plymouth's General Court condemned an "Indian, called Hoken, that hath bin a notoriouse theife," in absentia, and ordered in 1674 that if captured he be sold to Barbados "to free the collonie from soe ill a member."[11]

Such cases of enslavement for debt or criminality were rare before 1675, however, in part because as members of intact tribes native defendants had resources to draw upon to pay fines, and, often, sachems or white patrons to represent them in court. Initially, natives seemed no more likely to receive such sentences than other groups in colonial society. In several instances seventeenth-century Suffolk County courts ordered that white recidivist thieves, debtors, and unruly servants be sold so that the profits could be used to make restitution to their victims and their communities, and whites were sentenced to servitude by courts in early eighteenth-century Rhode Island as well.[12]

During King Philip's War, the colonists formalized and expanded upon these patterns of enslavement, with disastrous results for Native American communities in the region. Plymouth, Massachusetts, and Connecticut officials held mass public auctions of hundreds of Narragansett and Wampanoag captives at a time, as did the towns of Portsmouth and Providence in Rhode Island. Colonial governments assigned groups of captives to individuals as rewards for wartime service, and as a form of monetary restitution to war-battered English towns.

Previous loyalty to the English offered neutral Indians little protection. Kidnappers raided the coasts, indiscriminately seizing dozens of "friend" Indians for sale and export. In June of 1675, Plymouth's Council of War ordered that Indian children be removed from their families and forcibly apprenticed to white families. The resulting diaspora was extensive, as exporters sold many hundreds of New England captives—especially adult males—in the Wine Islands, Spain, England, and Jamaica. For example, Plymouth Colony authorities shipped 178 captives aboard a single vessel bound for Cadiz in October 1675.[13] Those who remained in North America might find themselves hundreds of miles from home and kin.

At the same time, the practice of enslaving New England Indians came under greater scrutiny during and after King Philip's War. The sheer scale of enslavement from 1670 to 1700 prompted a spate of legislation, both local and province-wide, regarding the status of Native Americans in southern and northern New England. But, from the Native American point of view, the outcome of this enhanced legal oversight was mixed, to say the least.

The first legislation concerning enslavement appeared while the war was still being fought. New England Indians never had a European public advocate of the stature of Bartolome de las Casas, but missionary John Eliot and Indian guardian Daniel Gookin privately begged colonial governments for help in protecting their charges from indiscriminate kidnappings. The colonists' own security concerns prompted a review of the practice as well, since many worried about the threat that a potentially hostile captive servant population represented. In response to these varied pressures, Massachusetts, Connecticut, and Rhode Island moved to bring captive Indians under more direct government control. At the onset of the conflict, Massachusetts and Plymouth passed Orders in Council against keeping adult Indian servants, although both permitted children under the age of twelve for males and fifteen for females to remain enslaved. Individual towns imposed their own temporary restrictions on enslavement. In March 1675, the inhabitants of Portsmouth, Rhode Island, banned the introduction of any new Indian slaves and servants into their community; Providence authorities did the same, briefly, in 1676. The Rhode Island General Assembly forbade enslavement *except* for debt in March of 1676; captive Indians and any non-combatants who surrendered were to be treated instead as indentured servants and, ideally, sold out of the area. Other laws followed that prohibited the extension of existing Indian indentures past contracted limits, the contracting of new ones, and the exportation of Indians outside of the region without the approval of local magistrates. A few West Indian governments, notably Barbados and Jamaica, forbade the importation of Indian slaves from New England in 1676, a stance which if enforced might have removed a profitable outlet for potentially dangerous male captives.[14]

Confusion over the legal status of Indian captives further complicated the picture. In earlier conflicts, colonists had clashed with Indians whom they recognized as members of distinct sovereign nations. By the time of King Philip's War, through conquest and treaty, colonial governments—particularly the powerful Massachusetts Bay—had come to view the Indians of southern New England as subject peoples answerable to colonial governments, courts, and laws.

Colonial declarations of war in 1675–76 placed orders to enslave captives in the context of a just, defensive war against a foreign aggressor, but they also accused the Indians of having "rebelled and revolted from their obediences"—in other words, of committing treason.[15] The charge of treason had consequences, since "rebel" Indians did not enjoy the legal immunity that soldiers in a sovereign army did, and could be punished for the civil crimes of treason, assault, and murder.[16] Indeed, field commanders, war councils, and, later, local courts executed some male captives on these grounds. But, for most captives the outcome was the same regardless of whether they were charged with murder, treason, or waging an unjust war, because the colonists justified enslavement or servitude as a lesser penalty for those guilty of a capital crime.

Identifying legitimate targets for enslavement remained complicated, however, given the blurred lines between friend and foe. Wartime hysteria led the United Colonies to intern many Christian Indians in camps on Deer Island and Long Island, ostensibly for their protection as well as for the colonists' security. Nonetheless, kidnappers raided the internment camps and Massachusetts authorized several individuals to forcibly draft Indian labor from these sites. Even families of those Indians who fought alongside English forces were vulnerable to capture and sale in the absence of male relatives. Three years after the war's end, relatives of John Sassamon, the pro-English Indian interpreter whose supposed murder by King Philip had sparked the conflict, were still seeking to free Sassamon's own sister from servitude. Shifting alliances during the war, divisions within tribes, and the English commanders' practice of drafting captured Indians into colonial military service created additional confusion. Were Indians (and their families) who had doubtless killed Englishmen before changing sides subject to punishment or sale?

Ironically, the Indians' very loss of autonomy put them in a position to challenge enslavement. The United Colonies' legal hegemony was a double-edged sword; as subjects or tributaries, the Indians had recourse to some of the privileges of citizenship—notably the petition and the courts. Unlike their counterparts earlier in the century, after 1675 captives and their relatives effectively used petitions, lawsuits, and other strategies to protest wrongful enslavement and to redeem some of its victims. Massachusetts indicted two men in November of 1675 under the manstealing law "for kidnapping Indians and selling them as slaves at Fyal," and sent agents to redeem some native captives who had been seized by Massachusetts trader Captain Richard Waldron in 1677 and shipped to the Azores.[7]

The most significant legislation passed during the war in 1675–76 in regard to Indian slavery was Rhode Island's outright ban. It provided only the barest protections, however, since its sliding age scale permitted binding children for up to thirty years—effectively a lifetime, given death rates for Indians. Most of the other prohibitory laws regarding Indian slavery were short-lived, unenforceable, and apparently had little effect on the movement of Indian slaves and servants. The Plymouth laws against keeping Indian slaves and servants did not prohibit exporting them, for example. In fact, once the immediate danger of war had subsided in a particular area, individuals and communities immediately protested the restrictions and sought exemption from the new laws on the grounds that removing the Indians would cause severe economic hardship. The same Rhode Island towns that earlier had banned the presence of bound Indians within their borders were holding public auctions of captives and distributing the profits at town meetings by the summer and autumn of 1676. Roger Williams himself presided over such a "Distribucion" in Providence in October of that year.[18] The legislation issuing from destination ports in the Caribbean appears to have been temporary and symbolic as well, and exporters found other receptive markets in the Atlantic Islands, Europe, and the Mediterranean. Still, King Philip's War had transformed the Indians of southern New England into subjects, and the cessation of conflict meant that ongoing enslavement of local Indians had ended.

Despite these changes, native slavery and involuntary servitude persisted and even flourished in the eighteenth century. Initially, New Englanders evaded the new barriers to enslaving local Indians by importing natives from outside the region. Tribes in northern New England—and the Indians from southern New England who took refuge with them—remained quasi-sovereign, independent entities. Continuing warfare on the eastern frontier even after Philip's death in August of 1676 meant that enslavement of prisoners of war and of non-combatant refugees continued in the upper Connecticut River valley, Maine, northern Massachusetts, and Lower Canada well into the early 1700s. In a single action, for example, Richard Waldron kidnapped approximately 200 Wampanoags and Pennacooks who had come to his Maine outpost under a flag of truce and offers of amnesty.[19] Massachusetts passed several acts at the onset of King William's War in 1689, in 1694, and again in 1704–1707 that used the taking and selling of Indian captives—especially women and children—as a means of recruiting and paying troops.[20]

Similarly, from the beginnings of settlement in the early 1670s English settlers in the Carolinas had been enslaving local Indians there. The desire for captives formed at least part of the motivation behind the wars against the Westos in 1680, the Yaddos in 1704, and the Yamasees in 1715. These conflicts, augmented by chronic English slaving raids on Indian missions in Spanish Florida, fed an exploding Indian slave trade in Charleston, one that exported captives throughout the British empire—including to New England.[21]

The trade eventually attracted government attention and regulation. The rapid influx of so-called "Eastern," "Spanish," and

"Carolina" Indians (whom New Englanders perceived as more war-like and less acculturated than the local Native Americans) began to worry authorities in the eighteenth century. As part of a 1709 law entitled "An Act to Encourage the Importation of White Servants," the Massachusetts General Court subjected the Indian slave trade to the same taxes as the trade in enslaved Africans. Later that year, authorities added a requirement that importers provide some proof that Indians had been legally enslaved in the plantation that exported them. Rhode Island passed similar laws, but the taxes apparently failed to discourage importers, because both assemblies eventually mandated the immediate re-exportation of any Eastern, Spanish, and Carolina Indians brought into the area on pain of a 50£ fine. The Rhode Island re-export law cited the "divers conspiracies, insurrections, rapes, thefts and other execrable crimes, [which] have been lately perpetrated . . . by Indian slaves" from other regions as a reason for ordering the new restrictions. Both colonies granted numerous exemptions to individual owners permitting them to keep their "Carolina Indians," however, and other importers simply ignored the law.[22] Newspaper advertisements from the decade after the 1712 law went into effect indicate that Carolina and Spanish Indians continued to be bought and sold in Boston through the early 1720s, in numbers comparable to Africans.

Moreover, colonists interested in controlling the labor of local Indians but barred in the absence of war from enslaving them outright could draw on another seventeenth-century precedent: the court-sanctioned sentencing of Native Americans to long periods of involuntary servitude. The sale of Indians for debt or in restitution for criminal penalties and legal fees, the legal and illegal extension of indentures, and the forcible apprenticeship of children all became even more prevalent after King Philip's War. A number of legal changes facilitated this turn to what I call "judicial enslavement."[23]

Daniel Mandell, Jean O'Brien, and other historians have ably described the radically changed world that the native inhabitants of southern New England faced in the late 1600s. In a series of moves that resembled the Spanish policy of *reconcentracion*, Massachusetts forcibly resettled most of the war-decimated "friend" Indians (except those already bound into labor) into designated enclaves—four towns in the seventeenth century, and four more after Massachusetts annexed Plymouth and Martha's Vineyard in 1691.[24] Rhode Island and Connecticut did not conduct a resettlement on this scale, but both colonies drew sharp boundaries between white settlements and the now shrunken Indian town and tribal land claims, essentially creating reservations in the Narragansett country and Sakonnet in Rhode Island and in southeastern and northern Connecticut. Still, with the growth of the English population and the expansion of settlement, white and Indian propinquity was a fact of life in provincial New England.

New England Indians continued to pursue traditional subsistence economies well into the eighteenth century, but their already decimated land resources declined steadily through sale and appropriation. The dwindling land base meant that natives depended on English markets and storekeepers for a variety of necessities: food, clothing, medical care. Some Indians resisted resettlement and continued to live in or near English towns, where they worked as day laborers or servants. Such individuals occupied a precarious position both economically and politically, however, since they lacked even the minimal protections that tribal membership afforded.

Meanwhile, proximity to white settlers increased the potential for charges of trespass, destruction of property by livestock, contention over the ownership of resources or goods, damages, assault, and other encounters. As a result, Indians began to appear more frequently before colonial courts immediately following King Philip's War, and this pattern continued throughout the eighteenth century. Many defendants now lacked the resources to pay their fines and debts, while many of the sachem-patrons who had protected Indians in New England courts in earlier generations had died or lost influence. This left Indian defendants in civil and criminal cases vulnerable to being sentenced to long terms of involuntary servitude.

Legal changes that ostensibly had nothing to do with native affairs made the situation worse. Between 1670 and 1700, all the New England colonies passed legislation that increased the damages defendants could claim in cases of theft to double or triple the value of the goods stolen, plus restitution. (The Plymouth law was an exception in that it singled out Indians for a harsher four-fold restitution penalty.) Courts also charged progressively higher legal fees and costs by the eighteenth century, which were folded into the defendants' fines and thus could translate into longer terms for Indians sold into service. Martha's Vineyard's 1672 legal code included a provision aimed at protecting the island's inhabitants from the evils of debtors' prison—but the law provided that in lieu of internment the debtor's "Person shall be sold for Satisfaction."

In some areas the shift to judicial enslavement was gradual, while in others it was dramatic. Of the twenty-two Indians convicted of trespass, theft, or assault in Martha's Vineyard between 1675 and 1687, only two received sentences involving servitude—one of twelve days, one of two years.[25] In January 1688 alone, however, the Dukes County Court convicted thirteen Indians of "killing Cattle and Shepe," or "Eatting of mottin [mutton] that was stolen"; each judgment included a rider providing that if the defendant failed to pay the fines and costs assessed, he or she should be sold into service for periods ranging from three months to seven years. Those who received sentences of over two years could be sold "in any part of ye kings dominyons."[26] This language became typical of sentences for Indian defendants in succeeding cases. The court bound eight more Indians to terms of six months to thirty years in 1689–90 for offenses that included stealing a handkerchief. Sometimes victorious plaintiffs assumed control of the Indians' labor, as in the case of Mathew Mayhew, who sold two Indians convicted of stealing about 8£ in money from him in 1693 to a buyer in Southold, Long Island, for seven-year terms.[27] Other plaintiffs chose to receive their restitution in cash, so Martha's Vineyard instituted a regular public "Vandue," or auction, of Indian convicts.

We know the fate of these Martha's Vineyard Indians because they enjoyed the right to jury trials at the quarterly Sessions Court there. In other parts of New England, Indians accused of debt or petty crime might never come before a jury. As part of the postwar reorganization of Indian communities, Massachusetts and, later, Rhode Island and Connecticut created a multi-tiered system of adjudication for cases involving reservation Indians. Massachusetts officials accepted the authority of Indian-run "courts" for mediation of disputes within a tribe or community, although Indian plaintiffs sometimes chose to appeal these verdicts or to bypass the Indian courts and resolve their differences in English courts. In criminal cases, or any civil case involving a white plaintiff or defendant, however, Indians had to appear before white authorities. In establishing Indian towns or reservations, colonial governments appointed Justices of the Peace— sometimes called "overseers," "guardians," or "trustees"—to supervise legal affairs. In counties near reservations the justices held court, took evidence, rendered decisions, and decided whether cases were serious enough to merit hearings in Superior Court or courts of Oyer and Terminer. This process meant that many petty civil and criminal cases involving Indians never went to juries, except on appeal.[28]

Unlike Sessions or Common Pleas court records, in many instances the Justices' Court papers were considered the private property of the men who held the office, so few of these records survive, making it difficult to determine how many Indians these officials sentenced to servitude. Some of the justices, such as Benjamin Church of Sakonnet, were sincere advocates for Native Americans. Although Church operated an *encomienda*-like estate, with numerous native dependents whom he expected to supply day labor and to follow him into war when the colony called, he also bitterly protested the mistreatment of Indians at the hands of local whites. Other justices evidently abused their authority. William Woddell and Thomas Thornton of Rhode Island were among several who appeared frequently as signatories on Indian indentures and bills of sale. Woddell clearly operated an Indian servant and slave clearinghouse, and Thornton's activities in illegally binding Indians to labor became so outrageous that several whites in Portsmouth petitioned the Assembly at Newport to intervene.[29] Despite the paucity of records from the Justices' Courts, however, evidence from Superior Courts and Courts of Common Pleas throughout New England indicates that Indians received sentences of servitude for non-capital crimes. For example, the Newport Supreme Court condemned at least fifteen Indian men, women, and children to terms of service between 1704 and 1725.[30]

Meanwhile, other New England natives, though technically free and not defendants at court, were becoming enmeshed in cycles of dependence with merchants, local landowners, and ships' captains that could lead to long-term servitude. Critics charged that many colonists intentionally encouraged Indians to pledge their credit for food, liquor, or funeral costs. Once in debt, it was almost impossible for Native Americans to clear their commitments. In some cases, these relationships resembled the kinds of relatively benign ongoing book-debt relations that many white New Englanders maintained with neighbors and storekeepers, with constant exchanges and credits for goods and labor that the Indians provided. In other cases, however, unscrupulous creditors coerced Indian debtors to contract their own labor or the labor of their children for terms of months and years. Daniel Vickers notes that whaling vessels operating out of Cape Cod, Martha's Vineyard, and Nantucket relied heavily on Indian labor, and he estimates that by the mid-1730s nearly three-quarters of the Indian whalemen of Nantucket turned over their entire earnings to white masters after every voyage.[31]

Both the ongoing enslavement of Indians from outside New England and the trend towards judicial enslavement met with opposition in the quarter-century after King Philip's War. Among the severest critics were the members of the King's Council and the Board of Trade, who asserted an even greater voice in colonial Indian policy after the new Massachusetts charter went into effect in 1692. For strategic reasons imperial policy dictated an anti-enslavement stance with regards to New England and Canadian Indians. The King's Commissioners for Plantations noted the prevalence of debt peonage and the Indians' loss of land when it sternly censured the Massachusetts General Court in 1701 for its "averseness . . . to establish laws" for the relief of its Native American subjects.[32]

These concerns for Indian welfare took on a new urgency once New England's northern frontier became a regular theater of war between England and France from 1689 onwards. Provincial officials, such as Lieutenant Governor Robert Treat of Connecticut, worried that enslavement threatened to drive the Eastern Indians into the arms of the French.[33] Indeed, the French used native fears of enslavement by the English to recruit Indian allies and contrasted their own behavior with that of the English. This was disingenuous, since French colonizers trafficked in Indian slaves in Louisiana, while authorities in French Canada permitted the enslavement of western "outsider" Indians captured in war, such as the Pawnees. Nevertheless, during the 1690s and early 1700s French leaders in

# The Changing Nature of Indian Slavery

Quebec vociferously protested enslavement as a violation of the rules of war, and threatened to retain English prisoners if New Englanders refused to abide by the rules of prisoner exchange and return Indians loyal to the French.[34] Native groups in northern New England and eastern Canada could make good on these threats. They represented a serious military challenge in the eighteenth century (in contrast to the Indians of southern New England), and they took white captives in retaliation for enslavement, as hostages, or merely for ransom.

Moreover, English military commanders and at least some provincial officials expressed concern that enslavement would hamper their efforts to recruit Indian soldiers at a time when such auxiliaries were becoming more crucial than ever.[35] During King Philip's War, New England Indians became integrated into provincial forces in unprecedented ways. After the war, colonial governments formally recruited Indians with special skills to augment English forces on the eastern frontier and in Canada. In the eighteenth century Indians typically composed 20% of the recruits mobilized by Connecticut, Massachusetts, and Rhode Island for wartime service. The King's Council recognized such interests when in 1749 and again in 1750 it ordered Massachusetts to release "all Abenakis Indian prisoners, and all slaves taken . . . in the late war."[36]

The Indians themselves also actively protested judicial enslavement. Simon Popmoney, George Wapock, and other Mashpee Indian leaders petitioned the Massachusetts General Court in 1700, complaining that "Thro Ignorance of the Law, weaknes, foolishnes, & Inconsideration some of us that are Elder, & severall of our Children have run in to the English mens Debts, and not being able, nor perhaps careful to pay att the time appointed; our Self & our poor Children, are frequently made Servants for an unreasonable time." The petitioners delicately accused white plaintiffs of abusing debt proceedings to control Indian labor.[37] In the end, Massachusetts

123

adapted the Indians' suggestions for amelioration in an "Act for Preventing Abuses to the Indians" passed later that year. The law acknowledged "the Executions and oppression which some of the English exercise towards the indians by drawing them to consent to covenant or bind themselves or Children apprentices or Servants for an unreasonable term on pretence of or to make Satisfaction for some small debt contracted or damage done to them."[38] Each indenture would now require the approbation of two or more Justices of the Peace, who were to review the contracts and ensure that they followed proper form. Contracts were to be finite in term, specific about the master's obligations, and signed by the Indian in question. Indians already bound into suspect indentures could petition local justices to review their cases.

English authorities applauded the move; yet, this law and others like it subsequently adopted in Connecticut and Rhode Island seem to have had little impact on the reality of judicial enslavement. The sentencing of Indians to servitude for debt and criminal activity continued unabated. The colonies passed more legislation in the 1720s and 1730s; finally the General Court forbade extending credit to Indians or bringing suit against Indians for any debt above ten shillings. The efficacy of laws against the illegal extension of indentures depended on the integrity of the justices who were supposed to enforce them and officials' personal interest in Indian labor, both of which varied.

Once indentured, Indians could find themselves bought and sold, separated from their families and taken from the region. Running away, stealing from one's master, and a host of other violations could double or triple the length of a servant's time obligation. Under such conditions, an indentured servant—especially a woman or a child— could easily become a de-facto slave. One example is that of "Ben," a Rhode Island Indian who petitioned the Pennsylvania Assembly in

1693. Around the time of King Philip's War, Ben had been made "in his Infancy a Servant unto William Coddington," a powerful Rhode Island planter. When Coddington died, his widow remarried and with her new husband (now Ben's owner), Robert Eaves, took Ben to Pennsylvania. In the process, Ben's position changed from that of a servant with a finite, specified term to that of a servant with an indeterminate life sentence—a slave. He requested either his freedom or a legal contract specifying his remaining obligation. Ben's case was by no means unique, as other litigation over the extension of indentures and the sale of servants into conditions of slavery attested. Another servant, Sarah Chauqum of Rhode Island, confronted a similar situation in 1733, when her master sold her as a slave to Edward Robinson of New London, Connecticut. Sarah won her freedom by establishing her Indian ancestry to the court's satisfaction—her mother resided in the Narragansett Indian reservation town of South Kingstown.[39]

One of the things that distinguished chattel slavery from servitude was its heritability. In the case of Indian indentured servants, however, it is difficult to determine the extent to which children automatically followed in their parents' footsteps. Scattered evidence suggests that at least some did. A servant named Alice on Martha's Vineyard and her master Samuel Norton appeared before local justices in 1695, locked in a dispute over the ownership of her child. In the end, Alice had to pay her master thirty shillings "in relation to her not allowing him to keep her child"; in effect, she had to purchase her own child's freedom, presumably through additional months or years of service.[40] Eighteenth-century probate inventories and advertisements for the sale of servants and slaves sometimes listed Indian women and their children together—indirect evidence that those children shared the status of their mothers. Occasionally, wills revealed the assumption that Indians were slaves for life, as in the case of Daniel

Coggeshall of Kingstown, Rhode Island, who left "my Indian woman and her sucking child Jeffery" to his wife and children "during the term of their natural lives." And whereas probate administrators and newspaper advertisements often noted the time remaining on the contracts of white servants, they omitted such information in entries for Indians.[41]

At a minimum such children probably served as forced "apprentices" until adulthood. Indentures of Indian children increasingly differed from those of their white counterparts over the course of the eighteenth century. Typically, Indian contracts began to omit the masters' obligations and lacked some of the usual provisions regarding training for a trade and education. Fewer parents appeared as signatories; instead, local justices commonly bound out such children, and parents' presence or absence as advocates for their children could be crucial in determining indenture provisions. The death of a parent might mean slippage into enslavement. In 1723 David Green of Jamestown, Rhode Island, bound "Hannah being a Girl half Indian and Half Negro" as an indentured servant to another master when her mother, his servant, died. Hannah was one and a half. The indenture refers to her as a "servant or slave," but tellingly, her indented master George Mumford was to return Hannah to Green upon completion of the indenture twenty years later, which suggests that Green planned to claim her labor for life.[42]

During this same period, the New England colonies were defining the legal parameters of the institution of slavery in ways that had enormous consequences for Indian servants. Between 1685 and 1720, colonial governments passed a spate of legislation regarding people of color analogous to the slave codes of Barbados, Virginia, and other slave societies. The New England laws specifically included Indian slaves and servants in their strictures, however, and in so doing they delimited a race frontier that separated whites from Africans *and*

Indians. Passed piecemeal by both localities and colonial legislatures, the laws ranged from anti-miscegenation restrictions to urban curfews for "Indian, negro, or mulatto servants and slaves" in Boston and other cities. New England officials also created separate penalties and processes, including summary courts—i.e. courts without juries—for "Indians, negroes, mulattoes, slaves or others" who stole or disposed of stolen goods. Blacks and Indians seem to have received harsher punishments than whites for identical crimes in the eighteenth centu- ry—for example, whippings *and* fines, rather than one or the other. And, as judicial enslavement became more common in cases involving Indians and Africans, it became less common for whites. Courts in all three colonies condemned a handful of white defendants—usually servants and often identifiable as Irish or members of "outsider" groups—to servitude in the eighteenth century, but cases involving Indians far outnumbered these scattered examples.

Even more ominous for bound native laborers, between 1696 and 1716 Massachusetts shifted the tax status of both Indian and black servants and slaves from that of persons subject to the regular poll tax—a category that included white servants—to that of personal property. These laws represented a conscious departure from a poli- cy that only a few years before had required Indian servants to pay a poll tax just as white servants did. Now, Indians and blacks were lit- erally to be "Rated with horses and Hogs."[43] Kathleen Brown and Peter Wood point to similar shifts in the tax status of Africans as crucial markers in the establishment of chattel slavery in Virginia and the Carolinas.[44]

Eventually these racialized laws had their own circular effect, espe- cially as the number of African slaves in New England increased in the eighteenth century. Color became associated with slavery, and slavery with color; in the process the very "Indianness" of many Native American servants came under attack. If one were a slave, then one must perforce be black. Court documents fostered ethnic slippage by designating Indian servants as mixed-race or black, often over their objections.[45] Racial designations had enormous significance, as the case of Sarah Chauqum illustrates. Enslaving Indians in Rhode Island was technically illegal, but her master had listed her as a "mollato" in the bill of sale to Edward Robinson. Sarah won her freedom by asserting her Narragansett Indian identity, but not all Indians were able to avoid passing from servitude into slavery.

Moreover, by the 1720s some New England Indians and their offspring *were* mixed-race, and this trend would only increase during succeeding decades. The demographic catastrophes wrought by war and enslavement left many tribes facing extremely skewed sex ratios, so Indian women found partners among free, servant, and enslaved African populations. Generally, children of such unions self-identified as Indians, but a mixed-race heritage made servants vulnerable to enslavement. Even choosing a black partner could have serious ramifications, as in the case of Patience Boston, an Indian servant from Cape Cod. Bound into "apprenticeship" to a white household by her father at age three, Patience was a self-described "mischievous and rebellious servant." She completed her term of service at age twenty-one, "happy that I had no Body to Command me." But, when she married an African servant or slave (the precise status of her husband, a whaleman, is unclear) she became "bound for life" to her husband's master.[46]

☆ ☆ ☆

Historians have long considered King Philip's War a turning point in Euro-Indian relations in New England; certainly it proved crucial to the evolution of Indian slavery and servitude. The war killed from ten to twenty-five percent of the native population, made possible the direct enslavement of many hundreds, perhaps thousands of Indians, and severely restricted the economic base of those who survived. At the same time, by bringing the remaining native population under the more or less direct administration of colonial governments, it transformed local Indians into subjects protected by law from some of the worst abuses of enslavement thereafter. Indeed, the outright enslavement of local Indians, debt peonage, and other private means of binding Indian labor were specifically banned in the New England colonies. Yet, such legal changes failed to prevent the continuing enslavement of Native Americans. In adjusting to this new world of postwar Indian relations, the colonists first turned to sources outside the region for a steady supply of Indian slaves. By the early eighteenth century, however, white New Englanders had found new vehicles—legislation and the courts—through which to control the labor of many local Indians.

The effects of these shifts were profound. By the mid-eighteenth century, bound Indian workers could be found throughout the region; they became especially concentrated in cities such as Boston, Providence, and New London, as well as the countryside of Narragansett, Cape Cod and Plymouth, Martha's Vineyard, southeastern Connecticut, Nantucket, and Maine. Not all Indians became slaves or involuntary servants; some farmed common lands, raised livestock, hunted, traded, worked as day laborers, contracted their own labor as whalemen, or produced finished goods for sale. Yet the first reliable census of a New England colony, the Rhode Island census of 1774, attests to the prevalence of Indian servitude on the eve of Revolution. At that time, 35.5% of all Indians in Rhode Island lived with white families; the proportion grows to over 50% if one excludes free Indians living in the largest Indian town, Charlestown.[47] Black and Indian workers helped construct the New England economy. Their significant presence also prompted the construction of racialized codes that put New England on common ground with the plantation societies of the south and the Caribbean.

# Notes

1.   See, for example, the essays in the special volume "Constructing Race," *William and Mary Quarterly* 54 (1997).

2.   David Eltis, "Europeans and the Rise and Fall of African Slavery," *American Historical Review* 98 (1993): 1399-1423, 1402 and n. 10; Gary Nash, *Red, White and Black: The Peoples of Early North America* (1974; repr. Englewood, N.J., 1992), 131-39. Almon Lauber's 1913 book, *Indian Slavery in Colonial Times within the Present Limits of the United States,* is the standard monograph on Indian slavery in North America, but regional studies by a number of scholars are now redirecting our attention to the magnitude and effects of enslavement on Amerindian and Euro-American societies. See Peter H. Wood, "Indian Servitude in the Southeast," Wilcomb H. Washburn, ed., *Handbook of North American Indians, Vol. 4: History of Indian-White Relations* (Washington, D.C., 1988); Daniel H. Usner, *Indians, Settlers, and Slaves in a Frontier Exchange Economy: The Lower Mississippi Valley Before 1783* (Chapel Hill, 1992); Alan Gallay, *The Indian Slave Trade: The Rise of the English Empire in the American South, 1670–1717* (New Haven, 2002); and two papers presented at the Seventh Annual Conference of the Omohundro Institute of Early American History and Culture in Glasgow, Scotland, July 2001: Juliana Barr, "A Trade in Women: An Indian Slave Market in the Eighteenth-Century Texas-Louisiana Borderlands," and Brett Rushforth, "Savage Bonds: Panis Slavery in Eighteenth-Century New France." Russell M. Magnaghi's *Indian Slavery, Labor, Evangelization, and Captivity in the Americas: An Annotated Bibliography* (Lanham, Md., 1998) offers a guide to some of the more recent literature.

3.  For an in-depth study of the history of Indian slavery in New England, see Margaret Ellen Newell, *"The Drove of Adam's Degenerate Seed": Indian Slavery in Colonial New England* (Cornell University Press, forthcoming). One exception to the scholarly silence about Indian captivity in New England is Jill Lepore, *The Name of War: King Philip's War and the Origins of American Identity* (New York, 1998), in which the author reminds us that New Englanders enslaved many Native American captives following King Philip's War in 1675–76, although Lepore sees the phenomenon as a singular occurrence rather than as a feature of New England society and economy. Two works that acknowledge the ongoing exploitation of native labor in New England include John A. Sainsbury, "Indian Labor in Early Rhode Island," *New England Quarterly* 48 (1975): 378-93, and Joshua Micah Marshall, "A Melancholy People: Anglo-Indian Relations in Early Warwick, Rhode Island, 1642–1675," *New England Quarterly* 68 (1995): 402-28.

4.  Israel Stoughton to John Winthrop, [c. June 28, 1637]; John Winthrop to William Bradford, July 28, 1637, *Winthrop Papers*, ed. Allyn B. Forbes and Malcolm Freiberg, 6 vols. (Boston, 1927–), 3:435-36, 456-58.

5.  John Winthrop, *Winthrop's Journal: "History of New England"* ed. James K. Hosmer, 2 vols. (New York, 1908), 1:227.

6.  For a request that Winthrop send some Indians to labor in Bermuda's nascent "Shuger workes," see William Berkeley to John Winthrop, June 12 and 25, 1648. Emanuel Downing recommended that the New England colonies seek Indian captives in order to exchange them for enslaved Africans; Emanuel Downing to John Winthrop, [c. August 1645]. All in *Winthrop Papers*, 5:38, 229, 232.

7.  On Bermuda, see "Grievances of the People in Bermuda," October 1622, in Vernon A. Ives, ed., *Letters from Bermuda, 1615–1646: The Rich Papers* (Toronto, 1984), 237. For the transportation of prisoners of war during the English Revolution, see Barbara Donagan, personal

communication; and Stephen Innes, *Labor in a New Land: Economy and Society in Seventeenth-Century Springfield* (Princeton, 1983), 9-10.

8.  For the runaway Pequot girl, see Richard Morris to John Coggeshall [May 1647], in *Winthrop Papers,* 4:164-65; "Petition of the Inhabitants of Hingham to the Council," December 21, 1676, Miscellaneous Bound Photostats, Massachusetts Historical Society.

9.  Roger Williams to John Winthrop, July 31, 1637, in *Winthrop Papers,* 3:459.

10. *Records of the Colony of Rhode Island and Providence Plantations,* ed. John Russell Bartlett, 10 vols. (Providence, R.I., 1856–65), 1:414-15 (hereafter cited as R.I. Recs.)

11. *Records of the Colony of New Plymouth,* 12 vols. (Boston, 1856–61), 5:151-52 (hereafter cited as PCR); James P. Ronda, "Red and White at the Bench: Indians and the Law in Plymouth Colony, 1620–1691," *Essex Institute Historical Collections* 110 (1974): 211.

12. *Records of the Suffolk County Court, 1671–1680,* ed. David Konig, 2 vols., *Publications of the Colonial Society of Massachusetts,* vols. 29-30 (Boston, 1983), 1:89, 113, 258, 259, 521, 557; 2:869, 1015, 1016, 1157.

13. PCR 5:173-74.

14. *The Early Records of the Town of Portsmouth,* ed. Clarence S. Brigham (Providence, 1901), 187-88; Lepore, *Name of War,* 170.

15. PCR 5:173; Governor Leverett's Certificate, September 12, 1676.

16. For a similar argument, see James D. Drake, *King Philip's War: Civil War in New England, 1675–1676* (Amherst, Mass., 1999), 112-14.

17. See, for example, "Petition of William Ahaton," MA 30:176, 207a; "Petition of Waban, Samuel Tomputawin, and other Indians of Natick and Punkapaugh," MA 30:229, all in the Massachusetts State Archives, Boston; "Petition from Joseph and William Wannukkow," September 5, 1676 and "Petition from severall Indians belonginge to Naticke and Punkapaugo," [November 1676?], Miscellaneous Bound Photostats, Massachusetts Historical Society; "Indictment for kidnapping Indians," November 2, 1675, Miscellaneous Bound Documents, Massachusetts Historical Society; "Petition of Bernard Trott to the Governor, Councill and Assembly," MA 31:1, Massachusetts State Archives.

18. *The Early Records of the Town of Providence, Vol. 15, Being the Providence Town Papers, Vol. 1, 1639–April 1682* (Providence, 1899), 151-54.

19. See Colin Calloway, *The Western Abenakis of Vermont, 1600–1800* (Norman, Okla., 1990), 81.

20. *The Acts and Resolves, Public and Private, of the Province of the Massachusetts-Bay,* 21 vols. (Boston, 1869–1922), 1:176 (1695), 530 (September 1703), 558 (October 1704), 594 (August 1706), 600 (March 1707).

21. Nash, *Red, White and Black*, 131-33, 136-37; Gallay, *The Indian Slave Trade.*

22. *Massachusetts Acts and Resolves,* 1:634, 696; R.I. Recs., 3:482-83, January 4, 1703/4; "An Act for preventing clandestine importations and exportations of passengers, or negroes, or Indian slaves into or out of this colony," February 27, 1711/12 session of the General Assembly, R.I. Recs., 4:131; "An Act for prohibiting the importation, or bringing into this colony any Indian servants or slaves," July 1715, R.I. Recs., 4:193.

23. Daniel Vickers has also used this term, although he focuses on debt peonage. See Vickers, "The First Indian Whalemen of Nantucket," *William and Mary Quarterly* 40 (1983): 560-83.

24. Daniel Mandell, *Behind the Frontier: Indians in Eighteenth-Century Eastern Massachusetts* (Lincoln, Neb., 1996), 29; Jean M. O'Brien, *Dispossession by Degrees: Indian Land and Identity in Natick, Massachusetts, 1650–1790* (New York, 1998), 65-71; Order in Council, March 19, 1689/90.

25. *William Southmound v. "Sassimmin an Indian"*; *Joseph Daggett v. Zackery Wonbosoott*, May 26, 1685, Dukes County Court Records, Quarterly Court of Sessions, vol. 1, 1675–1716, Dukes County Court House, Edgartown, Massachusetts.

26. "Spetiall Court at Edgartown January ye 14th 87/8," Dukes County Court Records, Quarterly Court of Sessions, vol. 1.

27. "Declaration against James Covell and Keoiape [Keipe] two indian youths," September 11, 1693, Dukes County Court Records, Quarterly Court of Sessions, vol. 1; Charles Banks, "unpublished notes re: Indian slavery," Banks Manuscripts, Box 174a, Folder 24, Martha's Vineyard Historical Society.

28. See Ronda, "Red and White at the Bench," 200-15, 214; Yasuhide Kawashima, "Jurisdiction of the Colonial Courts over the Indians in Massachusetts, 1689–1763," *New England Quarterly* 42 (1969): 532-50, 542-44.

29. "Petition for release of Grigory an Indian from indenture," October 1732, Petitions to the Rhode Island General Assembly, vol. 2, 1728–1733, item 69, Rhode Island State Archives, Providence.

30. *Rhode Island General Court of Trials, 1671–1730*, transcr. Jane Fletcher Fiske (Boxford, Mass., 1998), 221; Supreme Court of Newport, 1671–1724 [Newport Court Book A], mss., Rhode Island Judicial Records Center, Pawtucket, R.I.

31. Daniel Vickers, "The First Whalemen of Nantucket," in Colin Calloway, ed., *After King Philip's War: Presence and Persistence in Indian New England* (Hanover, N.H., 1997), 90-113, 105-6.

32. See Commissions for Plantations to Lord Bellomont, April 29, 1701, MA 40:689; also MA 47:227; 5:496; 31:692-93.

33. MA 2:210, 210a, Treat to Governor Bradstreet, July 31, 1689.

34. See MA 2:557, letters from D'Iberville and Villebon regarding Kennebec and Penobscot captives in Boston, 1696.

35. For more on Native American soldiers, see Richard R. Johnson, "The Search for a Usable Indian: An Aspect of the Defense of Colonial New England," *Journal of American History* 64 (1977): 623-51.

36. MA 5:496, 31:692-93.

37. "Petition to the Governor of Massachusetts from Simon Popmoney . . . on behalf of their neighbors asking to protect the Younger Indians," MA 30:456.

38. MA 30:460.

39. *Sarah [Chauqum] v. Robinson*, September 1724, Newport Supreme Court Record Book, vol. B, 1725–1741, and Washington, South Kingstown Justices' Court, July 1733 prosecution bond, Rhode Island Judicial Records Center. In earlier documents Sarah appears as "Sarah Mollatto."

40. "Meeting of the Justices, November 2, 1694," Dukes County Court House.

41. Sainsbury, "Indian Labor in Early Rhode Island," 386; Jane Fletcher Fiske, *Gleanings from Newport Court Files, 1659-1783* (Boxford, Mass., 1999), no. 658; *Boston News-Letter*, March 3-10, 1718.

42. Indenture, December 10, 1723 in the Shepley Papers, vol. 15, document 19, Rhode Island Historical Society, Providence. For a detailed compar-

ative study of Rhode Island indentures across racial lines, see the article by Ruth Wallis Herndon and Ella Wilcox Sekatau in this volume.

43. *Massachusetts Acts and Resolves,* 1:214, 240, 278, 714; *The Diary of Samuel Sewall,* ed. M. Halsey Thomas, 2 vols. (New York, 1973), 2:822.

44. Kathleen Brown, *Goodwives, Nasty Wenches, and Anxious Patriarchs: Gender, Race and Power in Colonial Virginia* (Chapel Hill, 1996); Peter H. Wood, personal communication.

45. Ruth Wallis Herndon and Ella Wilcox Sekatau also note the increasing tendency of Rhode Island officials to designate Narragansett Indian people as Negro or black, although they locate the shift in the latter half of the eighteenth century, especially in the post-Revolutionary period. See their "The Right to a Name: The Narragansett People and Rhode Island Officials in the Revolutionary Era," in Colin Calloway, ed., *After King Philip's War: Presence and Persistence in Indian New England* (Hanover, N.H., 1997), 114-43.

46. Patience was sold and resold several times after being tried for infanticide and acquitted; she was finally convicted in 1738 of killing the grandchildren of her then master, a minister in Falmouth, Maine. See Samuel and Joseph Moody, *A Faithful Narrative of the Wicked Life and Remarkable Conversion of Patience Boston* (Boston, 1738), in Daniel A. Cohen, *Pillars of Salt, Monuments of Grace: New England Crime Literature and the Origins of American Popular Culture, 1674–1860* (New York, 1993), 72-74.

47. Sainsbury, "Indian Labor," 379, 392-93.

# Colonizing the Children:

## *Indian Youngsters in Servitude in Early Rhode Island*

RUTH WALLIS HERNDON AND ELLA WILCOX SEKATAU

THIS ESSAY DESCRIBES HOW INDIAN CHILDREN in early Rhode Island were colonized through the practice of "pauper apprenticeship," whereby Anglo-American officials took legal orphans and also children described as "poor," "bastard," and "suffering" away from their parents and bound them to more prosperous masters until the children reached adulthood. On the surface, this kind of indentured servitude remedied perceived problems of poverty, bastardy, desertion, and death by raising supposedly vulnerable children in households that Anglo-American authorities considered more "respectable." But at a deeper level, this coerced servitude, rooted in English poor law, effectively secured the labor of particular youngsters to serve the needs of the community in general and larger property owners in particular. The system also enabled local officials and "respectable" inhabitants to impose their ideal of family organization on others by removing children from "improper" situations and placing them in "proper" households, where they would be maintained during their youth and trained for adulthood in ways deemed appropriate for their race, sex, and class.

"Pauper apprenticeship" was a system akin to but distinct from three other types of bound labor: gradual emancipation apprenticeships (by which children born to slaves in Rhode Island after March 1, 1784, remained under the control of their mothers' masters until adulthood); private apprenticeships (by which many middling sort parents voluntarily placed their children with neighbors or relatives for skills training); and immigrant indentures (by which many European adults obtained passage to North America). In contrast to these other forms of bound labor, pauper apprenticeship was arranged by Anglo-American officials responsible for the poor of the community, and the whole system rested on these officials' perceptions of "disorder" in the families within their jurisdiction. These perceptions are revealed most clearly in the paper contracts (indentures) that describe the children's family situations and stipulate the terms of the master-servant relationships into which they were thrust.

Pauper apprenticeship contracts reveal a prejudicial attitude on the part of Anglo-American officials towards those described as other than white, and for this reason it is necessary to evaluate the records in the light of oral tradition generated by the people most affected by the system. Ruth Herndon's analysis rests on a study of 1,200 indentures written into the Rhode Island town records between 1660 and 1860. The statistics reported below are drawn from a core subset of this body of evidence—some 759 contracts from the period 1750–1800, when pauper apprenticeship was at its height.[1] Ella Sekatau's analysis rests on the oral tradition of the Narragansett tribe, for which she is ethnohistorian, genealogist, medicine woman, and language teacher. From earliest childhood, she was trained in Narragansett customs and history stretching back over centuries to the time prior to contact with European settlers. Throughout her life, she has been an observer, listener, and keeper of confidences for the people of her tribe. Now in her seventies, she embodies Narragansett oral tradition.

The archival record and oral tradition, examined together, indicate that in early Rhode Island, pauper apprenticeship immobilized Indian and African American children—especially girls—at what authorities deemed to be their appropriate "station" in life. Children of color were highly overrepresented in pauper apprenticeship, constituting some 25 percent of these young laborers at a time when all people of color probably constituted around 10 percent of the region's general population.[2] Further, Indian and African American boys were often bound out for longer terms than Anglo-American boys, while simultaneously receiving lesser training and eventual payment. Indian and African American girls were particularly disadvantaged—bound out at younger ages than boys, for longer terms than Anglo-American girls, and for fewer benefits in education, training, and payment than all other bound children. Narragansett oral tradition corroborates these statistics by showing that many Anglo-American farmers, shopkeepers, and other householders profited from the system by enjoying long years of practically free menial labor performed by Indian youngsters.

In the larger context of colonialism, pauper apprenticeship functioned as a primary means of English dominance over the Narragansett and other native people who remained behind the frontier of contact. This form of bondage enabled Anglo-Americans to enslave Indians without calling it "slavery." Indian adults resisted enslavement, which they considered an insult and a violation of the sacred gender division of community labor; oral tradition informs us that many native people refused to labor, despite flogging, or fled bondage, seeding migrations of Narragansett to the north and west.[3] Indian children, however, were more easily ensnared and indoctrinated. By sliding these youngsters into servitude at an early age, one gen-

eration after another, Anglo-Americans effectively maintained colonial race and gender hierarchies and continuously reinforced the colonized status of Indian people.

This essay pays special attention to children specifically designated as "Indian" or "mustee" in the documentary record, but also takes
into account children designated as "black," "mulatto," "Negro," or
"colored." As used by eighteenth- and nineteenth-century town officials as a whole, racial labels do not always accurately reveal the ancestry of people of color, but they do reveal record-keepers' attempts to
create a divide between "white" and "other." Racial designations were
employed ambiguously throughout the 1700s and 1800s, effectively
conflating Native American and African into one undifferentiated
other-than-white group in the Anglo-American records.[4] In 1757, for
example, the Providence clerk described a child named Santee as
"Indian" in one copy of the boy's indenture and "molatto" in another copy.[5] A Portsmouth clerk described an eight-year-old child as
"molatto" in the text of her indenture but as "Indian" in a marginal
reference, and a Westerly clerk described Jehu Quocco as "mustee"
but labeled his brother "a black boy."[6] Since officials routinely
blurred racial distinctions in this manner, and since some children did
have mixed ancestry, this study includes all children who appear in the
records as other than "white" in order to discover their distinctive
treatment and experience.

Arbitrary and ambiguous racial labeling underscores a fluid state
of race relations in southeastern New England (as elsewhere in
Anglo-America) in the latter part of the eighteenth century.[7]
Revolutionary fervor resulted in the more frequent voluntary manu-
mission of slaves, and the gradual emancipation legislation of the
1780s promised to direct a steady stream of free young people of
color into the general population beginning in the early 1800s.
Further, both oral tradition and the documentary record tell us that

free Indian people continued to move about the region during this era in order to obtain work and maintain kin connections, drawing the attention of officials whenever the expanding Anglo-American population was inconvenienced by Indian lifeways.[8] There was thus a growing awareness of people of color on the part of Anglo-American officials, who worked more energetically than ever to regulate the lives of those they considered not "white." Indentured servitude, in particular, offered a convenient way to bring children of color under the control of "respectable" people.

In 1730, the Rhode Island colonial legislature passed a law designed to prevent "evil-minded persons" from "draw[ing] Indians into their debt, by selling them goods, at extravagant rates." This law specifically forbade private indentures that bound Indians "for longer time than is just and reasonable"; it further mandated that all such contracts be approved by two justices of the peace or other public officials.[9] When this law was renewed and updated in 1783, the state legislature noted once again that "unjust advantages are frequently taken of the Indians of the Narragansett tribe within this state" by non-Indians, ensnaring them in debt.[10] No such law prevented the involuntary servitude of Indian children, however; in fact, Rhode Island law encouraged such practice, by characterizing these youngsters as "poor," "liable to become chargeable," or otherwise subject to the dictates of town authorities.

In a typical pauper apprenticeship contract enacted in 1767, South Kingstown officials bound four-year-old "Indian boy" John, "son to Rexom," to widow Ann Mumford. John was to live with and labor for widow Mumford for a term of twenty years, until "he shall arrive to ye age of twenty four years." Widow Mumford, by convention, would supply John with all the necessities of life as deemed appropriate for an Indian child, and at the end of his indenture, he was to receive from her "one new suit of apparel throughout, besides his usual clothing from head to foot.["]11 In another typical contract, this time from 1784, the Warwick town council ruled that three-year-old Lucy, a "molatto or mustee" daughter of "one Diadami Spywood," was "likely to become chargeable"—that is, likely to need poor relief. Declaring it to be "for the interest of the Town to bind out the child," the councilmen offered a cash premium to whomever would take an indenture of her. William Burton of the neighboring town of Cranston came forward and "offered to take said child for nine pounds lawful money and bring it up until it should be eighteen years old," a fifteen-year contract. During that time, Burton was obligated to "find and provide for said child sufficient meat, drink, washing, lodging and apparel suitable to its station and degree." He also agreed to "learn said apprentice to read (if capable of learning)," and to give to her, at the end of her contract, "one new suit of decent apparel."12

The essence of all servitude contracts lay in such mutual obligations between servant and master. In typical fashion, John and Lucy were bound to live with and labor for their master and mistress, obey them, keep the secrets of their business, and refrain from running away or getting married. Masters were always obligated to provide room, board, and clothing, and were sometimes charged with providing basic literacy education and training in a particular skill.

Girls constituted a minority of these child servants. Overall, two-thirds of the indentures were for boys, although girls and boys were nearly at parity in the general population, according to the 1782 census;13 this dichotomy holds for both Indian and non-Indian children bound out in pauper apprenticeship. This does not mean that girls labored any less than boys, only that female labor was less frequently secured in a contract, regulated by outside authority, and recompensed with freedom dues, as meager as they might be. The documentary record is dotted with instances of Indian and African American girls working for Anglo-American masters without an official indenture, and oral tradition informs us that Indian girls took on such menial service as a means to earn a few pennies.

Town leaders usually bound out a child in response to a "complaint" lodged by a "respectable" member of the community concerning perceived poverty or disorder in the child's family. In many cases of children of color, the complainant was a person in whose household the child had already been living, so that indenture formalized an existing relationship. For example, in 1755 Peter Talman asked the Tiverton council for an indenture of an unnamed "mullatto" girl who had been living with him "several years."[14] Similarly, David Larkin asked the Warwick council for an indenture of eleven-year-old "black boy" George Mew, who had "lived at his house ever since he was about three years of age."[15] These and other requests for indenture were presented in the record as appropriate recompense for the cost of raising the child—Peter Talman wanted "satisfaction" for his "charge & trouble" and David Larkin for his "considerable expence" prior to an official contract. When Peleg Babcock asked the South Kingstown councilmen for a formal indenture of Sip, a fourteen-year-old "mulatto" boy who had been living with him for some unspecified length of time, Babcock received rights to Sip's labor until he was twenty-one, a handsome profit for his having cared for the boy in his early years.[16] Oral tradition asserts that such contracts were less concerned with real payment for the supposed costs of a child's maintenance than they were an opportunity for masters to co-opt labor as compensation for losses and injuries they had sustained at the hands of other Indians.

Significantly, the archival records often fail to reveal the whole story of how an Indian or African American child came to be lodged in a would-be master's household; the reader is left with the impression that these youngsters were parentless. In fact, as oral tradition asserts, many of the Indian and African American children who appeared so desirable as pauper apprentices had been living in Anglo-American households because their mothers labored there as servants. A careful piecing together of the documentary record shows this to be the case with Rexom and her son John, mentioned above. In 1746, twenty-one years before John was bound to Widow Mumford, John's mother Rexom, then three years old, was bound to Mumford's then-living husband, William. Rexom's mother was identified as "a mustee woman commonly called and known by the name of Mary Perry who lives at the house of Mr. William Mumford."[17] The family history was this: Mary Perry, servant to William Mumford, gave birth to Rexom, who was indentured to Mumford; a generation later, Rexom, still in service to Mumford's widow, gave birth to John, who was then indentured to Widow Mumford. Children such as Rexom and John were not neglected or orphaned; their mothers bore and raised them while laboring as servants.

The patriarchal tone of the records disguises both this process by which Indian and African American children came to interest potential masters and the associated process by which all young indentured servants were nurtured and trained. While servants were technically under the official "government" of the master, they were under the daily care and management of women in the master's household. It is patently unbelievable, for example, that Dr. John Chace of Providence instructed "mulatto child" Betsey Richmond how to perform "common household business," as her indenture specified; it was most certainly Chace's wife, other female relatives, or female servants who did the actual "instruction."[18] In some cases, pauper apprenticeship contracts indicate that child servants were going to a master "and wife," and in some instances the wife was explicitly mentioned as essential to the success of the indenture. If a master's wife died, for example, young servants—especially female ones—would quickly be taken out of the home where there was no longer a "proper person" to raise them.[19]

In many cases, an Indian or African American woman serving in an Anglo-American household actually proved to be the "proper person" to raise young Indian and African American servants, to tend to the children's daily maintenance and practical instruction. Understanding this reality and in a position to know the inner dynamics of households in their neighborhood, Indian mothers sometimes actively selected places for their sons and daughters, putting them where they would best receive the necessities of life and other care. The official records represent these actions as instances of Indian women "leaving" their children, the wording suggestive of abandonment or neglect on the part of the mothers. But when read with a knowledge of oral tradition, these records instead indicate a shrewd and thoughtful oversight on the part of the mothers. For example, in 1757, Indian woman Moll Pero "left" her five-year-old son in Joseph Underwood's household. Five years later, Underwood appealed to the Jamestown councilmen to give him an indenture of the boy, since the mother "though often called upon still refuses to bind him." In all likelihood, Pero had found a way to ensure the competent care of her son in a nearby household, probably one in which she labored periodically, without having to sign a formal indenture until absolutely necessary.[20]

A related family strategy of Indian mothers was to place two siblings together in the care of one master. For example, Dan Weeden asked the Jamestown councilmen to bind to him two Indian children, a four-year-old boy and a fifteen-year-old girl, whose mother, the Indian woman Betty Jack, had "left" them with him "for a maintenance" for the previous six months. Weeden viewed the indenture as "satisfaction" for the "extraordinary trouble" of feeding and clothing the children for six months; in fact, he probably had been well recompensed by the fifteen-year-old girl's labor during that time. In any case, Betty Jack apparently viewed the indenture as a way of making sure her daughter and son lived together in a household of her own choosing.[21] Similarly, "Indian" brothers Cesar and Jemmy (sons of Indian woman Tabitha) and "mustee" siblings Harry and Sarah (children of Indian woman Betty) were placed together in South Kingstown; "Negro" children Simon and Patience (children of Cesar Talbury) were placed together in East Greenwich; and "black" children John and Isabel (children of Rosanna Brown) were placed together in Exeter.[22] This recurring pattern corroborates the evidence of oral tradition—that watchful Indian mothers, unable to care for their children independently, deliberately placed them in the best non-Indian household available.

Whether watchful mothers, potential masters, or concerned neighbors instigated the process, the indenture itself was arranged by town leaders, whose right to bind out poor children was derived specifically from Anglo-American poor law, adapted in each colony and state from English precedent.[23] Such laws encoded a communitarian understanding of patriarchy, in which town "fathers" preserved order by governing all members of their public "family." These "fathers" understood hierarchy to be essential to good community order, and they saw themselves as doing the right thing when they took children from situations they deemed "improper" and put them under "proper" authority in other households.

Thus a child was indentured when town leaders perceived it to be necessary, and in many cases, they explained their action as the solution to a problem caused by a particular circumstance in the child's birth family.[24] Illegitimate or "bastard" children accounted for roughly one-fifth (18 percent, or 134 cases) of the indentures. Another fifth (19 percent, or 143 cases) were identified as "orphans" because their fathers had died or had abandoned them, although their mothers still lived.[25] Another 16 percent (119 cases) were described simply as "poor" without further elaboration, probably indicating illness or disability on the part of one or both parents. Most significantly, one quarter of the children were identified only by racial designation rather than by family circumstances, showing that officials used the terms "Indian," "mustee," "mulatto," "black," and "Negro" as synonyms for "poor," or "bastard," or "orphan."

This racial explanation for indenture invites scrutiny. The elision of poverty and Indian-ness indicates that communitarian patriarchy was overlaid by a colonialist view of Indians as "savages" who had previously been conquered and subjugated and who now stood in need of oversight by Anglo-Americans. But there is more here. By substituting racial labels for cause of indenture, officials avoided the necessity of explaining a child's family situation. Where did these "Indian," "mustee," "black," "mulatto," and "Negro" children come from? Who were their mothers and fathers? As we have shown above, many of these children were born to mothers already in indentured servitude or other forms of bondage; indeed, some of these children were sons and daughters of their masters.

Significantly, clerks avoided using the terms "bastard" and "orphan" to explain indentures of children of color. Young servant Lucy Spywood was not identified as an orphan, even though the record suggests that her mother had died;[26] in fact, children of color were *never* designated as "orphans," even though many were bound out when one or both parents died. Both oral tradition and archival evidence indicate that children of color were often bound out during disease epidemics, when a parent or grandparent died or was disabled. When Indian man Peter Norton and wife Rose died of smallpox in 1776, their two sons Richmond and Peter were bound out; when former slave Patience Havens died of yellow fever, her granddaughter Sophia was bound out.[27] Another frequent cause for indenture was a father's death in military service. When Indians Samuel Quince and Peter Cobb died "in ye late expedition against Cape Breton," the

Westerly council bound out their children to local residents who asked for indentures of the youngsters.[28] When Indian man William Brushet died while serving "as a soldier against his Majesty's enemies" during the French-Indian war, his two younger siblings were bound out by East Greenwich authorities.[29]

Nor was Indian boy John (described above) identified as a "bastard," even though his mother Rexom was not married (according to Anglo-American criteria) when she bore him.[30] Violet, a "mustee" child bound out in Warwick, was similarly born to unmarried parents but never referred to as illegitimate or "bastard."[31] In fact, only six indentures (of 759) identify a servant as being *both* a "bastard" and a child of color. "Bastard" and "orphan" imply a specific legal relation between a child and its father. The absence of these terms may indicate that authorities could not verify the identity of the child's father, the marital status of the parents, or the existence of an estate, which a child needed to be a legal "orphan" in order to inherit.[32] But the absence of the terms also substantiates what oral tradition tells us about these situations—that town authorities knew quite well when the mother's master was the father of her child, and that respectable Anglo-Americans did not want to sully each other's reputations by documenting intimate associations with "bastard" children. By keeping such family relationships vague, officials gave themselves room to treat the children as part of the great servant pool, to bind them out as if they were children of unknown fathers.

Whatever the reasons for omitting a cause for indenture in the case of *particular* children, it is clear that officials *generally* skipped an explanation because they assumed a right to manage the lives of Indian and African American children. Rhode Island town leaders scrutinized the private lives of people of color—even those who had never been enslaved or who had long since been set free—with an eye to placing them under supervision. Some Indians avoided the intervention of town authorities for a considerable portion of their lives, because they converted to Christianity, or minded their own business and worked hard, or had no children to interest or concern Anglo-Americans. Indeed, many Indians lived out of sight of the Anglo-American community and came to notice only when an epidemic or other catastrophe drove them to a state of need and higher visibility. Rhode Islanders made repeated attempts to remedy their incomplete knowledge of the numbers and circumstances of the Indians living in their communities. Middletown voters, for example, decided that all free "Indians and mulattos" should be under the management of the overseers of the poor; and Providence councilmen similarly ruled that a "list" be compiled of "all transient white people in poor circumstances, as also of the blacks of all descriptions whatever dwelling in this town."[33] Further, a number of towns authorized periodic "round-ups" that brought all people of color before the authorities to be counted, questioned, intimidated, warned out and/or put to labor. The Tiverton council ordered all "black people" who did not "belong" to the town to leave within one month; if they did not, the overseers of the poor would "take them up and put them in a workhouse and keep them to labor."[34] The Providence council advertised at one point for interested persons to take indentures of "a number of black men, women, & children now here and others expected."[35] In this atmosphere of oversight, taking particular Indian children under official management in indenture required little explanation or justification.

By the latter half of the eighteenth century, putting children of color into indentures had become routine in Rhode Island communities. The general terms of these contracts were set by custom, if not by law, leaving only three details to be negotiated by officials and potential masters: the "premium" a master might receive for taking on the indenture; the skill and literacy training he would provide; and the "freedom dues" he would pay the servant at the end of the contract.

The premium was designed to close the gap between the cost of the child's upkeep and the value of the child's labor. Some 16 percent of the indentures (116 out of 759) involved some sort of premium, usually offered in cases of very young or slightly disabled Anglo-American children. (The older the child at the time of the indenture, the lower the premium, and most children over the age of six brought no such allotment.) Most masters of Indian and African American children did not receive premiums; instead, authorities compensated them by lengthening the child's indenture past the typical age of freedom.[36] Thus John, son of Rexom, was bound out to age twenty-four instead of the usual twenty-one, highlighting what seems a deliberate strategy to secure the labor of children of color for the extended use of the master, and pointing up the similarity between this kind of indenture and slavery.

Also under negotiation were the skill and literacy training the master was to provide. Training clauses varied with the race and sex of the child, indicating that officials matched the child and the training so as to preserve what seemed to them natural distinctions of class, race, and sex. Girls and children of color were at a distinct disadvantage. In about one-third of the Anglo-American boys' indentures (124 of 373 cases), literacy clauses were recorded, and they were for "reading, writing and cyphering" in 83 percent of the cases (103 of 124, or 83.1%). Only 13 percent (16 of 124) of the African American and Indian boys' indentures contained a literacy clause, and those clauses were far less likely to include writing and cyphering.[37] About one-fifth of the Anglo-American girls' contracts (37 of 199) contained literacy clauses; about half of those clauses (17, or 45.9%) required reading only, and about half (18, or 48.6%) required reading and writing only; only one contract included cyphering. Only 14 percent (9 of 63 cases) of the African American and Indian girls' indentures contained a literacy clause, and two-thirds, of those were for reading only.[38]

Skills training clauses appear in 22 percent of all indentures (167 out of 759), and once again Anglo-American boys were promised the most benefits and Indian and African American girls the fewest.[39] One-third (126 of 374, or 33.7%) of the contracts for Anglo-American boys stipulated skills training and bound the boys to enter a variety of trades. About 9 percent (11 of 124, or 8.8%) of the indentures for Indian and African American boys stipulated training. Although these contracts limited the boys to less lucrative skills, such as coopering and shoemaking, the children usually were trained only in general farming.[40] Thirteen percent (26 of 199, or 13.1%) of the contracts for Anglo-American girls stipulated training, as did 6 percent (4 of 63, or 6.3%) of the contracts for Indian and African American girls. When training was specified for Anglo-American girls, it was generally in "housewifery" or "spinning," though occasionally a girl was to learn to be a "tailoress."[41] Particular training, even in that vague occupation "household business," was only rarely specified for girls of color. In a few cases, an Indian or African American girl was bound to learn the work of a "spinster" or to do "general housework"; more blunt was the stipulation in the contract of Sophia Havens, daughter of a "black" woman, that obligated her to do the work of a "house servant."[42]

Oral tradition informs us that the denial of literacy and skills training to Indian children—girls in particular—was a deliberate strategy to secure the cooperation of these youngsters in their own servitude. Young laborers who were unable to read, write, do basic math, or earn a competent living at a valuable skill or trade were likely to be dependent people. They were unlikely to realize when they were being cheated, unlikely to protest their situations, and unlikely to make demands upon their masters. Thus masters tried to maintain a "class" of people prepared to perform the menial tasks that Anglo-Americans themselves did not want to do. The lesser training of certain children was suggestively codified in the 1798 revision of the Rhode Island poor law, which gave town officials power "to bind out by deed indented or poll, as apprentices to be instructed and employed in any lawful art, trade or mystery, *or as servants to be employed in any lawful work or labour,* any male or female children."[43] This clause effectively created two classes of indentured children— those being *educated* in a particular skill and those being *employed* as "servants." Given this law's passage in an era of voluntary manumissions and gradual emancipation, it seems likely that it was designed to create distinctions between Anglo-American children and children of color.[44]

In reality, oral tradition reveals, most Indian children were learning traditional native skills along with their "white" training; they were not completely cut off from Indian ceremony and celebration, even if they lived in Anglo-American households, and they were frequently coached by older Indian domestic servants and day laborers. Nor were they as ignorant of "white" skills as their masters might have thought. Some became literate despite the master's neglect of this formal training. Some also developed skill in arithmetic (for which the Narragansett traditionally have an aptitude), figured out the value of their labor, and began to make demands of their masters.

The final element of pauper apprenticeship indentures comprised "freedom dues," the small payment a servant received when a contract ended and he or she was set free. This payment was always written into an indenture, and it varied widely in value, according to officials' assessment of a child's status when the contract was first forged.[45] Freedom dues almost always included clothing, which varied according to the servant's perceived rank: Anglo-American children generally received two outfits, children of color, one. The standard phrase for

Indian and African American children was "one new suit of apparel," without specifications concerning the quality or detail of the outfit. Contextual phrases reveal how that quality differed according to race. Lucy Spywood, mentioned earlier, was to receive "one new suit of decent apparel."[46] A "mulatto child" named only "Phebe" was to receive "one new suit of apparel throughout suitable for such a servant."[47] Isaac Gardner, son of a "black" woman, was to receive simply "a complete suit of clothing."[48] Such clauses left the master to determine what "decent" and "suitable" and "complete" might mean, according to his conscience and the custom of the region. Clearly, some newly-freed young adults walked away miserably clothed. It was so common for masters to try to send away former servants improperly attired for the season that some magistrates took care to specify that "freedom suits" include shoes, stockings, hats, and other apparel necessary for winter.[49] While Anglo-American children often received something more than clothing—a little money, livestock, or tools of the trade—as part of their "freedom dues," Indian and African American children rarely received anything else. It was highly unusual that twelve-year-old John Brown and six-year-old Isabel Brown, "black" children, were promised $10.00 plus interest if they completed their labor contracts without running away.[50]

The great majority of masters were "respectable" male Anglo-American taxpayers.[51] The wealthiest and most politically prominent men, who already had plenty of slaves and servants, occasionally also took indentures of children. More often, however, it was "middling" farmers and craftsmen who took on youngsters as bound servants. Oral tradition reveals that these middling sort masters were more likely than richer men to place severe restrictions on their servants, to make heavier demands upon them in an effort to derive maximum profit from their labors. In consequence, Indian children were more likely to run away from masters of modest means than from the more affluent.

Whatever their wealth, most masters were prompted to take on pauper apprenticeship indentures because they were economically profitable. Sometimes Anglo-American boys and girls were bound out because their masters felt a familial obligation, that of a grandfather taking on an orphaned or illegitimate grandchild, or a stepfather taking on the "bastard" child his wife brought to the marriage, for example.[52] But this was not the case with Indian and African American children. Missing from the record is any expression of "charity" or "pity" for a poor child of color, which sometimes appears in cases of Anglo-American children; and in no cases did their masters admit to being the father or grandfather of a child of color. Instead, masters of Indian and African American children appeared concerned with economics: keeping their costs to a minimum and controlling the child's labor for as long as possible. One man, for example, requested that the indenture of his "mustee" servant be rewritten, because the original contract had mistakenly bound the boy only to age twenty, when in fact, he should have been bound to age twenty-four.[53] Further, both archival evidence and oral tradition confirm that in South Kingstown, officials targeted children of color for indenture,[54] and the names of the masters are those of the large farmers and plantation owners, who bolstered their slave labor force with indentured labor, providing a transition to free labor in an era when public sentiment was turning away from slavery.

Children of all ages became indentured servants, from month-old babies to twenty-year-old young men, but the average age at binding was between six and eight years. At about this age, children usually made the passage into sex-segregated skills training; at six or seven, boys cast off childhood gowns, put on trousers, left their mothers' oversight, and joined their male relatives for day work in the fields or the workshop. Since the age at which a child was bound reflects this passage, the record suggests that parents exerted some control over the timing of indentures, and sheltered children from official management in their earliest years. It also suggests that masters waited to indent a child formally until they were sure he or she was capable of useful labor.[55] Here sex was the significant variable. The mean age at binding was 8.4 years for Anglo-American boys, 8.3 for Indian and African American boys, 7.2 for Indian and African American girls, and 6.2 for Anglo-American girls. These one- and two-year discrepancies suggest that girls were perceived as being ready for independent and productive labor earlier than boys.[56]

The age at which a servant became free also varied with sex and race. Indentures for Anglo-American children always ended at age 21 for boys and 18 for girls.[57] In contrast, indentures for Indian and African American children sometimes lasted until age 21 for girls and 24 for boys, and in South Kingstown, one-third of the indentures for children of color bound males past age 21 and females past age 18.[58] "Adulthood," it seems, was a malleable concept. For Indian and African American children, "freedom" did not correlate to a particular "coming of age," as it did for Anglo-American children. By delaying the freedom of young adult Indians, Anglo-American masters maintained extended access to their servants' labor and also, in the case of young men, preserved opportunities to send their servants off to do military duty in their place, a significant consideration in the Revolutionary era.

There is no doubt that this delayed freedom constituted a disadvantage for the servants. By keeping young men and women under contracts that forbade sexual activity and marriage, Anglo-American masters deprived them of the opportunity to follow openly native rites of passage—coming out ceremonies, sexual expression, marriage—when they were at the height of their sexual potency. The servant was frustrated; the servant's native culture was disrupted; and the master had under his power young people who were increasingly vulnerable to sexual exploitation as they grew to adulthood. Oral tradition tells us that in the seventeenth and eighteenth centuries, Narragansett girls usually began their menstrual cycles in their mid-teens. By keeping these girls in contracts that lasted longer than Anglo-American girls' contracts, masters effectively prolonged their access to Indian servants until they reached sexual maturity. It is not surprising, then, as oral traditional informs us, that some Indian servants defied the terms of their indentures and married in their own traditional fashion anyway. Masters had little legal recourse, since their servants had not married according to Anglo-American law.

Whatever their ages at binding and freedom, children were shunted into a system that kept them at the socio-economic level officials deemed appropriate for their "station," an ordering that depended heavily on race and sex. One-quarter of the contracts were for children of color, when people of color constituted around ten percent of the general population; two-thirds of the contracts were for boys, when the sex ratio was just about even. These disproportions suggest that boys of color were considered especially suitable subjects for bound labor. Further, the lesser training and fewer benefits received by children of color, and especially girls of color, indicate that indenture functioned to immobilize them as menial laborers.

The indentures tell us what the masters contracted to do, but they cannot tell us the realities of the labor their servants performed. What kind of work did three-year-old Lucy and four-year-old John actually undertake? Oral tradition tells us that bound youngsters assisted older servants at their tasks by stirring pots, washing clothes, scrubbing floors, emptying chamber pots, tending babies, carrying water, gathering kindling, chopping wood, feeding chickens, tending livestock, weeding crops, and mending tools. By the time they were ten or twelve years old, they would be laboring nearly at adult capacity.

Nor can the indentures tell us how indentured children were treat-ed within the families they served. Some Anglo-American children, no doubt, were virtually adopted into the family, particularly if they were relatives of the master. In the case of Indian and African American children, as discussed above, oral tradition tells us that older female servants or slaves in the household supervised their day-to-day care, and they were associated with the household as "ser-vants," not "family," a condition that is most compellingly evidenced in the matter of surnames. Oral tradition tells us that Anglo-American officials often rewrote Narragansett names to conform to European language patterns, or deliberately applied false names, as a strategy to write Indian family lines out of existence. Pauper appren-ticeship offered just such an opportunity to undermine Narragansett culture by renaming children. The indenture of Indian boy John, son of Rexom, is revealing in this regard. His grandmother was clearly named Mary Perry. But his mother, daughter of Mary Perry and ser-vant of William Mumford, became "Rexom Mumford" by the time her son was grown.[59] By renaming their servants in this way, masters were not claiming them as heirs or acknowledging their own paterni-ty of their servants' offspring; rather, the masters were trying to draw their servants forcibly into Anglo-American culture by separating them from their native families through the use of language.

The statistical evidence for this study has concentrated on a clus-ter of 759 Rhode Island indentures from the period 1750–1800. Both oral tradition and archival evidence make clear, however, that pauper apprenticeship of poor children began well before 1750 and carried on well past 1800. The seventeenth-century record is fragmentary, but the more complete early eighteenth-century record of pauper apprentice-ships includes Indian girls Hannah Tuntiahehu (1715), Thankful (1726), and Jenney Wompom (1728).[60] Pauper apprenticeship peaked in the late 1700s and then trailed off as state and local institutions assumed the care of poor and orphaned children. But as late as 1868, South Kingstown authorities continued to bind out children of color, as illustrated by the case of Alphonzo Watson, five-year-old "colored" child, who was removed from the town asylum and placed in an indenture that year.[61]

The human face of pauper apprenticeship can be glimpsed in the Mohegan and Narragansett family of Cummock/Fowler/Champlin, whose story threads through the town records of South Kingstown for the late 1700s and early 1800s.[62] Indian woman Mary Fowler Champlin and her children came to officials' attention when someone complained about them to the South Kingstown council in April 1796. The councilmen ordered the overseer of the poor to provide "suitable necessaries" for the family and then investigated the situation by questioning Mary Fowler Champlin and her mother, Mary Cummock Fowler, who had formed a household together with their children.

The elder Mary was the daughter of Sarah Cummock, "one of the tribe of the Indians in Charlestown." Mary herself was born in South Kingstown, was bound out at an early age to Caleb Gardner, and "served out all her apprenticeship." After becoming free, Mary lived for thirty years with "mustee" man James Fowler and "had ten children by him," but "never was married to him in the manner white people are married in these parts."

The younger Mary was the daughter of this union between Mary and James Fowler. The younger Mary escaped her mother's fate of being bound out, but she, like her mother, married a "mustee" man, John Champlin. She testified that she had lived with John Champlin for eleven years "as his wife" and had six children by him, "but never was married to him according to the form used by the white people in these parts." Both Marys used language that indicated the permanent and exclusive nature of their relationships, but officials neither understood nor honored these Indian marriages. Instead, they treated the children as illegitimate and suitable for indenture.

A year after this investigation, Mary Cummock Fowler—the elder Mary—who was at least in her middle 40s, gave birth to another child, Isaac, whom the town council declared a "bastard," despite Mary's testimony about her long-term relationship with her Indian spouse, James Fowler. In 1801, when Isaac was about four years old, the council ordered him bound out in a pauper apprenticeship contract to Jeffrey Watson, a local planter.

The Cummock/Fowler/Champlin family members disappeared from the South Kingtown records for a generation in the early 1800s; oral tradition tells us that they were then living in Mohegan country in eastern Connecticut. The family reappeared in 1838, when the South Kingstown council bound out as an indentured servant a girl named Lydia Champlin, "daughter of a colored woman, late Mary Champlin, since married to a man whose name is unknown." Lydia Champlin's mother may have been Mary Fowler Champlin—the younger Mary—who could have given birth to a child in the early 1820s. It is just as likely, however, that Lydia's mother was the namesake daughter of Mary Fowler Champlin, and that the girl bound out in 1838 was the granddaughter of Mary Fowler Champlin and the great-granddaughter of Mary Cummock Fowler. Like the names that parents passed on from one generation to another, pauper apprenticeship was visited upon the grandchildren and great-grandchildren of youngsters earmarked by Anglo-Americans for servitude.

Mary Fowler Champlin, by her own testimony, escaped pauper apprenticeship, probably by her mother's concerted effort to keep at least one child free from this sort of bondage. But she almost certainly labored, like her brothers and sisters, in the service of Anglo-Americans, since few other work options were available to Indians living behind the frontier. And like Mary Champlin, Indian children in the 1800s increasingly labored without contracts in the houses and on the farms of their Anglo-American neighbors. In 1832, the Narragansett tribal council reported to the Rhode Island state legislature that three-fourths of their number resided on the reservation in Charlestown; "the rest are absent; some go out on service."[63] In 1836, the Narragansett tribe petitioned for assistance in beginning a wintertime school for the tribal children, explaining that most of the young men could not attend a summer school, since they were off the reservation during the agricultural season, pursuing a livelihood as laborers on farms in the region.[64] After the Rhode Island state legislature peremptorily "detribalized" the Narragansett people in 1880 (in violation of federal law) and took away their reserved land, their Indian-ness was seldom acknowledged by European American authorities. Separated from their land, Indians were increasingly closed out of all labor except lowly work that non-Indians thought appropriate for mentally deficient, uneducated, and uncivilized people.

Pauper apprenticeship flourished in Rhode Island in the eighteenth century, when the Narragansett Indians struggled to maintain their communities against Anglo-American political and economic pressure in the wake of King Phillip's War. This system of indentured servitude functioned effectively as a means of removing Indian children from their mothers, training them to take their place as menial laborers in a society dominated by Anglo-Americans, and propagating the colonial relationship of "savage" but conquered Indian servant and "civilized" but paternal Anglo-American master. When the system of pauper apprenticeship declined, those in power found other ways to maintain the colonial relationship of servant and master through conventions of "service" shored up by limitations in the education, training, and work opportunities available to Indian children. When Indian children went out to service in the homes and on the estates of their European American neighbors in the 1900s, they were following a colonial pattern introduced in the 1600s and welded into mainstream culture in the 1700s. These youngsters were not learning skilled trades or academic subjects from their more privileged neighbors; they were continuing to provide a labor force for the unpleasant tasks of life.

This was not the whole story, however. Narragansett children, even those in bondage, continued to be taught by their Indian elders. They learned that a "white" education was not essential to preserving traditional ways or even providing adequately for themselves in the present. They learned that Indians could survive outside the social and economic world that non-Indians had created in Rhode Island. Further, many used the menial skills to which their masters set them as a bridge to occupational opportunities and job networks their masters never imagined. Had non-Indians been able to see, they would have observed what oral tradition reveals—the resourcefulness of Indians who combined old and new ways with pride in their tasks, caring for the earth as horticulturalists and farmers, caring for fellow humans as housekeepers, nurses, and midwives, creating human habitations as stonemasons and carpenters. Although Narragansett culture and religion went underground for a time, Narragansett children learned and preserved it while simultaneously making immeasurable contributions to Anglo-American culture through their service as pauper apprentices.

# Pauper Apprentices in Rhode Island, 1750–1800

Total indentures = 759, from a sample of 14 Rhode Island towns

| | Anglo-American Boys | Indian and African American Boys | Anglo-American Girls | Indian and African American Girls |
|---|---|---|---|---|
| Number of indentures | 373 | 124 | 199 | 63 |
| Percent of all indentures | 49.1% | 16.3% | 26.2% | 8.3% |
| Average age at binding | 8.4 | 8.3 | 6.2 | 7.2 |
| Any literacy education | 124 (33.2%) | 16 (13.0%) | 37 (18.5%) | 9 (14.3%) |
| Read, write, cypher | 103 (83.1%) | 9 (56.3%) | 1 (2.7%) | 0 (0%) |
| Read, write | 10 (8.1%) | 3 (18.8%) | 18 (48.6%) | 2 (22.2%) |
| Read only | 3 (2.4%) | 4 (25.0%) | 17 (45.9%) | 6 (66.7%) |
| Any skills training | 126 (33.7%) | 11 (8.8%) | 26 (13.1%) | 4 (6.3%) |

# Notes

1. These 759 contracts constitute all the indentures recorded between 1750 and 1800 in the towns of Cumberland, East Greenwich, Exeter, Glocester, Hopkinton, Jamestown, Middletown, New Shoreham, Providence, Richmond, South Kingstown, Tiverton, Warren, and Warwick. These fourteen towns comprised half the colony's population in 1780 and fairly represent the demographics, economic orientation and geographic characteristics of Rhode Island's thirty eighteenth-century towns, ranging from sparsely settled agrarian communities (New Shoreham), to "plantation" communities (South Kingstown), to thickly settled commercial towns (Providence).

2. According to a 1783 estimate by Anglo-Americans, African Americans made up 4.5 percent of Rhode Island's population and Indians made up 1.9 percent (Evarts B. Greene and Virginia D. Harrington, *American Population Before the Federal Census of 1790* [Gloucester, Mass.: Peter Smith, 1966], 67). These percentages are almost certainly inaccurate, reflecting *not* the self-designations of people of color, but rather Anglo-American officials' judgments of who was "black" or "Indian." Further, many people of African and Indian ancestry stayed out of sight of Anglo-Americans and were unknown to the census-takers. Lorenzo Greene calculated that African Americans made up 7.3 percent of Rhode Island's population in 1782 and 6.3 percent of the population in 1790 (*The Negro in Colonial New England* [New York: Atheneum, 1969], 87). Whatever the real totals of African American and Indian children, in the population of bound servants they were represented out of proportion to their numbers.

3.   Both oral tradition and archival sources describe the steady stream of Narragansett people out of Rhode Island in the 1700s and 1800s. Petitions made to the Rhode Island General Assembly by Narragansett relocated elsewhere document numerous instances of this migration. See especially the petitions of Simeon and Elizabeth Chapman (1828), Thomas Cummock (1840), Samuel Coyes (1841), and John D. Bats (1841), Folders 72, 107, 109, and 111, Documents Relating to the Narragansett Indians (hereafter DNI), Rhode Island State Archives. Many other Narragansett left without informing authorities or leaving a documentary trail, but the history of their departure is contained in tribal and family oral tradition.

4.   Ruth Wallis Herndon and Ella Wilcox Sekatau, "The Right to a Name: Narragansett People and Rhode Island Officials in the Revolutionary Era," *Ethnohistory* 44 (1997): 433-62.

5.   Town Council meeting (hereafter TCM), November 29, 1757, Providence Town Council Records (hereafter TCR), 4:163. The Town Council Records of each community are located in its town hall. Indenture of Santee, November 29, 1757, Providence Town Papers (hereafter PTP), 1:139, Rhode Island Historical Society.

6.   Indenture of Joseph Peleg alias Anthony, TCM, November 5, 1763, Portsmouth TCR, 5:108; TCM, March 30 and May 25, 1789, Westerly TCR, 5:42, 45. Numerous adults were similarly labeled ambiguously in the town records. See, for example, the case of Winsor Fry, who appeared in the East Greenwich town records as "an Indian man" in 1790 but as a "black man" in 1795 (TCM, January 30, 1790, and November 28, 1795, East Greenwich TCR, 4:110, 235.) This habit of blurring racial designations was not peculiar to Rhode Island record-keepers. For example, Lucy Garrett, a five-year-old child bound out in 1797 by the Stonington, Connecticut, selectmen, was described as "molatto" in the text of the indenture but as "Indian" on the label (Indenture of Lucy Garrett, September 4, 1797, Stonington Town Accounts, MS 70286, Connecticut Historical Society).

7.  For an excellent discussion of race anxiety in southern New England in the late eighteenth century, see Joanne Pope Melish, *Disowning Slavery: Gradual Emancipation and "Race" in New England, 1780–1860* (Ithaca: Cornell University Press, 1998).

8.  Herndon and Sekatau, "The Right to a Name," 447-50.

9.  "An Act to prevent Indians from being abused by designing and ill-minded Persons, in making them Servants," *Acts and Laws of the English Colony of Rhode-Island and Providence Plantations* (Newport, R.I.: Samuel Hall, 1767), 150.

10. "An Act to prevent Impositions upon Indians of the Narragansett Tribe," *The Public Laws of the State of Rhode-Island and Providence Plantations* (Providence: Carter and Wilkinson, 1798), 615-16.

11. TCM, July 13, 1767, South Kingstown TCR, 5:184.

12. TCM, February 9, 1784, Warwick TCR, 3:152. For most of the eighteenth century, English currency was the official money of exchange and account in Rhode Island. One pound (£1) equalled twenty shillings (20s), and one shilling (1s) equalled twelve pence (12d). Throughout this period, 3 shillings (roughly equivalent to 50 cents) was a typical daily wage for a common laborer, £1 (roughly equivalent to $3.30) was a little more than a week's wage, and £40 was a solid year's wage.

13. According to the Rhode Island 1782 census, the sex ratio for children 0-15 years of age was 103.6 males for every 100 females (Jay Mack Holbrook, *Rhode Island 1782 Census* [Oxford, Mass.: Holbrook Research Institute, 1979], ix.) Of the 572 indentures for Anglo-American children in this study, 373 (65.2%) were for boys and 199 (34.8%) were for girls. Of the 187 indentures for children of color, 124 (66.3%) were for boys and 63 (33.7%) were for girls.

14. TCM, January 6, 1755, Tiverton TCR, 2:78.

15. TCM, September 12, 1791, Warwick TCR, 4:303-4.

16. TCM, July 12, 1784, South Kingstown TCR, 6:106.

17. TCM, April 14, 1746, South Kingstown TCR, 4:94.

18. TCM, May 2, 1785, Providence TCR, 5:313.

19. See the case of John Langworthy, who "broke up housekeeping" and gave up the indentures he had for six-year-old Martha Deake and seven-year-old Mary Deake because "his wife not retaining her common reason," he could no longer provide a proper home for the girls (TCM, February 15, 1768, Hopkinton TCR, 1:117). In another circumstance, the Cumberland town council bound Eunice and Elihu Jones to Jabez Whipple of North Providence in 1779, but three years later Whipple's wife died and the council ruled that there was "no proper person in his family to instruct and bring up the said Eunice." The council left Elihu in Jabez's charge, indicating that a boy past a certain age could be raised properly without female care, but it bound Eunice to another master, who presumably was married (TCM, April 21, 1779, and August 5, 1782, Cumberland TCR, 3:4, 68).

20. TCM, March 27, 1762, Jamestown TCR, 1:143-44. Another particularly illuminating case is that of Marcy Scooner, who "left" her daughter Hannah at the household of Matthew Greenhold before Scooner departed the town to pursue work elsewhere (TCM, September 3, 1766, Jamestown TCR, 1:229). This placement strategy occasionally had an air of desperation, as in the case of two-year-old "Indian" girl Sarah, who was "left" at George Babcock's house by an "Indian squaw" who was "unknown" to Babcock; the South Kingstown council bound the toddler to Babcock until she was twenty years old (TCM, April 9, 1770, South Kingstown TCR, 5:228).

21. TCM, August 27, 1754, Jamestown TCR, 1:75-76.

22. TCM, September 13, 1742, and October 13, 1772, South Kingstown TCR, 3:176 and 6:7; TCM, March 27, 1773, East Greenwich TCR, 3:142-43; TCM, July 4, 1800, Exeter TCR, 6:200.

23. For eighteenth-century Rhode Island laws pertaining to indenture, see *Acts and Laws of His Majesty's Colony of Rhode-Island and Providence Plantations* (Newport, R.I.: J. Franklin, 1745), 48-51; *Acts and Laws* (1767), 228-32; and *Public Laws* (1798), 352-58.

24. Eighteenth-century Rhode Island law gave town officials wide latitude in indenture, empowering them to "bind out to apprenticeship poor children, who are likely to become chargeable to the town wherein they live" (*Acts and Laws* [1767], 232). In 1798, the law was revised so that town officials could bind out any children whose parents were "chargeable" to the town, appeared "unable to maintain" their children, or were being supported "at the charge of the state" (*Public Laws* [1798], 350-51).

25. Nearly one-third of the "orphans" (42 of 143) had a father who was described as having "absconded" or who had been "absent" for a long period of time. Because the record-keepers frequently called these children "orphans," we have folded them into that larger category.

26. See the examination of Betsy Spywood (TCM, March 4, 1799, Providence TCR, 7:330) who referred to her mother "Dianna" (the clerk's rendering of Diadami) in the past tense.

27. Ruth Wallis Herndon, *Unwelcome Americans: Living on the Margin in Early New England* (Philadelphia: University of Pennsylvania Press, 2001), 106-9 and 125-29.

28. TCM, December 29, 1746, Westerly TCR, 4:92.

29. TCM, August 29, 1761, East Greenwich TCR, 3:76.

30. TCM, July 13, 1767, South Kingstown TCR, 5:184.

31. TCM, October 8, 1759, Warwick TCR, 2:181.

32. Oral tradition tells us that Indians began to have non-Indian marriage ceremonies, which would be legally recognized by Anglo-Americans, in order to protect their future offspring from being designated "fatherless" and therefore subjected to town magistrates' official management.

33. Town meeting, May 11, 1757, Middletown Town Meeting Records (hereafter TMR), 1:63; TCM, November 8, 1800, Providence TCR, 7:576.

34. TCM, March 6, 1786, Tiverton TCR, 1:np. In 1783, Tiverton taxpayers purchased and renovated the dwelling house of resident Esther Manchester to use as "a workhouse for the poor of this town" (town meetings, October 6 and December 13, 1783, Tiverton TMR, 2:157-58). The record does not indicate if this workhouse was still in use three years later. The wording of the 1786 council order suggests that the overseers intended to segregate "black people" into a separate workhouse, to be put to whatever labor the overseers deemed beneficial for the town.

35. TCM, November 28, 1800, Providence TCR, 8:6.

36. In two exceptional cases, premiums were paid to the masters of children of color. The Warwick town council ordered that Simon, an eighteen-month-old child abandoned by his "molatto" mother and "negro" father, be bound out to "any of the inhabitants of this Town, who shall see cause to take him" with the added "incouragement" of £40 (TCM, March 20, 1752, Warwick TCR, 2:100). And Ephraim Church, three-year-old "mustee" son of an "Indian squaw," was bound to Joseph Hix, who received £100 for taking the boy's indenture (TCM, March 14, 1764, Warwick TCR, 2:241-42). In both cases, the amount of the premium in Rhode Island Old Tenor (£40 in 1752, £100 in 1764) was equivalent to £4.5 sterling, the equivalent of a month's wages for a laborer.

37. In those 16 cases, four stipulated reading only; three stipulated reading and writing, and nine stipulated reading, writing, and cyphering.

Sampson Spywood's contract was typical: the master of this fourteen-year-old "black boy" was bound to "learn him to read" but not to write or cypher (Indenture of Sampson Spywood, TCM, March 11, 1782, Warwick TCR, 3:113).

38. Lesser literacy training for girls was standard practice in New England. *The Town Officer*, a manual published in 1791 to assist town officials in their duties, provided a model indenture for use in binding out poor children. A male Anglo-American child was presupposed, and the indenture form included the phrase, "read and write, and cypher as far as the rule of three"; but the author advised that "If the apprentice be a girl . . . leave out the words 'and cypher as far [as] the rule of three.'" No special provisions for indenting children of color are included (Samuel Freeman, *The Town Officer; or the Power and Duty of Selectmen, Town Clerks . . . and other Town Officers* [Portland, Maine: Benjamin Tiscomb, Jr., 1791], 35). Until 1798, Rhode Island law required no literacy education for indentured servants; that year, Rhode Island revised its laws to conform to Massachusetts standards and gender distinctions: "And provision shall be made in such deed for the instruction of male children so bounden out, to read, write, and cypher, and of females to read and write" (*Public Laws of Rhode Island* [1798], 351). No provision in the law indicated that this standard might be adjusted for children of color.

39. Freeman recommended as a standard element of an indenture the phrase "promise and agree to teach and instruct the said apprentice, or cause him to be taught and instructed in the art[,] trade or calling of [blank to be filled in]" (*The Town Officer* [1791], 35). He indicated no special adjustments if the "apprentice" were a girl or a child of color. The Rhode Island indenture agreements, which are recorded in fragmentary form in the town council minutes, do not always indicate what skill the child was to be taught, perhaps reflecting hurried or sloppy record-keeping. Even so, clerks omitted this information more often in the case of girls and children of color, which suggests that this data was considered of less importance in their contracts.

40. The three exceptions were boys of color bound to be trained as a cooper, a shoemaker, and a boatbuilder.

41. Indenture of Elizabeth Pearce, TCM, September 13, 1762, Warwick TCR, 2:215.

42. Indenture of Sophia Havens, August 7, 1797, PTP, 28:48.

43. *Public Laws* (1798), 350; emphasis added.

44. Until 1798, Rhode Island town authorities were empowered simply "to bind out to apprenticeship poor children," without any mandatory requirement that those children learn a specific skill (*Acts and Laws* [1767], 232).

45. Rhode Island law made no stipulation about freedom dues, indicating that local authorities had a free hand to distinguish among servants in this matter. Samuel Freeman prescribed that at the end of indenture, the servant receive "two suits of wearing apparel, one suitable for Lord's Days, and the other suitable for working days," making no distinction according to a child's racial designation (*The Town Officer* [1791], 35). However, in Rhode Island, children of color usually received only one suit of clothing.

46. TCM, February 9, 1784, Warwick TCR, 3:152.

47. TCM, May 9, 1763, South Kingstown TCR, 5:142.

48. TCM, July 14, 1813, South Kingstown TCR, 7:101-2.

49. See, for example, the indenture of Thomas Berry, July 4, 1761, Warwick TCR, 2:205.

50. TCM, July 4, 1800, Exeter TCR, 6:200.

51. The vast majority of masters were male, though occasionally a child was bound to a single woman who practiced a trade or to a widow who carried on her husband's business. In the model contract provided by Samuel Freeman, 'master' alone is mentioned, but there is an addendum for a female child: "to the word *'master'* add *'or mistress'*" (*The Town Officer* [1791], 35).

52. Even in these cases of family indenture, economic issues were significant. In 1755, the Rhode Island General Assembly passed a law requiring parents and grandparents to support their children and grandchildren financially, and vice versa ("An Act declaring how far Parents and Children are liable to maintain each other," *Acts and Laws* [1767], 201). However, some persons evaded this statute by pleading they were not "of sufficient ability" to take care of their family members in distress. The common practice of demanding indentures of one's own grandchildren appears to have been part of a larger crisis in family relations that necessitated this law.

53. TCM, August 20, 1753, South Kingstown TCR, 4:237.

54. South Kingstown bound out 49 Indian and African American children between 1750 and 1800, representing 53 percent of its total indentures (93) and 10 percent of the town's Indian/African American population (485). Warwick bound out 47 children of color, representing 32 percent of total indentures (149) and 27 percent of the population of color (173). Children of color were far less likely to be bound out in Providence, where only 17 were indented, representing 12 percent of the town's total indentures (145) and 5.8 percent of its entire population of people of color (291).

55. In one illuminating exchange, a prospective master told the Jamestown council that a boy who had come to him as a five-year-old "several years" earlier had now "grown fit for business" and was ready to be bound (Indenture of Moll Pero's "mustee" son, TCM, March 27, 1762, Jamestown TCR, 1:143).

56. Perhaps this was because girls did not undergo the transition from maternal to paternal supervision; instead, from their earliest years they labored steadily at household tasks of food and clothing preparation under the supervision of older females.

57. Rhode Island law did not mandate the ages at which freedom would be granted until 1798, when the age was set at 21 for boys and 18 (or upon their marriage) for girls, with no variations for children of color (*Public Laws* [1798], 351). Freeman's model indenture ended the contract at 21 years of age for boys and prescribed that if the child were female, "for *twenty-one* say *eighteen*," with no variations for children of color (*The Town Officer* [1791], 35).

58. In most of these contracts, the child was less than five years old when bound. Such longer-than-normal indentures were probably town officials' way of compensating masters, without paying a premium, for taking on children too young initially to contribute significantly to the household economy. Typical cases were those of "a Negro boy named Richard" bound to a Newport boatbuilder until the child "arrives to the age of twenty-four years"; and "Mary a black child," daughter of an indentured servant, who was bound to her mother's master "until she shall arrive to the age of twenty years" (TCM, September 21, 1772, Middletown TCR, 2:53; TCM, December 29, 1770, East Greenwich TCR, 3:127).

59. TCM, April 12, 1784, South Kingstown TCR, 6:102.

60. Indenture of Hannah Tuntiahehu, June 1715, PTP, 1:1:39B; Indenture of Jenney Wompom, July 25, 1728, PTP, 2:3:7; TCM, February 14, 1725/26, South Kingstown TCR, 2:27.

61. TCM, July 13, 1868, South Kingstown TCR, 8:431.

62. The story can be traced through the following records: Examinations of Mary Cummock Fowler and Mary Fowler Champlin: TCM, May

14, 1796, South Kingstown TCR, 6:229-30; TCM, April 11, May 9 and 14, 1796, April 10, 1797, February 9, 1801, September 11, 1837, September 10, 1838, South Kingstown TCR, 6:227, 229, 230, 243, and 7:2, 325, 331; and Holbrook, *Rhode Island 1790 Census*, 48. For a full narrative, see Herndon, *Unwelcome Americans*, 60-62.

63. Remonstrance against report of Dr. Daniel King, January 1832, Folder 89, DNI.

64. Petition from Narragansett Indian tribe for money for a school, June 1836, Folder 98, DNI.

# Recovering Gendered Political Histories:

## Local Struggles and Native Women's Resistance in Colonial Southern New England

TRUDIE LAMB RICHMOND AND AMY E. DEN OUDEN

## Introduction

I
N THE OPENING SECTION of his *Historical Collections of the Indians of New England* (1674), missionary Daniel Gookin includes the following brief commentary on the creation stories of the indigenous people of New England:

> I have discoursed and questioned about this matter with some of the most judicious of the Indians, but their answers are divers and fabulous. Some of the inland Indians say, that they came from such as inhabit the sea coasts. Others say, that there were two young squaws, or women, being at first either swimming or wading in the

water: The froth or foam of the water touched their bodies, from whence they became with child; and one of them
brought forth a male; and the other, a female child; and
then the two women died and left the earth: So their son
and daughter were their first progenitors. Other fables and
figments are among them touching this thing, which are
not worthy to be inserted. These only may suffice to give
a taste of their great ignorance touching their origin[s].[1]

For Gookin, this account of indigenous origins must be a "fable
and figment" because it has been related through oral tradition;
indeed early in *Historical Collections*, Gookin discredits any accounts by
natives of their own past, dismissing his Indian informants as "ignorant of letters and records of antiquity."[2] Thus, he concludes, "any
true knowledge of their ancestors is utterly lost among them."[3] Surely
more "fabulous" to Gookin than oral tradition, however, were the
central figures of the native women who, having mingled with the elements of the earth, became cultural creators: the forebears of a people and a way of life. Such an origin would not only be an affront to
the masculine Christian god, but an intolerable cultural opposition to
seventeenth-century Puritan colonists, for whom the planting of the
earth (with crops, colonies, and Christian souls)—and thus the pro-
liferation of culture—was properly the work of men. Finally, what
may have been as troubling for Gookin as the indigenous emphasis on
the multifaceted reproductive powers of the wading women was the
notion that native histories and identities had emerged from, and
remained rooted in, the very landscape that English colonists had
claimed as their own "homeland." Hence Gookin's opening section
of *Historical Collections*, entitled "Several Conjectures on their Original
[origins]," argues that Indians did not arise from the lands of America,
but rather wandered there, having been either banished from their pre-

sumed ancestral territory by the Christian god, or disowned by their "original," non-American ancestors.[4]

Implicit in Gookin's origins fable is the relationship between the processes by which native peoples of New England have been dispossessed of their land, and those by which indigenous women have been obscured from history. For Gookin's assessment of "Indian origins" points to the less than subtle way in which native women's pasts, like indigenous knowledges, were overwritten by a colonial discourse on Indianness, and thus obscured from the "American" landscape. To some extent, Euroamerican historiography of colonial New England, which has focused heavily on "culture contact"[5] and the so-called "Indian Wars" of the seventeenth century, has sustained this discourse. For one thing, the emphasis on the seventeenth century has conveyed the notion that the only significant struggles waged by native people over land and political autonomy occurred on military battlefields (a predominantly male arena) and ended in 1676 with "King Philip's War."[6] Indeed, as historian Colin Calloway has recently noted, "it seems that Indians figure in [American history] only when they offer violent resistance. Indians are 'the frontier'; once their armed resistance is overcome, once the 'frontier' has passed them by, they no longer seem to count."[7] Not only has the conventional focus on seventeenth-century warfare and early "contact" minimized the significance of those forms of native resistance that continued beyond the period of English military conquest; it has also tended to obscure the varied means by which colonialism—as a "cultural project of control"[8] —intruded into the lives of native women and men long after 1676, engaging them in struggles that tested the limits of colonial authority.

This essay attempts to understand the cultural knowledge and historical experiences that informed those struggles, investigating the ways in which notions of gender—and native women's resistance to colonial domination—shaped the lives and historical possibilities of indigenous peoples in colonial southern New England. The essay is divided into two sections: in Part I, Trudie Richmond provides an overview of native women's political and cultural influence in their own communities, and examines the particular ways in which native women in southern New England resisted and adjusted to colonization and its varied attempts to silence or extinguish local indigenous identities. In Part II, Amy Den Ouden focuses on the relevance of gender in the long-running land dispute between Mohegans and the colony of Connecticut, highlighting the ways in which Mohegan resisters contested the colonially imposed notions of gender hierarchy and cultural legitimacy that had been employed to undermine the land rights of their reservation community.

By exploring the ways in which gender, and indigenous notions about the nature of women's power, shaped colonial power relations during and beyond the period of military conquest, we may better understand the complexity of the political struggles waged by native people in an unsettled colonial world. Equally important, we may gain further insight into the specific, local knowledges that continued to bind native women and men to their homelands and sustain their identities.

## Part I:
### Native Women's Resistance—A Path to Survival

*I am a Schaghticoke woman from northwestern Connecticut and one of only five families living on the Schaghticoke Reservation. It has been my home for over 15 years. However, my life there has not been without struggle, sacrifice, and an intense determination to maintain the visibility of my people and protect our heritage. It has been the homeland of my ancestors for several thousand years. Yet, our continued presence honors the ancestors, emphasizes our commitment to our land, and states very clearly: "We are still here." Therefore, it is my intention to re-examine native women's roles in colonial southern New England in order to address several key issues: (1) how native women were identified by others and how they identified themselves in the seventeenth and eighteenth centuries; (2) how Christianity impacted the positions of Algonquian women; and (3) how native women's strategies of resistance ensured the survival of native identities and communities.*

Native women have always been an important part of the cultural landscape; however, early colonial writers often made them seem invisible simply by ignoring them. At best, the authors failed to provide a great deal of vital information that would have added to our understanding of the diversity of women's roles in pre-colonial native societies. Women lived differently among distinct native nations, as well as within their own communities. They played key roles in all aspects of economic life: as sachems, shamans, healers, horticulturists, and traders. In colonial society, however, women were not held in high esteem. English women fell under the authority of their fathers or their husbands and had no rights to their children or their property. Nor were English women even meant to be "visible," and they could suffer harsh consequences if they were thought to have behaved inappropriately, particularly in public. It should come as no surprise, then, that native women's roles and influence in their own societies were obfuscated and disparaged by colonial chroniclers.

Although Roger Williams, in his *A Key into the Language of America* (1643), interpreted the term *sunksquaw* to mean "Queen or Sachem's wife," he failed to acknowledge that the women carrying the title wielded significant political authority within their own communities.[9] However, there is considerable evidence of female political leadership among coastal Algonquian women of the seventeenth century, which indicates that female sachems, or *sunksquaws*, played an active role in decisions concerning matters most crucial to their communities, such as colonial land transactions. In addition, there were those among them who were unafraid to take on the role of warrior women

178

and lead armed resistance to safeguard their people. While notions of gender and power varied among the native societies of the northeast, in southern New England *sunksquaws* were figures of political influence and authority in their own right. Some inherited the office of sachem, sometimes succeeding a father, a brother, or even a husband; however, as anthropologist Robert Grumet observes, "this does not mean that every 'sunksquaw's' husband or brother was a leader. Many women sachems were married to men who had no pretension to leadership."[10]  Indeed, in colonial southern New England, *sunksquaws* remained leaders in their communities because they proved themselves capable and competent.

Weetamoo, a Pocasset *sunksquaw*, was already a woman of considerable power and authority when she married Alexander (Wamsutta), son of Sachem Massasoit. Weetamoo had inherited the right to rule upon the death of her father and had control of a great deal of land as well as a large quantity of surplus corn. As Grumet notes, she "served as a war chief commanding over 300 warriors" when she joined forces with King Philip (Metacomet) in the war of 1675.[11] Likewise, Quaiapan (also known as Matantuck[12]) was an influential *sunksquaw* of a Narragansett village. She was married to Mixanno, son of the Narragansett sachem Canonicus, and her brother, Ninigret, was a Niantic sachem. A strong supporter of Philip during the war of 1675, Quaiapan presided over "Queen's Fort," which lay at the heart of Narragansett ancestral territory.[13] According to archaeologist Patricia Rubertone, during King Philip's War Queen's Fort had become "a formidable pocket of [Narragansett] resistance to colonial advancement," precisely because of Quaiapan's "steadfast refusal to sell land to English entrepreneurs and settlers."[14] Quaiapan was killed in battle by English colonists in 1676.[15]

These are just a few of the women sachems whose power shaped native-Anglo relations in seventeenth-century southern New

England.[16] They lived at a time when, within the hierarchy of local leadership, the position of sachem went to the most eligible and proficient, including women. This position, it must be remembered, was not one of dictatorial power; rather, it was won by those who exhibited wisdom and admirable traits of character, and who demonstrated the ability both to resolve disputes and to maintain and strengthen alliances.[17] Since marriage and kinship ties were equated with political alliances, women in native communities—particularly those in the matrilineal societies of coastal southern New England—were always a visible political force. Thus *sunksquaws*, like male sachems, well understood the significance of the alliances that permeated their societies and bolstered the authority of local leadership.

Colonization worked to disrupt and undermine indigenous societies and intra-community relations in ways that directly impacted native women's lives. In his important examination of the diversity of women's roles in coastal Algonquian societies in the seventeenth and eighteenth centuries, Robert Grumet stresses the adaptive dimensions of the native response to European intrusion.[18] As Grumet explains, coastal Algonquian peoples managed to maintain an independent existence in the midst of a pervasive and often hostile European presence. To a great extent, this was due to the deeply ingrained cultural importance of land, and to practices of cultural renewal and economic production that had always prominently included women. In the seventeenth century, women's power and status were based on their control over land and agricultural production. The cultivation of corn began in southern New England about 1000 A.D.,[19] and by the sixteenth century, agriculture had become fundamental to indigenous subsistence, with corn, beans, and squash constituting the principal crops.[20] Women were responsible for planting and caring for agricultural fields, and because of their skills and knowledge as agriculturalists, large quantities of crops could be harvested and stored; women thus provided the bulk of subsistence and became a dominant economic force in these agricultural societies.[21] Corn surpluses, then, were an important source of women's power in their own communities, as well as an important commodity to be traded by some native women.[22] No less important, the economic primacy of corn certainly reinforced women's cultural relationship to the land: because women were the primary agriculturalists in their communities, their intense use of land established and maintained their rights to it.

Nonetheless, seventeenth-century colonists often failed to grasp the larger political and economic significance of native women's activities. Roger Williams seemed to describe native women as drudges when he observed that they "constantly pound their corn" and "carry heavy loads."[23] Yet Williams's interpretation of what he saw reflected a profound cultural misunderstanding. Native women's daily labor embodied their true power: power over the reproduction of community life as well as the subsistence economy. Women cared for their planting fields as they cared for their children, and the product of this labor was exhibited in the persistence of native communities and identities in the colonial world. Thus while Williams appears to have ignored native women as leaders, perhaps without realizing it, he did describe the source of their economic power, noting that "the woman of the family will commonly raise 2, 3 or 4 heaps of 12, 15, or 20 bushells a heap, which they drie in round broad heaps and if she have help, of her children or friends, much more."[24]

In redefining native women's roles and their increased value in food production and village stability in southern New England, archaeologist Russell Handsman evaluated the importance of women's mortars within the context of the story of Chanameed, a mythic character whose gluttony represented the consumptive and wasteful forces of colonization. Chanameed convinced a young Mohegan woman to come away and live with him; she agreed, and the only possession she wished to take with her was her mortar and pestle for grinding corn. But when Chanameed began leaving her alone for longer and longer periods, she decided to leave him and return to her people. Significantly, she used her mortar and pestle to impede Chanameed's effort to recapture her, and thus she ensured her escape. As Handsman explains, the story suggests that the mortar and pestle—a native woman's tool of production—symbolizes her identity and signifies her resistance to colonialism.[25] The Mohegan woman's actions compel us to understand that women's subsistence activities were an articulation of important cultural beliefs, embodying what Handsman calls a language of resistance and preservation, one that was particularly significant in the context of a struggle between two societies that differed drastically in morals and beliefs.[26] Just as agriculture, and women's economic labor, had transformed native societies, so too could they serve to affirm and maintain social and cultural identities—to tell a story, in effect, about the enduring importance of native life ways.

Indigenous languages in southern New England also quite literally expressed the centrality of women's roles. Anthropologist Kathleen Bragdon has observed that "links between [Algonquian] people and their surroundings were marked in language use, which in turn reinforced expectations and understandings about the 'naturalness' of experience."[27] A look at Algonquian terms in southern New England that refer to the reproduction and source of life lends insight into the nature of women's roles and how they were interpreted within native communities. In the Algonquian dialect of southern New England, the word *ohke* or *auke* means "the earth" and "that which produces or brings forth life."[28] Not coincidentally, the word for "mother" is *okasah*, from the same root as *ohke*.[29] The words for "home" and "bride" come from the same root: *wetu* (*Weetauomonat*, for instance, means, "to take a mate" and "to marry").[30] The word *wetu* symbolizes more than living space: it designates that which shelters and strengthens the spiritual ties that embrace the earth. As they nurture and gather plants, and sustain their families and communities, women continually sustain the connection between their people and the spirit world. Like the earth, they are the progenitors of life. It was in this manner that native women in southern New England identified themselves, and were valued, in their own communities.

Colonialism, however, would have a destructive impact on gender relations and women's power in the indigenous societies of southern New England, particularly as it operated through the Christianizing mission. It is well documented that reducing the status of Indian women within their nations was a task that European colonizers were eager to undertake in order to weaken and destabilize indigenous societies. Systematic efforts to erase the cultural practices of indigenous people and displace them from their land base—the source of their economic livelihood as well as a spiritual foundation—were intended to ensure control over native populations.[31] The missionary endeavor clearly served to undermine native women's status and power in many communities as the process of colonization ensued, and as indigenous people experienced "conversion," both voluntarily and involuntarily. With regard to the varied impact of Christianity on native women throughout northeastern North America, some scholars have argued that conditions in some indigenous societies, particularly those in which women did not enjoy equal status with men, facilitated missionaries' efforts to convert women.[32] Kathleen Bragdon points out that, in certain cases, Christianity "reinforced a preexisting gender division and underscored the 'private' nature of women's activities."[33]

By the early eighteenth century, native peoples in southern New England had endured colonization and Christianity for nearly 150 years. Many indigenous communities had been rendered landless, while others were confined to reservations. Moreover, colonial authorities had utilized a particular cultural strategy to undermine the economic roles of native women and to separate them from their traditional positions of authority. As native ways of using the land were being forcibly undermined, many indigenous women and men were compelled to conform to colonial prescriptions for "proper" gender roles.[34] As historian Jean O'Brien has explained, English colonists sought to transform native men into agricultural laborers, while native women were to be trained in colonial "domestic" skills such as weaving and spinning;[35] "once the principal producers of the crucial agricultural element of their subsistence economies," native women in eighteenth-century New England "were expected to sever the vital connection they had to the soil as its principal cultivators and nurturers."[36]

Missionaries continued to take a central role in imposing such changes on native women and their societies in the eighteenth century. In 1735, for example, John Sergeant, a Yale-educated minister, was appointed by the Society for the Propagation of the Gospel in New England to work with the Housatonic Indians at Stockbridge, Massachusetts. After convincing some Mahicans of the Hudson River to join them at Stockbridge, Sergeant worked to create a "civilized" Christian community in a six-square-mile village, where he hoped to prepare his native converts for a changing world.[37] Sergeant was soon concerned to increase the number of converts, and, believing that Indian habits and culture were deeply ingrained from childhood, he thought he might achieve better results by creating boarding schools for native children, where he could work to force early conversions. Sergeant was devoted to "reforming" Indian girls as well as boys: boys were to cultivate the land, while girls were to be in charge of colonial domestic duties such as weaving and housekeeping.[38]

In 1747 approximately 50 Mahican families lived in Stockbridge, and 35 were members of the church. The imposition of colonial gender roles on these native families was not a task to be easily accomplished, however. Sergeant complained that native women spent a good deal of time gathering wood, planting, and weeding, and not enough time engaged in the activity of "housekeeping."[39] Further, while Sergeant observed that native children learned English quickly, he found indigenous people to be obstinately attached to their own ways, as he pointed out in a letter to George Drummond of the Society for Propagating Christian Knowledge: "The Indians in general are a people difficult to be reformed from their own foolish, barbarous and wicked customs." [40]

Despite continuing resistance, colonizers' efforts to Christianize and "civilize" indigenous people took their toll on native women and men in southern New England. In the mid-eighteenth century, the religious revival known as the "Great Awakening" prompted the conversion of considerable numbers of native people. By this time, the structures of native societies had been obscured, and in some cases destroyed, by the processes of colonization and the "civilizing" mission. In the face of increasing economic pressures and cultural domination by Euroamerican society, however, indigenous people found creative ways of resisting alienation from their homelands and the erasure of their cultural identities.

In certain contexts, women remained a powerful social and political presence in their communities and demonstrated their ability to become a significant force for resistance. These women acted with a wide range of motives and from a multitude of perspectives, as a careful assessment of native women's cultural and political activities in the eighteenth and nineteenth centuries reveals. The specific cases addressed below provide further insight into the particular ways in which native women, as figures of power and progenitors of life, worked to ensure the survival of their communities.

## *Narragansett*

Following King Philip's War, the native people of coastal southern New England experienced economic devastation, political disruption, and geographic relocation. Native communities, families, and individuals responded differently to the turmoil in their lives. The Narragansett people struggled to maintain traditional ways and to co-exist with their English "neighbors," while combating poverty, discrimination, and disease. Many Narragansett people, influenced by the Great Awakening and seeking spiritual support, decided to build their own church. In 1750 the Narragansett Indian Church was built, and the Narragansett people obtained their own Indian minister. Located on tribal lands in Charlestown, Rhode Island, the church became the center of Narragansetts cultural as well as religious life: there they maintained church records and preserved Narragansett history through family records and the documentation of tribal activities. The Narragansett Church served as a meetinghouse where, very often, important decisions and survival strategies were developed. On three separate occasions the church burned down, but each time it was rebuilt. Indeed, by the late nineteenth century the Narragansett Church had become a crucial source of cultural identity and autonomy, helping Narragansetts to endure the attempt by the state of Rhode Island to "detribalize" them, and thus declare them "extinct," in 1880. While Euroamericans continued in their efforts to erase Narragansett identity, particularly through the racial categorization of Narragansett as "colored" or "black,"[41] hardship and oppression served to strengthen the resolve of the Narragansett people to maintain traditional ways and remain within their homelands. In many instances it was Narragansett women who served as the culture bearers, passing down history and cultural knowledge, and thus maintaining historical continuity in the lives of Narragansett people.

Narragansett elders, like medicine woman and historian Ella Wilcox Sekatau, have been vital to the perpetuation of Narragansett oral tradition. For countless generations, such elders have been training the young people to listen carefully to Narragansett accounts of history in order to learn their people's unwritten laws and ceremonies. Today, it is the knowledge and teachings of Ella Sekatau that serve to sustain oral tradition and cultural identity among her people.

### Mohegan

During the seventeenth century, Mohegans, particularly their sachem Uncas, were allies with English colonizers. In an effort to maintain a friendly relationship with colonial authorities, Uncas transferred a great deal of land to colonists. Ultimately, like other native communities who had survived the impact of European diseases and colonial warfare in the seventeenth century, the Mohegan people were confined to an ever-diminishing reservation and a life of poverty and discrimination. In 1827, an aspiring missionary from Norwich, Connecticut, Sarah Huntington, felt compelled to "do something for the sadly neglected Mohegans, to improve their moral condition and build a suitable place of worship."[42] Huntington subsequently organized the "Society for the Improvement of the Mohegan Indians," and, as a result, the Mohegan Church was established and dedicated in 1831. As was the case for Narragansetts, the Mohegan Church came to represent the core of Mohegan people's cultural heritage, and Mohegan women played a central role in establishing and maintaining the cultural significance of the church. The green in front of the church became the spiritual center of life at Mohegan, for that was where the annual Wigwam Festival, sponsored by the Mohegan Ladies' Sewing Society, was held each summer.

An event that continued for over 100 years, its purpose was to raise funds to support the church; but the Wigwam Festival also contributed to the cultural survival of the Mohegan people. The gendered division of labor in the preparations for this event revealed both the changes and continuities in Mohegan cultural life. Each year Mohegan men worked together to erect a wigwam-like arbor, constructed from white birch saplings. Men also brought forth their families' wooden mortars, and some helped to pound corn, parch it, and make the traditional *yokeag*. "Pounding the yokeag was an activity performed by each generation of Mohegans. It connected them with those who had gone before."[43] The women also made several native dishes for the event, including succotash, clam chowder, and oyster stew, as well as a variety of pies and cakes. In addition, Mohegan women sold the splint baskets, beadwork, and woodcarvings they had made. As Mohegan tribal historian Melissa Fawcett has explained, the Wigwam Festival was an opportunity to "learn to be Muhukiniuk," which means "one with the spirit of Mohegans."[44] The planning and preparation for this event not only emphasized the importance of complementary gender roles, but also celebrated the role of elders in cultural preservation, providing them with an opportunity to share the oral traditions and the history of the people. The Mohegan Ladies' Sewing Society, which worked to keep this event at the center of Mohegan community life, met throughout the year, and also provided an opportunity for mothers, daughters, and granddaughters to share family stories and to preserve their cultural beliefs.[45] Today, Mohegan women are considering restoring the Ladies' Sewing Society.

## Schaghticoke

Colonists often justified the taking of indigenous lands in southern New England by denying that they were in fact native homelands, describing and devaluing them as a "vast wilderness." Likewise, local histories of the towns in northwestern Connecticut reduced the existence of the native people of that region to a few short paragraphs. For instance, in his *History of the Indians of Connecticut* (1852), nineteenth-century Connecticut historian John W. De Forest wrote that the state, "now inhabited by a populous, civilized and Christian community, was once entirely possessed by a few barbarous tribes of a race which seems to be steadily fading from existence."[46] As De Forest and other Euroamerican historians of the era have suggested, if it were not for the presence of the "civilized" population, the land would have remained a "desolate wilderness." The map of Connecticut in 1630 that De Forest included with his text depicts the northwestern region of the state as an empty space, ignoring and omitting the indigenous communities—including Weantinock, Schaghticoke, Mahican, and Pootatuck—whose ancestors had lived along the Housatonic River for thousands of years. In effect, the map offers a justification for the taking and "settling" of the land.

The Housatonic River was a source of great power and majesty to the native peoples who inhabited that region of what is now western Connecticut. For centuries, many native communities built their villages on or near the riverbanks. The Schaghticokes and Paugussetts of contemporary Connecticut are among those whose ancestors lived along the Housatonic. These communities had a true partnership with the land, and their cycle of subsistence was regulated by generations of spiritual tradition. However, that belief system was threatened repeatedly in the eighteenth century by the imposition of Euroamerican technology, the pressure of Christianity, and disease. The encroachments of colonists from New England to the east and New York to the west contributed to the weakening of native social and political systems in the region. Thus native women and men were faced with difficult choices for survival: accommodate or boldly resist.[47]

It was not until the early eighteenth century that the northwestern corner of Connecticut was invaded by colonizers. The town of Kent was established in 1739, and within a decade a reservation had been created for the Schaghticoke people. Their leader, Gideon Mauwee, approached the town officials for support, requesting a school and teachers for the education of Schaghticoke children, but he was refused. Subsequently, when the Schaghticoke community was visited by Moravian missionaries from Germany, Mauwee invited them to stay. Unlike the English, the Moravians sought to accommodate the native lifestyle, and lived and worked among Schaghticoke people without conflict. They remained for nearly twenty years, and even built a stone mission as a site for conversions, baptisms, and worship. Because the Moravians kept extensive daily dairies, which included descriptions of Schaghticoke activities as well as examples of resistance, they preserved important fragments of Schaghticoke cultural history.

During the period of the Moravian presence, Schaghticoke life flourished, and the Moravians encouraged them to continue some of their traditions, such as the production of carved bowls and spoons, canoes, baskets, and braided corn husk mats, the sale of which might allow Schaghticokes to adjust better to the colonial economy. Whether converts or not, Schaghticoke people worked to preserve elements of their culture. Moravian records indicate that expressions of their cultural traditions and values persisted in the Schaghticoke community. Periodically, Schaghticoke converts requested permission to be absent from evening services because they were participating in traditional sweathouse activities. To Schaghticoke people, such activities had both physical and spiritual value, not only by curing illness but by purifying the spirit as well. Moravians urged Schaghticokes to alter their customary way of harvesting materials for their crafts, attempting to convince Schaghticokes that if the women remained at home engaged solely in craft-making while the men went out onto the land to collect the resources, they could more efficiently produce their crafts for the marketplace. The Schaghticoke people stubbornly refused; they were unwilling to change the communal nature of men's and women's labor as producers of crafts.[48]

These glimpses into natives' lives during and beyond the colonial period reveal that in many important ways, women's traditional political and economic roles continued to shape the histories of indigenous peoples in southern New England long after the arrival of colonists, and despite the varied forms of cultural and economic domination that infused their lives in the seventeenth century and beyond. As a final tribute to the histories of native women in southern New England, I would like to introduce two Schaghticoke women who engaged in resistance—both passively and aggressively—and who never denied their identities or their connection to their homeland, even in the face of discrimination and prejudice. The first, Eunice Mauwee, was born in 1759, the daughter of Joseph Mauwee and the granddaughter of Gideon Mauwee, a Schaghticoke sachem and the last traditional chief among his people. Although Eunice was born a few years after the Moravians left, her family had adopted many Euroamerican ways. Eunice recounted one of the most revealing events of her life in a story of her girlhood when she was no more than eight or nine years old. One day, when her grandfather and several of his friends came to visit her father, their "wild" appearance frightened her: they had dressed in the "Indian" manner—perhaps in animal skins and adorned with tattooed designs on their bodies and faces. The presence of these "real" Indians caused Eunice to hide in the bushes; they were undoubtedly perceived as "menacing" by this little girl, albeit an Indian herself, who was wearing a cloth dress and high-buttoned shoes. Having been born into a Christianized society, she had been separated from the natural and spiritual world of her ancestors.

*Eunice Mauwee*

But Eunice did not grow to be a woman detached from her cultural heritage. She lived to be over 100 years old, and is considered by Schaghticoke people today to be the "grandmother of us all," the strength of her people. Eunice survived most of her life as a basket maker, traveling about the countryside selling her crafts. Other native women of the time shared her experience; indeed, by the mid-nineteenth century the principal basket makers in southern New England were women. When she was 85 years old, she decided to join the Congregational Church and to stay at home and share the old stories. Too old to travel, she passed down tribal history through her storytelling, as she had been taught. When she died, the headlines of her obituary misleadingly read, "The Last of the Pequots, an elder basket maker." Finally, she had become "visible" in Euroamerican society, as if her longevity were now her only claim to fame. What Euroamericans would have been unlikely to see, however, was that Eunice was a sociocultural authority among her people.[49] She was neither a leader nor a political force, but her basket making was symbolic of the transfer, and the power, of cultural knowledge and Schaghticoke identity. Eunice's baskets represent the "internal qualities of culture"[50] and are preserved and exhibited in museums and homes throughout the country. Eunice was a *real* Indian.

Julia (Cotsure) Coggswell was another influential Schaghticoke woman of the nineteenth century. Born in 1860, not long after Eunice died, Julia never knew her great-grandmother. But she experienced the same racism and identity struggles as her relatives. She also lived in a time when even families with restricted incomes and little money for luxuries believed that they might best preserve who they were through photography. Moreover, having one's picture taken seemed to instill a sense of pride in one's identity. Like many Schaghticokes, Julia was motivated by such sentiments when, dressed in her best Euroamerican attire, she went to a local photographer. The photographer, however,

*Julia Coggswell*

decided that he wanted to take a second photograph (seen here). He draped a blanket with an Indian design around her shoulders, had her take down her hair, and then placed a toy bow and arrow in her hands. The expression on her face is one of sadness and remorse. She was a proud, gentle woman, who never denied who she was, but this was not the way she identified herself.[51] This was not how she captured her own "Indianness." Yet, in her eyes a look of passive resistance is preserved.

## Part II:
### Gender, Culture, and Power in the Mohegan Land Struggle, 1704–1738

The overview of native women's histories in Part I emphasizes the fact that cultural processes and political struggles are often propelled by the ostensibly mundane activities of daily life: subsistence activities, for instance, and the routinized interactions between women and men as they worked to sustain their communities in an increasingly oppressive colonial world. Such forms of "passive" resistance were crucial to the reproduction of native identities, and to the continuity of native histories. But there were also dramatic moments of overt resistance to dispossession and cultural domination in the post-"Indian War" period in southern New England. Remarkably, one of the most significant instances of such resistance is found in the eighteenth-century history of a native people who have long been cast as a major colonial ally. Indeed, under the leadership of Uncas, Mohegan men participated in the English massacre of Pequots at Mystic in 1637; and it is undoubtedly that historical moment that has preserved Mohegans' name in popular (Euroamerican) accounts of colonial history. However, just as it cannot be assumed that indigenous people's historical possibilities were elided by military conquest, neither can Mohegan history during the colonial period be reduced to that of a "colonial ally." [52] In fact, throughout most of the eighteenth century, Mohegans were engaged in an intense and complex legal dispute with the colony of Connecticut over rights to their reserved land.[53]

At a crucial moment during this dispute, Mohegans engaged in an act of protest against the Connecticut government that emphasized their own ideas about gender, political authority, and the enduring importance of their cultural connection to their ancestral lands. On September 10, 1736, Mohegans held a ceremony on their reservation in New London to name Anne, daughter of deceased Mohegan sachem Cesar, as *sunksquaw*[54] in opposition to Ben Uncas II,[55] a Mohegan leader who had complied with the Connecticut government and failed to defend Mohegans' land rights.[56] This ceremony, characterized by Connecticut Governor Joseph Talcott as an attempt by rebellious Mohegans to "set up a queen or imposter,"[57] marked an important moment in the history of Mohegans' relationship with the colony of Connecticut. For the leadership ceremony was not only an assertion of Mohegans' land rights, but an expression of their resistance to the Connecticut government's efforts to manipulate their cultural beliefs and political affairs.

In order to begin to unravel the significance of gender in the context of the Mohegan land struggle, one must first acknowledge that the women and men who comprised reservation communities[58] in eighteenth-century Connecticut were possessed of a political and historical consciousness, and were fully engaged in the colonial world precisely because their remaining lands were perpetually threatened by encroachers. In the aftermath of King Philip's War, native histories in Connecticut were shaped by local struggles against dispossession, and by reservation communities' efforts to retain some measure of cultural and political autonomy. Natives' petitions to the Connecticut government, through which they sought redress against encroachers, preserve important details of these struggles, revealing the devastating impact of colonial encroachment on reservation economies while also expressing the cultural and historical importance of reservation lands to the women and men who sought to protect them. Mohegans, like the neighboring Niantic, Eastern Pequot, and Mashantucket Pequot reservation communities in New London County, contended with the intensifying pressure of an expanding Angloamerican population and its demand for land in the early eighteenth century.[59] In an October 1703 petition to the Connecticut General Assembly, Mohegan leaders Owaneco, Ben Uncas I, and Mahomet I detailed the extent to which colonial land hunger had undermined Mohegans' subsistence economy, and called upon the colonial government to acknowledge the history of agreements between Mohegan leaders and the colony regarding Mohegans' land rights. "As to our Boundaries," they reminded colonial legislators:

> they have been established by youre fathers & ours. Your records declare the same and what was by them Done we acknowledged and the articles made by them we own . . . [but] you have Suffered your people to Doe us wrong in seteing upon our Lands notwithstanding our complaints from time to time.[60]

The petition then explained that Mohegans had been threatened "to be Killed" by townspeople of Colchester

> whoe are settled upon our Land without our consent . . . and they have burnt our Hunting house that we Dare not goe to hunting upon our own Land for feare of being Killed by them and we forced to defend ourselves. [And] the Governr. [Fitz-John Winthrop] did in a time of snow Last winter turne our women & children of[f] our planting fields Claiming it for his own and the people of

N[ew] London did take away great part of our planting Land far above theire bounds which have been known between them & us for many years and Last May your courte granted to New London & Coulchester all the Rest of our Lands s[o] that we have noe Land eithere to plant or hunt upon. we have [claimed] nothing but what your own Records Declare and now we heare by the scouts that are out that the English up Conecticot River threten to take our Scalps and the pequots and make money of them acording to boston Law.[61]

The Mohegan reservation, referred to by the Connecticut government as the "sequestered land" and the "Mohegan fields,"[62] was known by colonial officials to be the place where the majority of Mohegan people "dwell and plant."[63] At the time of this petition, the reservation encompassed a thirty-two-square-mile tract of land between the towns of New London and Norwich. In May of 1703, however, the Connecticut General Assembly's "Act for the enlargement of New London township" incorporated Mohegans' sequestered land within the town's boundaries. Neither this act nor the 1704 New London patent that followed it acknowledged any specific boundaries for the Mohegan reservation,[64] and thus they offered implicit incentive for encroachment.

Despite the dire conditions of life described in the 1703 petition, Mohegans, like other reservation communities in early eighteenth-century Connecticut, persisted in their efforts to preserve their remaining lands. As the colonial records indicate, reservation communities' struggles against encroachment at times had a considerable influence on legislative debates over land rights, and in some instances caused the Connecticut government to be at odds with the English crown as well as with its own Angloamerican constituency. In their protests, reservation communities not only asserted local understandings of land rights and historical continuity, but also strategically employed colonial law to question the legality of particular acts of dispossession that Connecticut officials and colonial encroachers sought to legitimize.[65]

Reservation communities' resistance to dispossession elicited specific, culturally salient efforts on the part of the Connecticut government to "quiet" natives' complaints against encroachment, as it was commonly phrased by colonial officials. While the colony's fundamental reservation law, established in 1680, held that lands reserved for a particular native community were to "remayn to them and their heirs for ever,"[66] the Connecticut government initiated practices that served to justify and perpetuate colonial encroachment on reservation lands. By the early eighteenth century, the Connecticut General Assembly's legislative decisions regarding natives' rights to reservation land began to reflect an effort to evade the 1680 law, and to interpose, instead, colonial assessments of the cultural viability of reservation populations. Thus, in its response to natives' complaints against encroachment, colonial legislators began to appoint investigatory committees that tended to scrutinize reservation communities rather than the actions of colonial encroachers. An overview of both the General Assembly's orders to such committees and the committees' own reports indicates that their investigations into native complaints against encroachment were primarily concerned with assessing the size of the reservation population in question (and particularly the number of resident adult men in the community), and the reservation communities' "improvements" of their land according to colonial cultural standards. Disparaging reservation communities on cultural grounds—depicting them, for instance, as poor caretakers of the land, or as imminently "disappearing" from the landscape due to an insufficient number of men visible among them—became an effective means of circumventing the 1680 reservation law and legitimating ongoing processes of dispossession.[67]

Thus, in the context of native-Anglo struggles over rights to reservation land in early eighteenth-century Connecticut, it was not simply territorial boundaries that were contested, but particular notions about the cultural and political legitimacy of reservation populations. The Connecticut government's handling of the Mohegan land dispute serves as a crucial example of this newly significant strategy of colonial rule in the post-"Indian War" period. At the onset of the Mohegan land dispute, events foretold that colonial ideas about gender hierarchy were to figure prominently in the Connecticut government's efforts to justify its appropriation of Mohegan reserved land. In 1704, when Mohegan sachem Owaneco petitioned the English Crown in protest of the colony's appropriation of Mohegan lands in New London and Colchester, Queen Anne responded by establishing a commission to investigate and resolve the dispute.[68] The commission met in Stonington, Connecticut, in 1705, and ultimately ruled in favor of the Mohegans' complaint, determining that the colony had unjustly "granted away" their planting and hunting lands and ordering that those lands be restored to Mohegans.[69] Connecticut refused to acknowledge the 1705 decision, however, charging that the imperial commission lacked the authority to decide the case.[70] In its appeal to the Crown, the Connecticut government also attacked the 1705 decision on the grounds that Mohegans were not worthy of such consideration: as described by Connecticut's attorney, Sir Henry Ashurst, Mohegans were *"inconsiderable Indians"* who had *"but very few men."*[71] Hence a characterization of the Mohegan people as a politically and culturally unviable entity was introduced into the legal debate over Mohegan land rights. As the dispute wore on, gendered disparagements of Mohegan identity and cultural life would become increasingly important to the Connecticut government's efforts to silence Mohegan resisters and avoid enforcing the 1680 reservation law.

The colony's failure to comply with the 1705 decision did not serve to quash Mohegan resistance, however, nor did it deflect imperial scrutiny. As Connecticut's Governor Saltonstall reported to his Assembly in 1713, the Queen intended to look again into the "Affair of the Indian Lands."[72] Not surprisingly, subsequent colonial legislation concerning reservation populations and their land rights, passed in 1717, reflected the Connecticut government's interest in tightening its control over natives' lives and lands, this time under the aegis of the Christianizing mission. The 1717 act, referred to as "measures for Bringing the Indians in this colony to the knowledge of the Gospell," was directed primarily at Mohegans.[73] Ostensibly intended to "civilize" indigenous communities in Connecticut more effectively, the act specified that native populations were to be confined to "settlements in convenient places, in villages after the English manner" and identified the town of New London as the appropriate place to begin the endeavor, since it was there that the largest native community in the colony-that is, the Mohegan reservation community—resided.[74]

Perhaps the most significant provision of the act was its directive concerning the precise nature of the proposed native "settlements": they were to comprise "suitable portions" of land assigned to individual native families, the rights to which were to *descend from the father to his children*, the more to encourage them to apply themselves to Husbandry."[75] Seventeenth-century Indian law in Connecticut had not made such a pointed attempt to impose gendered prescriptions regarding land tenure on reservation populations,[76] and this particular stipulation suggests that nearly a century of colonial domination in southern New England had not eradicated native women's role as the primary agriculturalists in their communities. Given that dispossession, the undermining of indigenous subsistence economies, and service in the imperial border wars compelled many native men in southern New England to leave their communities in the eighteenth century, it is likely that women, or matrilineal kin groups, controlled agricultural plots on reservation lands and sustained community life.[77]

In attempting to impose a patriarchal and privatized system of land tenure on reservation communities via the 1717 "measures," colonial legislators sought not only to sever native women's cultural and economic connection to their lands, but also to deny the communal nature of landholding among reservation populations (and at the Mohegan reservation in particular). Conversely, the colony's 1680 reservation law asserted that rights to reservation land were to be held collectively, by a "parcel of Indians . . . and their heirs for ever."[78] Thus, the 1717 act may well have been intended to legislatively terminate *both* the Mohegan reservation and the reservation community itself. Obscuring the vital presence of native women on reservation land would have been a necessary first step in legitimating such an effort.[79]

A committee of colonial officials sent to implement the 1717 legislation met with immediate resistance from Mohegans, who had refused to acquiesce to encroachment on their reserved planting land. The General Assembly responded in 1718 by appointing another committee to investigate Mohegans' continuing complaints;[80] but, as was often the case in native-Anglo land disputes in eighteenth-century Connecticut, the appointment of an investigatory committee by no means ensured that native complainants would receive a fair hearing or "just" treatment in the colonial legal system, as Mohegans learned all too well. Indeed Connecticut officials who set upon the task of "quieting" such disputes were likely to be more concerned with protecting the interests of other colonial landholders than with preserving native rights to reservation land.[81] When Mohegan leaders Cesar and Ben Uncas I met directly with Connecticut Governor Gurdon Saltonstall in October 1720, they may have hoped for a better governmental response to the ongoing problem of encroachment on their sequestered land. In this instance, they provided Saltonstall with the names of particular colonists who had pressured Mohegan leaders to sell portions of their land.[82] More important, according to Saltonstall's own report on the meeting, Cesar and Ben Uncas expressed their concern for the land rights of future generations of Mohegans, having "declared, that the Land was not theirs to dispose of, but it was to descend to their Children."[83]

Despite these protests, by 1721 the Connecticut General Assembly reduced the Mohegan reservation to approximately five thousand acres, or one-fourth of its original size.[84] It had been Mohegans' government-appointed "guardians," colonists James Wadsworth and John Hall, who recommended that the Assembly so reduce the sequestered land as a means of resolving the dispute between Mohegans and colonial encroachers.[85] Through that act, Wadsworth and Hall secured Mohegan lands for a number of New London residents, among them six men who had been named as encroachers by Cesar and Ben Uncas I in their meeting with Governor Saltonstall in the previous year.[86] But this legislation had broader implications for the colony's Indian policy as well, since it introduced the politically expedient notion of imminent Indian "extinction" into the official legal discourse on native land rights. As it was phrased in the General Assembly's 1721 order, Mohegans' diminished reservation "shall forever belong to the Moheagan Indians . . . *so long as there shall be any of the Moheagan Indians found, or known alive: and when the whole nation, or stock of said Indians are extinct . . . [the reservation] shall for ever belong to the town of New London.*"[87] Hence it was the idea of Mohegans' inevitable disappearance from the landscape that, in effect, trumped the 1680 reservation law and signaled the emergence of a form of colonial surveillance intended to assess the presumed "degeneration" of those "stocks" of land-holding Indians. Indeed, it might be argued that this act fore-shadowed the "racialization" of Euroamerican discourse on Indianness, and its emphasis on evaluating the legitimacy of native identities and native rights in terms of the notion of Indian "racial purity" (i.e., "blood quantum").[88]

This legislative action must also be viewed on another level, how-ever, one which acknowledges that Mohegan resistance to dispossession had indeed made a significant impact on the shapers of colonial Indian policy. For it is certain that, in this instance, colonial officials and encroachers alike had sought to silence Mohegans' very pointed assertions of their land rights, which had served in 1704 to capture the ear of the Crown and had not yet been muted by the impoverished, if not desperate, conditions of reservation life. And thus, in this extreme reduction of Mohegans' reserved planting land, and in legislators' overtly stated prediction of impending doom for the Mohegan body politic, the 1721 action superceded the 1717 "civilizing measures" as an attempt by colonial officials to bring both the dispute over Mohegan lands, *and Mohegans themselves*, to an end. Nonetheless, as their leaders made clear to Governor Saltonstall in October 1720, Mohegans did not envision themselves as a vanishing people. Fifteen years after the 1721 action—and despite the hardships that act had wrought for the reservation community—Mohegans managed to persist; moreover, they had not succumbed to the authority of the Connecticut government. By January 1736, after Connecticut Governor Joseph Talcott learned that Mohegan leader Mahomet II, grandson of Owaneco, was making his way to London to present a second petition to the Crown,[89] Mohegans' legal case against the colony was reignited. Since Mohegans' complaints had been heard by external authorities whose interest in the matter might serve to be troubling for the Connecticut government (for example, the Society for the Propagation of the Gospel, as well as the Crown),[90] the controversy over Mohegan land rights had become something of a public relations problem for Connecticut, one that had focused attention on the legality of the colonial government's actions during the course of this dispute. Such attention was clearly warranted: the colony had disregarded the 1705 decision of the imperial commission as well as its own 1680 law. A November 1735 letter from the Reverend Benjamin Colman of Boston, a Commissioner for the Society for the Propagation of the Gospel in New England, to Eliphalet Adams of New London, the Society's "agent with the Indians in the eastern part of Connecticut,"[91] suggested that it was the legitimacy of the Connecticut government that was now at stake in the dispute. Indeed, Colman warned Adams that Mohegans' complaint "will fall heavy at Last upon your colony, for the Injury done the Indians in their Laws." Colman continued:

> I have as high a Resentment of such Injustice as any one, and Againe am as loath to apply home [to England] in any complaint for a Relief to the poor Natives, always friendly and faithfull to us, never to be Enough Acknowledged by us. We have complained to Your Gov[ernment] in Vaine. I know nothing more threatening to your charter than a wrong of this Nature, well proved, but what heart or hand can I willingly have in a piece of Justice which may bring on you so heavy a Revenge. What would it be for Your Province to do the Indians Right, and bear the loss among them [?][92]

Colman had raised the thorny issue that had been addressed by the 1705 commission: "to do the Indians Right" would require the restoration of their land. Such an argument against Connecticut's position in the matter, from an external authority, required a response, but it was to be a response that diverted attention from the central question posed in Colman's letter.

In 1736, Governor Talcott initiated a campaign to discredit Mahomet II and those Mohegan resisters who supported him. In a January 1736 letter to Massachusetts Governor Jonathan Belcher, Talcott sought support for Connecticut's cause in the matter, and argued that Mahomet II was not the legitimate sachem of the Mohegan people, but was rather "a tool" of Captain John Mason, a longtime friend and advisor of Mohegans whom Talcott had cast as the land-hungry instigator of the dispute.[93] But Talcott intended to do more than simply promote the Connecticut government's own position in the controversy to influential outsiders; he was also concerned with more effectively and directly controlling the Mohegan reservation community itself, and that required the cultivation of a Mohegan leader who would do the colony's bidding. Thus Talcott worked to legitimize the authority of Ben Uncas II, who had inherited his leadership position from his father but had been rejected, as Talcott himself was to learn, by his own community.[94] Although Talcott had assured Belcher that it was not Mahomet II, but Ben Uncas II who was "now in the full possession of the [Mohegan] Government, and has the hearts of his people,"[95] in February Talcott employed Captain Benajah Bushnell of Norwich to interrogate Mohegans on the reservation for the purpose of obtaining evidence that might be used to discredit Mahomet II, and to prove that Ben Uncas II was Mohegans' rightful sachem.[96]

In his February 1736 report to Governor Talcott, Bushnell explained that he could acquire from Mohegans "no Evidences of there Discarding of Mahamit the 2."[97] In fact, Bushnell noted that the Mohegans he encountered during his investigation had not readily submitted to his inquiries, and that some of those he had questioned about Mahomet II simply refused to talk to him, telling Bushnell "that they did not care to Declare or say anything about it, *without the People were all together.*"[98]  In the face of colonial assumptions about impending Mohegan extinction, Mohegan women and men thus proclaimed their political autonomy and the legitimacy of Mohegan community life.  Nevertheless, Bushnell's report went on to conclude that Mohegans' disappearance was imminent, and depicted the reservation community as existing in a state of cultural and political decay. As Belcher argued, this alone rendered Mohegans unworthy of the Crown's concern:

> I have Examined Several of the Indians, Concerning the number of all the ffamelies that belong to the whole Tribe of them . . . and Cant make more than 28 of them, & Several of them are non Residents, and seldom Live there. And there are several Widdows that keepe house, which they Reckoned as ffamelies. And they are not only a few but miserable pore, that I think if our Sovereign Lord the King knew their Circomstances well he would hardly put himself much out of his waie to obtain an alliance with them.[99]

Bushnell's contempt for Mohegans is obvious enough, and his assessment of the Mohegan reservation community indicates how the ostensibly mundane practice of *counting Indians* became an effective silencing maneuver, central to both the justification of dispossession and the obfuscation of natives' own ideas about what sustained community life. Among Mohegans, households headed by women—even destitute widows—were "reckoned as families." Indeed, their presence may well have become increasingly important during the course of the land dispute, as Mohegans contended with encroachers and the effects of dispossession on their means of subsistence.  Talcott reported later in 1736 that the Mohegan reservation community included "47 men 12 and up, and 48 women 12 and up."[100] Thus Mohegan women would have been extremely important to community life not only economically, as food producers, and as bearers and nurturers of children, but as a presence representing Mohegans' enduring connection to their homeland. Subsequent events of 1736 suggested that Bushnell's report obfuscated the cultural and political relevance of Mohegan women to the reservation community's struggle to preserve their collective land rights.

Despite Bushnell's failed investigation, by April of 1736 Governor Talcott had in hand two documents, both written in the colonial legal parlance of the time, which he would offer as evidence of Mohegans' own denial of Mahomet's legitimacy as a political leader, thus discrediting Mahomet's petition to the Crown as well. One of the documents, entitled "Declaration of Ben Uncas, Sachem of Mohegan," proclaimed the alliance between Ben Uncas II and the Connecticut government, and denounced previous complaints against the colony.[101] The other, a purported "Declaration of 9 of the Prime Mohegan Indians," was intended to defame Mahomet II by asserting that his political illegitimacy was rooted in an unsavory parentage. The document claimed not only that Mahomet I had been "banished" by his father, Owaneco, for his "Cruelty and barbarity," but that Mahomet I had, likewise, "banished" his own son, Mahomet II, because he was not born of "a Woman of the Royall Blood," but rather was the "issue" of "*a Concubine of a Mean Extract.*"[102] This parentage, the document alleged, rendered Mahomet II "a Stranger & an Alien" to Mohegans.[103]

This gendered construction of Mahomet's political and cultural "illegitimacy" brings into relief a crucial aspect of the Mohegan leadership ceremony that took place several months later. During this ceremony Mohegans not only contested the authority of Ben Uncas

II and his alliance with the colonial government, but also challenged colonial beliefs regarding gender hierarchy and political authority that had been made explicit both in the 1717 "civilizing" measures and in Governor Talcott's subsequent campaign against Mahomet II. Indeed, colonizers' distinctly patriarchal and class-based notions about land rights and political leadership were embodied in the opposing phrases *"Woman of the Royal Blood"* and *"Concubine of a Mean Extract."* This colonial construction of Mohegan political, cultural, and indeed biological "legitimacy" was intended to disqualify Mahomet II as a leader as well as a *Mohegan*; but it also disparaged indigenous women, particularly those who were impoverished, in a far more insidious fashion than had Belcher's contemptuous characterization of widow-headed households in the Mohegan community. Indeed, this effort to root legitimate Mohegan identity—*and thus Mohegan land rights*—quite literally in the wombs of women of (colonially concocted) Mohegan "Royal Blood" hinted at the possibility of far more Mohegans being disqualified, or "unrecognized," via the government's own calculations of the presence of such "blood" in the reservation community.

Mohegans' September 1736 leadership ceremony offered a dramatic counterpoint to the gendered tactics of colonial domination that the reservation community had endured. The sole account of the 1736 ceremony was given by colonists Jabez Crocker and Joseph Tracy Jr., of Norwich, who had witnessed the event. According to their testimony, on September 10 of that year "a very great number of Moheagan Indians" gathered "on the Indian land at Moheagan [i.e., the Mohegan reservation in New London]," for "a meeting which they call a black dance."[104] During the ceremony, Mohegans proclaimed their support for Mahomet II and his complaint against the colony, and "entirely denied Ben Uncas [II] to be their Sachem." Most important, Mohegans explained to Crocker and Tracy that, "the one principal cause of their meeting or dance was to establish Anne the daughter of Caesar . . . to be their ruler until Mahomet returned."[105] Crocker and Tracy's account thus indicates that Mohegans had not yet learned that Mahomet II had died of small-pox in England in the previous month. Governor Talcott had been informed of the event, however, by the colony's agent in London, who expressed in a letter to Talcott his hope that with Mahomet's death "an end is put to the Affair."[106]

The September 1736 ceremony indicated to the Connecticut government that Mahomet's death alone would *not* end the affair, for there was another leader, Anne, to whom Mohegan resisters had already looked. As Governor Talcott's response to the ceremony suggests, Anne's leadership presented a considerable political threat to the colony by confronting Connecticut officials with the likelihood that Mohegans' legal case would go forward.[107] Talcott subsequently instructed missionary Jonathan Barber to warn Mohegans not to "set up a queen or imposter," for if they did, the colonial government "would protect only Ben [i.e., Ben Uncas II] and his family, with those that adhered to him."[108] As Barber later testified, this was no idle threat to Mohegans at the time, since after the September leadership ceremony, a timely and perhaps colonially contrived rumor had circulated that the so-called "Eastward Indians" (that is, Abenakis) were planning to attack Mohegans. According to Barber, the rumor "caused the [Mohegans] a very great fear, even so great that they did many of them begin a fort for their defence."[109]

Connecticut officials also sought a more direct, and surely more "traditional," means of silencing Anne: an arranged marriage. As colonist Samuel Avery later explained, "some time in the Year 1737 it was Proposed and Thought Convenient that Ben Uncas, Junr. [son of Ben Uncas II], who was then an Indented Apprentice . . . in the Province of Massachusetts, should be Sent for . . . And Marryed unto

Sachem Cesar['s] daughter."[110]  In his petition to the Connecticut
General Assembly requesting reimbursement for his services, Avery
stated that he had retrieved the son of Ben Uncas II as ordered,
and according to colonial accounts, Anne's forced marriage did
take place.[111]

Thus Anne's sachemship appears to have been effectively undermined by the Connecticut government; subsequently, her name virtually disappeared from the historical record. Nonetheless, Mohegans
continued to denounce Ben Uncas II, explaining in a May 1737 petition to the General Assembly that he had assisted encroachers whose
livestock damaged Mohegan crops, and that he "utterly Denies to ask
us any Council in any of [our] affairs but Does as he is Directed by
them whome we think to be our Trespassers."[112]  By this point, however, colonial officials were intent upon ignoring Mohegans' protests
against the actions of Ben Uncas II. When a second imperial commission sat in Norwich, Connecticut, in May 1738 to review the
Mohegan case, the majority of the commissioners, who were from
Rhode Island, declared Ben Uncas II to be Mohegans' legitimate
sachem and overturned the 1705 decision.[113]  In July 1738, Governor
Talcott assured the colony's agent in London, Francis Wilks, that the
"proper Moheags" continued to support their rightful "King," Ben
Uncas II.[114]  From the Connecticut government's perspective, then,
only those Mohegans who did its bidding—which included Ben
Uncas II and his few followers—were to be acknowledged as "proper," that is *legitimate*, Mohegans. Although Mohegan resisters appealed
the 1738 decision, by 1773 the Crown ruled on behalf of the colony
and the legal case was brought to a close.[115]

The final legal outcome of the dispute notwithstanding, the 1736
leadership ceremony was a crucial moment in Mohegans' dispute with
the Connecticut government, for it signaled the enduring importance
of land, and local knowledge, to a community shaped by a history of

struggle. In one sense, the event seems to have been a means of commemorating the previous three decades of Mohegans' resistance to dispossession, for indeed Anne's name recalled the English queen who had established the first commission to hear Mohegans' complaint against the colony in 1705. Thus Anne's leadership may have suggested a compelling irony, invoking imperial authority to remind the Connecticut government of its failure to acknowledge the 1705 decision.

At the same time, however, the 1736 ceremony was a forceful expression of Mohegans' own beliefs and practices regarding political authority and land rights. It asserted that Mohegan leadership was a local matter, its legitimacy rooted in the reservation community— and in Mohegan land—rather than in the halls of the colonial government. And if Mohegans did in fact refer to the event as a "black dance," that name too may have had a timely political and cultural significance: evoking as it does the colonial notion of Indian "savagery" as a diabolic, anti-Christian force, such a designation suggests that the ceremony expressed Mohegans' rejection of the multiple cultural trappings of "civilization," not simply the patriarchal strictures of colonial rule. Given Governor Talcott's attempt to undermine Mohegan leadership and deny Mahomet's Mohegan identity, Mohegan resisters may have intended for the "black dance" to emphasize Mohegans' *otherness*, to articulate Mohegan identity in terms of a *gendered* opposition that defied both colonial understanding and governmental control.

Finally, it is also important to note the significance of the season during which the ceremony was held. Since late summer was the time of harvesting green corn, this gathering at Mohegan on September 10 may well have coincided with the Green Corn Ceremony, a celebration that highlighted the importance of women's role as agriculturalists.[116] Thus the naming of Anne as *sunksquaw* may have been a means of reaffirming the importance of women within the reservation community—not only as cultivators of corn, but as reproducers of community life and purveyors of Mohegans' cultural ties to their reserved land.

The September 1736 ceremony thus embodied a complex critique of colonial power, challenging colonizers' patriarchal notions about land rights and the legitimacy of reservation communities, and affirming the local knowledge and practices that bound members of the Mohegan reservation community to each other and to their homeland.

## Conclusion

Gendered beliefs and practices played a powerful role in natives' strategies of resistance and accommodation in colonial southern New England. By unraveling the significance of gender in indigenous struggles for land and political autonomy, we may come to better understand the complexity of native women's lives during and beyond the period of military conquest. Moreover, examining the particular ways in which ideas about gender shaped relations of power in the post-"Indian War" colonial world, we may release from obscurity a broader field of historical actors, among them those native women and men who may not have been sanctioned by colonial officials as "legitimate" leaders, or whose voices and experiences may not have been acknowledged by Euroamerican historiography, but whose actions nonetheless sustained their communities, and their histories.

# Notes

1.  Daniel Gookin, *Historical Collections of the Indians in New England* ([1674]; repr. New York: Arno Press, 1972), 6-7.

2.  Gookin, *Historical Collections*, 6.

3.  Gookin, *Historical Collections*, 6.

4.  Gookin, *Historical Collections*, 4-6.

5.  The trend in the historiography of colonial New England to cast conquest and colonialism as seventeenth-century phenomena consisting of "culture contact" or "cultural encounter" tends to obscure the complexities of colonial domination as a multifaceted system of control, in the context of which the production of knowledge about culture, and indeed about history itself, were (and remain) implicated in relations of power. As anthropologist Bernard Cohn has explained, the colonial situation "is not to be viewed as 'impact,' nor as 'culture contact,' nor is it to be viewed through a methodology that seeks to sort what is introduced from what is indigenous." Rather, the colonial situation must be understood as a context in which both colonizers and indigenous peoples "were constantly involved in representing to each other what they were doing," and in which forms of knowledge and representations of the past thus shaped, and were informed by, relations of domination. Bernard S. Cohn, *An Anthropologist Among the Historians and Other Essays* (Delhi: Oxford University Press, 1987), 44-45. See also Bernard S. Cohn, *Colonialism and Its Forms of Knowledge* (Princeton: Princeton University Press, 1996); Nicholas B. Dirks, "Introduction: Colonialism and Culture," in *Colonialism and Culture*, ed.

Nicholas B. Dirks (Ann Arbor: University of Michigan Press, 1992); Frederick Cooper and Ann L. Stoler, "Tensions of Empire: Colonial Control and Visions of Rule," *American Ethnologist* 16 (4) (1989): 609-21; and Peter Pels, "The Anthropology of Colonialism: Culture, History, and the Emergence of Western Governmentality," *Annual Review of Anthropology* 26 (1997): 163-83.

6.   The historiography of colonial southern New England has long indicated that King Philip's War marked the end of significant political resistance for the Native peoples. Historian Harold Clayton Bradshaw referred to it as "the last great stand of the Indians"; more recently, historian Harold Selesky called it "the last Indian challenge." Similarly, ethnohistorian Laurie Weinstein has argued that as a result of the 1675 war "New England Indians [were] defeated in their efforts to protect their lands from further colonial encroachment," and that "there were no more barriers to colonial settlement of New England." Harold Clayton Bradshaw, *The Indians of Connecticut: The Effect of English Colonization and of Missionary Activity on Indian Life in Connecticut* (Deep River, Conn.: The New Era Press, 1935), 52; Harold Selesky, *War and Society in Colonial Connecticut* (New Haven: Yale University Press, 1990); and Laurie Lee Weinstein, "Indian vs. Colonist: Competition for Land in 17th Century Plymouth Colony" (Ph.D. diss., Southern Methodist University, 1983), v. However, a close look at the land struggles of reservation communities in eighteenth-century Connecticut (see below) reveals that such depictions do not reflect the way in which Native people themselves understood their past, or envisioned their historical possibilities.

7.   Colin G. Calloway, "Introduction: Surviving the Dark Ages," in *After King Philip's War: Presence and Persistence in Indian New England*, ed. Colin G. Calloway (Hanover: University Press of New England, 1997), 4.

8.   Nicholas B. Dirks, "Introduction: Colonialism and Culture," 3. In the past several decades, feminist ethnohistory and other critical studies in colonialism have contributed much to our understanding of the varied cultural mechanisms by which colonial powers imposed and

maintained authority. Among the most important for this essay has been the work of anthropologists Irene Silverblatt and Ann Laura Stoler. See Irene Silverblatt, "Interpreting Women in States: New Feminist Ethnohistories," in *Gender at the Crossroads of Knowledge; Feminist Anthropology in the Postmodern Era*, ed. Micaela di Leonardo (Berkeley: University of California Press, 1991); and Ann Laura Stoler, "Rethinking Colonial Categories: European Communities and the Boundaries of Rule," *Comparative Studies in Society and History* 31 (1) (1989): 134-61.

9.  Robert S. Grumet, "Sunksquaws, Shamans, and Tradeswomen: Middle Atlantic Coastal Algonkian Women During the 17th and 18th Centuries," in *Women and Colonization: Anthropological Perspectives*, ed. Mona Etienne and Eleanor Leacock (New York: Praeger, 1980), 49.

10. See Grumet, "Sunksquaws, Shamans, and Tradeswomen," 49.

11. Grumet, "Sunksquaws, Shamans, and Tradeswomen," 51.

12. See Patricia E. Rubertone, *Grave Undertakings: An Archaeology of Roger Williams and the Narragansett Indians* (Washington: Smithsonian Institution Press, 2001), 122.

13. Rubertone, *Grave Undertakings*, 122.

14. Rubertone, *Grave Undertakings*, 122-23.

15. Grumet, "Sunksquaws, Shamans, and Tradeswomen," 51.

16. For other relevant discussions of the role of sunksquaws in native-Anglo political struggles in seventeenth-century southern New England, see for instance Anne Marie Plane, "Putting a Face on Colonization: Factionalism and Gender Politics in the Life History of Awashunkes, the 'Squaw Sachem' of Saconet," in *Northeastern Indian Lives, 1632–1816*, ed. Robert S. Grumet (Amherst: University of Massachusetts Press, 1996), 140-65; and John Menta, "Shaumpishuh,

'Squaw Sachem' of the Quinnipiac Indians," *Artifacts* 16 (3-4) (1988): 32-37.

17. In John Trumbull's "Natick Dictionary," the word sachem (*sohkom*) is translated as "he has the mastery" and "he leads." James Hammond Trumbull, "Natick Dictionary," *Bureau of American Ethnology Reports,* Bulletin 25 (1903).

18. Grumet, "Sunksquaws, Shamans, and Tradeswomen."

19. See Carolyn Merchant, *Ecological Revolutions: Nature, Gender, and Science in New England* (Chapel Hill: University of North Carolina Press, 1989), 69.

20. Peter Nabokov and Dean Snow note that by the time of Columbus's invasion, "techniques for growing and storing vegetables had been developing in the Northeast for four or five centuries." Peter Nabokov and Dean Snow, "Farmers of the Woodlands," in *America in 1492: The World of the Indian Peoples Before the Arrival of Columbus,* ed. Alvin M. Josephy (New York: Alfred A. Knopf, 1992), 126. On indigenous women as the primary agriculturalists in New England, see Merchant, *Ecological Revolutions,* 69-81.

21. A number of scholars have offered important insights into the nature of native women's labor and economic power in northeastern North America. Among the most important to the present discussion are: Joy Bilharz, "First Among Equals? The Changing Status of Seneca Women," in *Women and Power in Native North America,* ed. Laura F. Klein and Lillian A. Ackerman (Norman and London: University of Oklahoma Press, 1995); Joan M. Jensen, "Native American Women and Agriculture: A Seneca Case Study," in *Unequal Sisters: A Multicultural Reader in U.S. Women's History* (New York: Routledge, 1994); and Russell G. Handsman, "Algonkian Wigwams: An Invisible Presence, Political Spaces," *Artifacts* 17 (4) (1989).

22. Grumet, "Sunksquaws, Shamans, and Tradeswomen."

23. Roger Williams, *A Key into the Language of America* ([1643] ; repr. Detroit:

Wayne State University Press, 1973), 121.

24. Williams, *Key into the Language*, 171.

25. Russell G. Handsman, "Chanameed and A Mohegan Woman's Mortars," *Artifacts* 16 (3-4) (1988): 11-27.

26. Handsman, "Chanameed," 25.

27. Kathleen J. Bragdon, *Native People of Southern New England, 1500–1650* (Norman: University of Oklahoma Press, 1996), 135. Mohegan Tribal Historian Melissa Fawcett has elaborated on this notion. In her recent book, *Medicine Trail: The Life and Lessons of Gladys Tantaquidgeon,* Fawcett records the teachings of Mohegan elder and medicine woman Gladys Tantaquidgeon on a variety of matters, including the way in which language expresses particular aspects of the leadership roles of men and women. According to Tantaquidgeon, "in the Mohegan language, the spirit of rocks is acknowledged in the names for our leaders. A male leader is called sachem, which means rock man and a woman leader is referred to as sunksquaw, which means rock woman. It has been passed down that the rocks are the bones of Mother Earth." Melissa Fawcett, *Medicine Trail: The Life and Lessons of Gladys Tantaquidgeon* (Tuscon: University of Arizona Press, 2000), 21.

28. Trumbull, "Natick Dictionary," 102.

29. Trumbull, "Natick Dictionary," 104.

30. Trumbull, "Natick Dictionary," 187.

31. See M. Annette Jaimes Guerro, "Civil Rights versus Sovereignty: Native American Women in Life and Land Struggles," in *Feminist Genealogies, Colonial Legacies, Democratic Futures*, ed. Jacqui Alexander and Chandra Talpade Mohanty (New York: Routledge, 1997).

32. Kathleen Bragdon provides an excellent overview of the literature on

the impact of the Christianizing mission on native women and gender relations in colonial New England. Kathleen Bragdon, "Gender as a Social Category in Native Southern New England," *Ethnohistory* 43 (4) (1996): 573-92.

33. Bragdon, "Gender as a Social Category," 575.

34. See Jean M. O'Brien, "Divorced from the Land: Resistance and Survival of Indian Women in Eighteenth-Century New England," in Calloway, ed., *After King Philip's War*.

35. O'Brien, "Divorced from the Land," 145-49.

36. O'Brien, "Divorced from the Land," 149.

37. Russel G. Handsman and Trudie Lamb Richmond, "Confronting Colonialism: The Mahican and Schaghticoke Peoples and Us," in *Making Alternative Histories*, ed. Thomas C. Patterson (Santa Fe: School of American Research Press, 1995).

38. Electa Jones, *Stockbridge, Past and Present: Records of an Old Mission Station* (Springfield: Samuel Bowles and Co., 1894), 70.

39. See Patrick Frazier, *The Mohicans of Stockbridge* (Lincoln and London: University of Nebraska Press, 1992).

40. Shirley Dunn, *The Mohican World, 1680–1750* (Fleischmanns, N.Y. Purple Mountain Press, 2000), 130.

41. Ruth Wallis Herndon and Narragansett Tribal Historian Ella Wilcox Sekatau have examined the impact of imposed racial categories on Narragansett history and identity in the eighteenth and nineteenth centuries. Ruth Wallis Herndon and Ella Wilcox Sekatau, "The Right to a Name: The Narragansett People and Rhode Island Officials in the Revolutionary Era," *Ethnohistory* 44 (3) (1997): 433-62.

42. Henry Baker, *History of Montville, Connecticut, Formerly the North Parish of*

*New London, from 1640–1896* (Hartford: Press of the Case, Lockwood, and Brainard Company, 1896), 65.

43. Fawcett, *Medicine Trail*, 48.

44. Fawcett, *Medicine Trail*, 54.

45. Documents and personal papers relating to the history of the Mohegan Ladies' Sewing Society are housed at the Mohegan Archives, Mohegan Tribal Office, Uncasville, Connecticut.

46. John W. De Forest, *History of the Indians of Connecticut from the Earliest Known Period to 1850* ([1852]; repr. Hamden, Conn.: Archon Books, 1964), 1.

47. For further discussion of the history of Schaghticoke resistance, see Trudie Lamb Richmond, "A Native Perspective of History: The Schaghticoke Nation, Resistance and Survival," in *Enduring Traditions: The Native People of New England*, ed. Laurie Weinstein (Westport, Conn.: Bergin and Garvey, 1994).

48. For a more detailed discussion, see Trudie Lamb Richmond, "Spirituality and Survival in Schaghticoke Basketmaking," in *A Key into the Language of Woodsplint Baskets*, ed. Ann McMullen and Russell G. Handsman (Washington, Conn.: American Indian Archaeological Institute, 1987).

49. The notion of native women as sociocultural authorities in their communities was introduced by Mohegan Tribal Historian Melissa Fawcett. Melissa Fawcett, "Sociocultural Authority: The Mohegan Case," in *Rooted Like the Ash Trees*, ed. Richard Carlson (Naugatuck, Conn.: Eagle Wing Press, 1987), 52-53.

50. See Fawcett, "Sociocultural Authority," 53.

51. In *Partial Recall: Photographs of Native Americans*, Lucy Lippard discusses

the impact of photographic images on Native American identities, revealing how photography has shaped Euroamerican society's idea of Indianness while it has also obscured native histories and identities through both romanticism and dehumanization. Julia had clearly experienced the dehumanizing aspect of portrait photography. Lucy R. Lippard, "Introduction," in *Partial Recall*, ed. Lucy R. Lippard (New York: The New Press, 1992), 13-45; see also James C. Faris, "Photographing the Navajo: Scanning Abuse," *American Indian Culture and Research Journal* 20 (3) (1996): 65-81.

52. The idea that Mohegans' history during the colonial period can be reduced solely to that of colonial "ally" reflects the persistent power of colonial discourse, and of colonial divide-and-rule policies, most dramatically evinced in colonists' cultivation of relationships with specific native leaders for the purpose of carrying out the 1637 massacre and thereby acquiring Pequots' much-coveted lands. This particular notion has also shaped the way native people in Connecticut view their histories today. Anthropologist Jack Campisi has observed that it is not uncommon for Mashantucket Pequots, when talking about the colonial past, to remark that Pequots and Mohegans "had not had much contact" since Mohegans "join[ed] the English in the massacres and enslavement" of Pequots in 1637. Jack Campisi, "The Emergence of the Mashantucket Pequot Tribe, 1637–1975," in *The Pequots of Southern New England: The Rise and Fall of an American Indian Nation*, ed. Laurence Hauptman and James Wherry (Norman: University of Oklahoma Press, 1990), 117. Contrary to the claims of colonial discourse, however, seventeenth-century divide-and-rule tactics did not result in a permanent disaffection and disconnection between native communities that were embroiled, and opposed, in seventeenth-century colonial warfare. As Amy Den Ouden discusses elsewhere, Pequots and Niantics—whose reservations, like Mohegans, were besieged by colonial encroachers—participated in Mohegan leadership ceremonies in the eighteenth century and supported Mohegans in their legal dispute with the colony over rights to their reservation land. As Den Ouden points out, such alliances between reservation communities suggest that kin ties, local cultural

beliefs, and the common historical experience of struggle against dis-possession, continued to bind native peoples to each other, despite the political dissension wrought by military conquest in the seventeenth century. Amy E. Den Ouden, "Against Conquest: Land, Culture, and Power in the Eighteenth-Century Histories of the Native Peoples of Connecticut" (Ph.D. diss., University of Connecticut, 2001).

53.  Den Ouden, "Against Conquest," 182-263.

54.  There is evidence that *sunksquaw* was the term Mohegans used to describe Anne's position of leadership. Testifying before the imperial commission of 1743, which was charged with reviewing the Mohegan case and the proceedings of the previous commission in 1738, colonist Samuel Leffingwell of Norwich testified that he "heard, when Mahomet [II] was in England, that some of the Indians were about to set up Anne, the daughter of Caesar, to be Sunkee Squaw." *Governor and Company of Connecticut, and Mohegan Indians, by Their Guardians. Certified Copy of Book of Proceedings Before Commissioners of Review, 1743* [hereafter *Book of Proceedings*] (London: W. and J. Richardson, 1769), 204.

55.  Cesar was the son of Owaneco and grandson to Uncas; Ben Uncas II was the son of "Major" Ben Uncas (Ben Uncas I, the brother of Owaneco) and also grandson to Uncas. Mahomet II (son of Mahomet I and nephew of Cesar) and Anne were great-grandchildren of Uncas. See "Uncas Genealogy" in *The Talcott Papers: Correspondence and Documents during Joseph Talcott's Governorship, 1724–1741*, vol. 2 (1737–1741), *Collections of the Connecticut Historical Society*, vol. 5 (Hartford: The Society, 1896).

56.  Den Ouden, "Against Conquest," 233-54.

57.  *Book of Proceedings*, 237.

58.  My use of the term *community* here refers to native women and men who share a land base and economic resources, and who are bound by kin ties and a common historical experience. In using this term, I do

not intend to imply that, by the eighteenth century, there were no longer native sociopolitical entities that can be termed *nations*. Rather, what I mean to specify is that reservation communities did (and do) not necessarily comprise the entirety of a native nation or people. The harsh economic realities of the eighteenth century required that native men, for instance, often had to seek work away from their communities as wage laborers (in the whaling industry, for example), and that parents might have had to send their children out as indentured servants in Euroamerican households.

59.   All four of these reservation communities were located within New London County and were engaged in struggles to protect their remaining lands in the eighteenth century. Each petitioned the Connecticut General Assembly several times during the first half of the eighteenth century to seek redress against colonial encroachers. Den Ouden, "Against Conquest," 264-67; 327-34. The combined population of Mohegans (351), Mashantucket Pequots (321), Eastern Pequots (218), and Niantics (163) equaled approximately 3/4 of the total indigenous population (1,400-1,600 individuals) as estimated by Gov. Joseph Talcott in 1725. Thus New London County, a main hub of colonial society in Connecticut, contained the largest concentrated population of indigenous people in the colony at the time. *Talcott Papers*, 2: 397-402. In 1730, Talcott reported that the total native population in the colony was "about 1600, of both sexes and all ages," and that the total Euroamerican population in Connecticut was 38,000, with a significant increase having occurred between 1720 and 1730. *Public Records of the Colony of Connecticut* [hereafter CPR], ed. J. H. Trumbull and C. J. Hoadley (Hartford: Press of Case, Lockwood & Brainerd, 1850–1890), 7:580-84.

60.   *Indian Papers*, Connecticut State Archives, Papers and Correspondence of the General Assembly, 1st ser., doc. 52.

61.   *Indian Papers*, 1st ser., doc. 52.

62.   See *Book of Proceedings*, v; *Indian Papers*, 1st ser., doc. 122.

63. *Indian Papers*, 1st ser., doc. 122.

64. *Book of Proceedings*, 27-28; 177-81.

65. For a detailed discussion of the cultural and political facets of these struggles over reservation land in eighteenth-century Connecticut, see Den Ouden, "Against Conquest."

66. CPR, 3:56-57.

67. See Den Ouden, "Against Conquest," chaps. 6-7.

68. Owaneco's 1704 petition initiated the legal case known as *Mohegan Indians, by their Guardians v. The Governor and Company of Connecticut*. Legal scholar Mark D. Walters provides an excellent overview of the legal case, and of the views held by colony and Crown with regard to native sovereignty, but his article does not include an analysis of the role of Mohegan resisters themselves as important political actors during the course of the dispute. Mark D. Walters, *"Mohegan Indians v. Connecticut* (1705–1773) and the Legal Status of Aboriginal Customary Laws and Government in British North America," *Osgoode Hall Law Journal* 33 (4) (1995): 785-829. Other discussions of the legal case, none of which address the significance of Mohegan resistance, include: E. Edwards Beardsley, "The Mohegan Land Controversy," *Papers of the New Haven Historical Society* 3 (1882): 205-25; David W. Conroy, "The Defense of Indian Land Rights: William Bollan and the Mohegan Case in 1743," *Proceedings of the American Antiquarian Society*, vol. 103, pt. 2 (1994); and Joseph Henry Smith, *Appeals to the Privy Council from the American Plantations* (New York: Columbia University Press, 1950). As argued here, Mohegans' political strategies and cultural knowledge were a driving force of the legal case and offered an important critique of colonial authority and colonial claims to native land.

69. *Book of Proceedings*, 28.

70. *Book of Proceedings*, 33. See also Walters, *"Mohegan Indians v. Connecticut,"*

804-11. Another important argument in the colony's appeal, and one that continued to be articulated throughout the course of the legal case, was that all Mohegan lands were "conquest lands," having been acquired, it was claimed, via the "Pequot War" of 1637, during which "the Pequots and all theire Adherents and Subjects, whereof all the Mohegans were a part, were Conquerred." Likewise, the Mohegan sachem Uncas, who had been allied with colonial leaders against Pequots in 1637, was rendered a "subordinate" sachem in this argument, one who had only "pretended to the Proprietary of a smale Territory Called Mohegin." *Indian Papers*, 1st ser., doc. 61.

71. *Book of Proceedings*, 153-55.

72. *Indian Papers*, 1st ser., doc. 79.

73. *Indian Papers*, 1st ser., doc. 87; CPR, 6:31-32.

74. CPR, 6:31-2.

75. CPR, 6:32.

76. The 1680 reservation law, for instance, included no stipulation regarding the necessity of patrilineal inheritance of rights to reservation land. CPR, 3:56-57.

77. That women were important to alliance-making between native communities, and to community formation itself, in the post-Pequot War period is evinced in the efforts made by Niantic and Mohegan male leaders to marry Pequot women in the aftermath of the massacre. Seventeenth-century colonist Roger Williams reported to colonial officials that the Eastern Niantic Sachem Wequashcook had married the mother of the dead Pequot sachem Sassacus and was harboring a number of Pequot refugees after the massacre. As historian Glenn LaFantasie explains, the marriage "strengthened Wequashcook's rights to [Niantic] lands that overlapped into the Pequot Country, gave him added rights to incorporate Pequot survivors into his band,

and allowed him, at the very least, to demand hunting rights in the Pequot territory." Roger Williams reported, as well, that Uncas, in marrying the sister of Sassacus, "hath drawn all the scattered Pequts to himselfe and drawne much wealth from them." Glenn LaFantasie, ed., *The Correspondence of Roger Williams*, 2 vols. (Hanover: University Press of New England, 1988), 117, 121, 146. At least part of the "wealth" men like Uncas and Wequashcook acquired through marriages to these women, in addition to the economic benefit of access to Pequot lands and the political benefit of strengthening the numbers within their own communities, was cultural capital. For indeed, native women were not simply tokens of kinship or producers of offspring; they were perpetuators of cultural identities and cultural ties to land. There is also the overlooked likelihood that these women were sought after by Wequashcook and Uncas because they had considerable political savvy and political power in their own right.

78. CPR, 3:56-7.

79. An early eighteenth-century petition to the General Assembly from Eastern Pequot *sunksquaw* Mary Momoho serves to illuminate the complexity of natives' responses to colonial efforts to undermine the position of native women within their own communities. Her petition informed legislators of threats to her reservation community from several residents of Stonington, Connecticut, who "tell us that when one or two more of us be dead the [reservation] Lands will fall to them again." In response to this suggestion that Eastern Pequots were near extinction, Mary Momoho argued, "we suppose that there will be some pleas made that wee are almost all dead & indeed so we be but yet wee have Thirty three men yet alive which belong to Momoho besides woemen & Children therefore we would begg the Honoured Courtt that they would take prudent care of us as to Lett no Country Grants to be Laid upon our Lands." The petition is concluded with the line, "these from the sunk squaw which was the wife of Momoho and her men." In emphasizing the precise number of men in the reservation community—as well as her own, and her community's, continuing allegiance to the deceased male sachem

Momoho—Mary Momoho's petition indicates that she understood the necessity of deferring to colonists' patriarchal notions about land rights and political authority. Yet clearly her petition does not wholly acquiesce to the demands of colonial power. Indeed, it opens with a reminder to the Connecticut government "of the former unity which was betwixt you and our Nation [during King Philip's War]," and that "Momoho was then the Pecot Saysjum and had sixty men under him and att all your expeditions of War was ready to serve you & doubtless was a guard to your nation." Her petition's concluding line, which indicated that the male members of the Eastern Pequot reservation community were *"her men,"* was surely an assertion of her authority by her own community's standards, not those of colonial society. In the record of the General Assembly's response to her petition, however, she is referred to as "Momoho's Squaw," rather than as a sachem or *sunksquaw* in her own right. Connecticut State Archives Collection, Early General Records of Connecticut: Papers and Correspondence of the General Assembly, the Governor and Counsel, and other Colony or State Officials, *Indian Papers*, 1st ser., doc. 73.

80. CPR, 6:78.

81. The same was often true with regard to the government's appointment of colonial "guardians" or "overseers" of reservation communities. See Den Ouden, "Against Conquest," 135-81.

82. *Indian Papers*, 1st ser., doc. 90.

83. *Indian Papers*, 1st ser., doc. 90.

84. *Book of Proceedings*, 189-91; De Forest, *History of the Indians of Connecticut*, 315; Mohegan Tribe, Petition for Federal Recognition, vol. 1, (1984), 79.

85. Den Ouden, "Against Conquest," 219-29; CPR, 6:148-49.

86. *Book of Proceedings*, 189-91; Den Ouden, "Against Conquest," 221-29.

87. *Book of Proceedings*, 194; emphasis added.

88. Later in the eighteenth century, and beyond, the Connecticut government's surveillance of reservation communities and evaluation of
their land rights would come to be cast in distinctly racialized terms.
Den Ouden, "Against Conquest," 27-42, 343-72.    On the
Euroamerican racial notions of "Indian blood" and "blood quantum" as the standard means of assessing, and disparaging, Indian
identity as well as native land rights in the nineteenth, and twentieth-
century U.S. , see Ward Churchill, "The Crucible of American Indian
Identity," *Z Magazine*, January 1998, 47-51; M. Annette Jaimes,
"American Racism: The Impact on American Indian Identity and
Survival," in *Race*, ed. Steven Gregory and Roger Sanjek (New
Brunswick: Rutgers University Press, 1994); Pauline Turner Strong
and Barrik Van Winkle, "'Indian Blood': Reflections on the
Reckoning and Refiguring of Native North American Identity,"
*Cultural Anthropology* 11 (4) (1996): 547-76.

89. *Talcott Papers*, 1:330.

90. *Talcott Papers*, 1:310, 339.

91. *Talcott Papers*, 1:107n.

92. *Talcott Papers*, 1:327-28.

93. *Talcott Papers*, 1:329.

94. It is difficult to ascertain precisely how it was that Ben Uncas II came
to cooperate with the Connecticut government in its effort to bring
an end to the land dispute.  In fact, when Ben Uncas II became
sachem in 1726, after the death of his father Ben Uncas I, he petitioned the Connecticut General Assembly to announce that he had
named four Mohegans as "Trustees or over seers for the Moheag
Indians," and that he had made a Mohegan man, Jo Weebucks, the
"True and Lawfull Attorny . . . for all the Mohegen Indians." The

task Ben Uncas II had assigned Weebucks was to "Recover and Require . . . Any Land Rents or herbage" that New London residents owed to Mohegans. Thus Ben Uncas II indicated early in his leadership that he was to press for Mohegans' land rights by demanding payment from colonists who had "leased" or encroached upon Mohegan reservation land, using it, for instance, for grazing their livestock. In addition, his naming of *Mohegans* as "trustees" or "overseers" for the reservation community defied the Connecticut government's practice of appointing colonial "guardians" as decision-makers for reservation communities. Yet, while Ben Uncas II had asserted Mohegans' political autonomy in his September 1726 petition, the General Assembly acknowledged neither the appointment of Jo Weebucks as Mohegans' attorney nor the complaint against ongoing colonial encroachment; instead, colonial legislators reappointed Wadsworth and Hall as Mohegans' official "guardians," empowering them to "take care of the sd Indian Affairs in the sd Mohegan Country by leasing out their Lands for their best benefit and advantage." *Indian Papers*, 1st ser., docs. 128, 129. For Ben Uncas II, then, it may have seemed that any effort to affirm Mohegans' political autonomy, and their land rights, against the wishes of the Connecticut government would in the end prove fruitless, and thus he may have opted to comply rather than resist. Whatever the case may have been, by 1736, Ben Uncas II was touted as the sole legitimate sachem of Mohegans by Governor Talcott, but clearly was not regarded as a leader by many, if not most, of his own people. See Den Ouden, "Against Conquest," 231-60.

95.  *Talcott Papers*, 1:339.

96.  *Talcott Papers*, 1:350.

97.  *Talcott Papers*, 1:350.

98.  *Talcott Papers*, 1:350; emphasis added.

99.  *Talcott Papers*, 1:350-51.

100. *Talcott Papers*, 1:377.

101. *Talcott Papers*, 1:361-63.

102. *Talcott Papers*, 1:365; emphasis added.

103. *Talcott Papers*, 1:365.

104. *Book of Proceedings*, 235-36.

105. *Book of Proceedings*, 235-36.

106. *Talcott Papers*, 1:374.

107. At this point, Governor Talcott was also troubled by a further political complication that would potentially impact the Mohegan case: the fact that Pequots and Niantics had joined Mohegan resisters in denouncing Ben Uncas II in 1736. According to Talcott, when Mohegans appeared before the next imperial commission to hear the case in 1738, they were joined by Pequot and Niantic supporters. Talcott sought to dismiss this political alliance as a mere contrivance, arguing that Pequots and Niantics "have Nothing at all in the Controversy." *Book of Proceedings*, 218; *Talcott Papers*, 2:54. But since Niantics, Mashantucket Pequots, and Mohegans had brought formal complaints against encroachers to the Connecticut General Assembly during his tenure as governor, Talcott well knew that these communities had a shared interest in protecting reservation land and in urging the government to enforce the colony's 1680 reservation law. Den Ouden, "Against Conquest," 252-60, 264-67, 326-34.

108. *Book of Proceedings*, 237.

109. *Book of Proceedings*, 237.

110. *Indian Papers*, 1st ser., doc. 236.

111. *Indian Papers*, 1st ser., docs. 236 and 173g; *Talcott Papers*, 2:198.

112. *Indian Papers*, 1st ser., doc. 158; *Book of Proceedings*, 218.

113. *Book of Proceedings*, 7.

114. *Talcott Papers*, 2:63.

115. Walters, *"Mohegan Indians v. Connecticut,"* 812-13; Smith, *Appeals to the Privy Council*, 439.

116. Trudie Lamb Richmond, who has researched and written about the Green Corn Ceremony in seventeenth-century native New England, notes that it occurred "usually five days after the full moon during the month of the ripening corn—when it is still green but edible (late August or early September)." Trudie Lamb Richmond, "Out of the Earth I Sing: The Story of Corn," *Artifacts* 19 (2) (1991): 13. Richmond explains that the "great preparation of corn" entailed in the Green Corn Ceremony was carried out by women: "their mortars and pestles continually grinding corn," and thus representing "native people's relationship to all living and growing things." Trudie Lamb Richmond, "'Put Your Ear to the Ground and Listen.' The Wigwam Festival is the Green Corn Ceremony," *Artifacts* 17 (4) (1989): 25. See also Carolyn Merchant, *Ecological Revolutions*, 72-74. It is important to note that the Green Corn Ceremony continues among Mohegans today, known now as the Wigwam Festival. Melissa Jayne Fawcett, *The Lasting of the Mohegans: The Story of the Wolf People* (Ledyard, Conn.: Pequot Printing, 1995), 54.

# "This Once Savage Heart of Mine"

## Joseph Johnson, Wheelock's "Indians," and the Construction of a Christian/Indian Identity, 1764–1776

TAMMY SCHNEIDER

Great Wonder! even marvelous in my Eyes, or rather the admiration of my soul that I, a hell deserving cursed Creature has been suffered to live in this World so long, Sinning, offending, and provoking the God of holiness, and the God of justice, and the God of vengance, and what is the joy of my Soul the God of love, and the God of mercy, through his dearly beloved and only begotten Son, the Lord Jesus Christ, who is admired by all them that believe, and in whom I humbly hope, I have been enabled by the Spirit of the living God, to put my whole trust & confidence, for time and for Eternity. O! that I might see more and more of my own wretchedness, and insufficiency, that Jesus Christ might be more and more precious to my Soul. Oh! I am nothing. Should I have the boldness to tell you, that I am hopefully converted, I should tell a news that I am not certain of. For since I first thought so myself, I have often doubted. I percieve Sin to be lurking within. Sometimes I greatly fear that I am altogether in my Sins, even under the power and Dominion of Sin, if so I am wretched wretched poor miserable creature sill, notwithstanding the World calls me blessed, notwithstanding I pass for a true Christian among all setts, and Denominations, as it were.[1]

## The Rhetoric of Confession

For those of the Reformed faith, an ideal way to measure spiritual progress was through the act of writing. Writing allowed Reformed Christians to keep a permanent record of their thoughts and actions as each progressed in a personal quest for spiritual salvation. Equally important were the rhetorical devices these writers used to illustrate the authenticity of their desire to live in a state of grace. Such devices could include dramatic flourishes, repetition, anaphora, chiasmus, and parallelisms, among others. Similar rhetorical devices appear in many conversion narratives of well-educated New England ministers, trained in theology as well as the art of writing. What makes the above letter particularly interesting is that it was not written by a New England minister, but by a young Native American man engaged in the constant soul-searching common among his white, Euroamerican colonizers.

Joseph Johnson was a Mohegan Indian preacher and schoolteacher under the auspices of Eleazar Wheelock. His letters to Wheelock, an ordained minister of the Second Congregational Church at Lebanon Crank, Connecticut, and headmaster of Moor's Charity School, span a period of twelve years from 1764 through 1776. These letters are an interesting scene of writing, illustrating for the reader a struggle in power relations between a dominant European civilization and a colonized people.

Looking at the above-quoted letter with twentieth-century eyes, one may find Joseph Johnson's abjection and self-loathing to be off-putting, but the reader must bear in mind that religious doctrine required Christians to humble themselves before God and before their spiritual community. Nonetheless, there is still an element of discomfort when one is aware of Johnson's position as an Indian in eighteenth-century colonial America. It is these two elements—Johnson as *Christian* and as *Indian*—that are of paramount significance to this work.

Johnson's correspondence helps us to recognize the complex and problematic relationship that existed between Wheelock and the Indian students. The definition of that relationship was, as Johnson's letters illustrate, of critical importance to Johnson's struggle to unite two seemingly oppositional or incompatible identities: those of Christian and Indian. This paper will trace Johnson's struggles to construct an identity through his appropriation of rhetorical Christian discourse and his interpretation of Reformed theology. Although both Christian discourse and theology were firmly embedded in Western civilization, Johnson was able to manipulate certain rhetorical and theological devices that made visible the power relations between him and Wheelock.

Most importantly, the correspondence reveals how Johnson, and others like him, responded to the imposition of Christianity on the Indian nations located within and around colonial America. Johnson's letters and writings illustrate a refashioning of Christian doctrine that made it fundamentally different from the doctrine of Wheelock. The difference was founded not in race, but rather in understanding. Johnson's definition and comprehension of regeneration tended toward Arminianism, Wheelock's toward Calvinism.[2]  Johnson, and other students of Moor's Charity School, stated on several occasions their *choice* to take part in activities deemed both improper and heretical. Many of these activities, as in Johnson's case, took place after the writer had undergone a spiritual experience. Therefore, choosing to act in an improper manner meant that one was able to refuse a divine decree, the very point over which Arminians argued with Calvinist theologians.

On several occasions, Johnson bemoaned his failure to live a Christian life, yet consistently took responsibility for his own actions. In a letter written to Wheelock in 1774, Johnson asserted that he had "in times past *crucified* as it were, the Lord of Glory, even the Son of God, *afresh* and put him to an open shame."[3] Johnson's words denoted action on his part: he *crucified* both God and Christ, not once, but many times *afresh*.

In laying claim to his actions, Johnson addressed a major dilemma inherent in Protestant doctrine: the relation between will and reason. According to Perry Miller, if will were to follow a regenerated reason, then grace would become no more than an intellectual exercise. On the other hand, if will were not subject to reason, then the Christian would be able to refuse God's grace. Both views, according to Miller, were equally repugnant to Calvinists: the former discounts faith, the latter discounts divine decree.[4] Yet, as we shall see, the writings of Wheelock's Indians continually addressed one's will as it related to the acceptance or refusal of God's grace.

## Eleazar Wheelock and the Function of Power

In order to examine the writings of Johnson and other members of Moor's Charity School, I have turned to the work of both James C. Scott and Michel Foucault. Foucault and Scott chart the way in which subjugation and resistance are both material and discursive processes. Scott's work focuses on two kinds of discourse that take place between the dominant and the subordinate: the public discourse, or transcript, and the critique of power that occurs "behind the back of the dominant," the *hidden transcript.*[5] Foucault, in both *Discipline & Punish* and *The History of Sexuality*, focused on the body as a site of power relations. The body is controlled through regimentation and surveillance. As we will see, Eleazar Wheelock's civilizing mission included the strict control of activity, the constant gaze of authority, and the extraction of the confession.

In Johnson's letters we can see the workings of Scott's *public* and *hidden transcripts* as well as the workings of Foucault's *panopticism* and his theory of the confession as a discourse firmly embedded in a power relationship, all of which contribute to the formation of Johnson as a colonized subject. In *The History of Sexuality*, Foucault wrote that confession is one method on which Western society relies for the production of truth; confession plays "a central role in the order of civil and religious powers."[6] By forcing Johnson and the others to confess their sins publicly, Wheelock constantly strengthened his power over them. Furthermore, these letters served as a permanent record of the students' transgressions, allowing the confession to be alluded to repeatedly in order to reinforce the notion that the students were deficient in character and to cement the hierarchy of English over Indian.

Johnson's letters illustrate that the formation of his subjectivity was not a steady affair. A closer look at them reveals a man who was trying to position himself in a changing world. And it is here, in the interpretation of Johnson's letters, that I differ from James Scott. Scott argues that hidden transcripts take place away from, and outside of, dominant society's observation. Johnson's letters refute Scott's argument, since they function as both public and private discourse: public because of their material existence, and private because they are the written conversation (confession) between pupil and mentor.

This essay will demonstrate that a careful reading of these letters undermines one's assumptions about the power relations that at first glance seem so obvious. Johnson was excruciatingly aware of the social hierarchy within his community. He attempted to come to terms with the racialist ideology of those in power and simultaneously construct an identity that would allow him to function fully in both the Indian and the white worlds, an identity that one cannot label Christian, in the Wheelockian sense, nor "Indian," in the Krupatian sense.[7]

For European settlers in colonial America, the Christian school became a site for civilizing Native Americans. Wheelock, whose goal was to convert the Iroquois,[8] founded the Indian Charity school, commonly known as Moor's Charity School, in 1754; in its final incarnation, it became Dartmouth College. He referred to his efforts as a *Great Design*[9] and was compelled as much by religious motives as he was by political and economic imperatives. France and England were in constant competition to win the allegiance of the Indians, and Wheelock believed that if half the money used to build and man fortifications had been spent on missionaries and schoolteachers, the "converted Indians 'would have been a far better defence than all our expensive fortresses.'"[10]

Although a liberal thinker, Wheelock maintained that Indian conversion required a strictly regimented school day and constant surveillance:

> They are obliged to be clean, and decently dressed, and be ready to attend Prayers before Sun-rise in the Fall and Winter, and at 6 o'clock in the Summer. . . . [T]he School begins with Prayer about 9, and ends at 12, and again at 2 and ends at 5 o'clock with Prayer. Evening Prayer is attended before the Daylight is gone &c. They attend the publick Worship, and have a Pew devoted to their Use in

the House of God. On Lord's-Day Morning, between and after the Meetings, the Master, or some one whom catachises them, discourses to them &c. . . . And in general they are orderly and governable.[11]

Wheelock was creating what Foucault termed the "docile body." During the eighteenth century, the body was identified as an "object and target of power." Institutions such as schools and the military found that a body that is "manipulated, shaped, [and] trained" is, in turn, compliant, responsive, and proficient.[12] Although Foucault restricted his study to Europe, one can apply his theory to Wheelock's methodology as it pertained to his Indian students.

By strictly regimenting the actions of his students, Wheelock increased the utility of the Indians' bodies while decreasing their autonomy. In other words, he forced their obedience in order to increase their productive capability. If one substitutes Moor's Charity School for the Gobelins school, Foucault's analysis of pedagogical discipline summarizes Wheelock's goal:

> [Moor's Charity School] is only one example of an important phenomenon: the development, in the classical period, of a new technique for taking charge of the time of individual existences; for regulating the relations of time, bodies and forces; for assuring an accumulation of duration; and for turning to ever-increased profit or use the movement of passing time.[13]

The motivation behind Wheelock's strict regimentation of the Indian body was to transform the "savage" into a reasonable facsimile of an English citizen. The important word here is "facsimile." Wheelock strongly believed that an Indian could never disregard his true "nature"; it could only be controlled through confession and surveillance. Therefore, when Joseph Johnson left school to begin his missionary work, Wheelock received reports of his progress in Johnson's own letters and in letters from others, including Samuel Kirkland, a white student of Wheelock's, and Ralph Wheelock, Eleazar's son.

## Writing as Public Transcript

Wheelock promoted the idea of using his Indian students as missionaries to the more remote tribes, believing that they had an advantage over English-speaking missionaries, given the similarities in their language and their knowledge of Indian culture. However, as Laura Murray points out, Wheelock's motives were not purely philanthropic: he sought students as a financial supplement to his meager salary.[14] Wheelock sent his students to work on nearby farms several days a week, causing one of his students, Hezekiah Calvin, to level charges of theft and misuse against the Reverend. In a letter to Wheelock, Edward Deake, a white teacher in Rhode Island, listed Calvin's allegations:

> you use y$^e$ Indians very hard in keeping of them to work, & not allowing them a proper Privelidge in y$^e$ School. . . . That Mary Secutor, & Sarah Simon has been kept as close to work, as if they were your slaves, & have had no privelidge in y$^e$ School since last Fall, nor one Copper allow'd y$^m$ for their Labour. . . . So y$^t$ y$^e$ Indians are ready to conclude, that their Fellow-Indians will never receive any great Benefit of y$^e$ Large sums of Money contributed by good People to promote so good a Cause.[15]

In addition to questioning the sincerity of Wheelock's philanthropic motives, Calvin's accusations illustrate the importance of the written word as it applied to the Indian student and his teacher. Evidently

Calvin was unable to express his anger and frustration with Wheelock through a more direct communication such as a face-to-face confrontation or a personal letter. However, Calvin felt comfortable enough among his friends to express his concerns.

Another important aspect of Calvin's accusations, as they relate to Joseph Johnson and the students of Moor's Charity School, is the very survival of these accusations in the written record. Wheelock was extremely careful in preserving the letters his students wrote to him, but few of his responses exist. Deake's letter allows us a rare glimpse into Wheelock's character and his relationship to his Indian students. As this essay will demonstrate, letters from Kirkland and Ralph Wheelock that inform Wheelock of Johnson's behavior and actions were likewise preserved.

Letters written by the Indians who attended Moor's Charity School were extremely important to Wheelock's fundraising efforts, which is why the Reverend took such pains to save them. Wheelock often sent copies of the letters to patrons in England and Scotland as proof of his capability to educate and convert the "savage and brutish" Indians.[16] Johnson and his fellow students were aware of Wheelock's methods, as the postscripts of letters from Johnson and David Fowler indicate. In a letter sent to Wheelock in May of 1765, Fowler closed with the following: "Sir, I hope you won't let this letter be seen, I have no Table to write upon, besides I have not writ so long my Hand's out of order."[17] In February of 1768, Johnson wrote a lengthy letter to Wheelock, adding, "Please sir to overlook my hast, an the many Blunders which I Suppose are in the paper. I have no time to write it over or correct it. Dont Expose it."[18] Thus, Johnson and his peers were aware that they were writing for a larger audience and that their "performance" affected Wheelock's purse.

If Johnson and his peers were aware of their *power* over

Wheelock, albeit limited, why this willingness to participate in his *Great Design*? To answer this, one must return to Scott's work on power relations and resistance. Scott divides social subordination into two distinct, but related, areas: the *public transcript* and the *hidden transcript*. The *public transcript* is the open interaction between the dominant and the subordinate. The *hidden transcript*, as defined previously, characterizes subordinate discourse that "takes place 'offstage,' beyond direct observation by powerholders." Hidden transcripts thus "confirm, contradict, or inflect what appears in the public transcript," which Scott defines as "subordinate discourse in the presence of the dominant."[19] If one only looks at the public transcript, one fails to see the complete workings of power relations. For example, in the following quotations from Johnson and Fowler, one may discern little more than deference and consent.

> And may the Blessings of Heaven rest on you &c &c and continue you a long and rich Blessing in the World, may the Heathen in the Wilderness feel the goodness of thy Labours. May you have Double Measure of the Spirit of God, and fill your Heart with Love of God and Compassion to poor perishing Souls, and may the Giver of all things, give Strength and Health, Wisdom and Authority to rule govern and teach those who are commited to your Care in Fear of the Lord: which is the sincere Prayer of him who desire the Continuance of your Prayers.
>
> your affectionate
> tho: unworthy Pupil,
> David Fowler[20]

Rev^d and Hon^d Doct^r.

Suffer me as an Indian and a good for nothing one, to Subscribe myself your dutifull Pupil, or one that will Endeavour to be dutifull, for time to come.

Pray that he would grant me wisdom from on high, Such as none but a God can give; that he would grant me wisdom So to behave myself as not to dishonour or bring to Religion, that he would make me a blessing to the Children which he has commited to my charge.

This is the true and Sincere, hearty desire, of me, thy Dutifull tho Unworthy Pupil.

Joseph Johnson[21]

But was this deference a tactic used to appease Wheelock? Is the obsequiousness that runs throughout Johnson's letters a true indication of his relationship with Wheelock? Both questions can be answered in the positive. As Murray points out in her study of the letters of Calvin and Fowler, the relationship between Wheelock and the Indians was intense and complex.[22] Following Scott's argument, it is imperative that the subordinate fulfill the expectation of the dominant society. Scott goes on to state that "the public transcript will typically, by its accommodationist tone, provide convincing evidence for the hegemony of dominant values . . . "[23] Therefore, the public transcript between Johnson and Wheelock on its own shows Johnson playing the role of social subordinate.

Johnson's first letter to Wheelock was written in 1764, while he was still attending the Indian Charity School. The circumstances surrounding the letter indicate that some type of altercation had occurred between Johnson and Eleazar Sweetland, a fellow student.

Rev^d & Hon^d Sir

With A great deal of consideration would I inform you Sir what past between Eleazar Sweetland & I. This is the true meaning According to the best of my Memory, that as we was playing the Misfortune was this that Sweetland took up A Stone, Gourdains being present and he Sent the Stone not knowing that the dog was there. Gourdain told me of it.

In a mean & Sordid Manner I told him that I would do the Same to him, As he would do to the dog, But All in Jest, Sweetland Witnesses to it.

And I Also threw him down not Violantly & there held him down About A quarter of An-hour he Witnesses himself. In A shorst time After I had got him down I Asked him what if I keept him All the Night then he said he would not Stay here 2 hours longer. Then I told him I did not Intend he Should. Then he said he would not Stay one hour longer. Then I Askd him how he could help himself In no Anger but All in Jest Eleazar Sweetland witnesses.

Your Humble Servant<br>Joseph Johnson[24]

Although Johnson's letter *was* a confession, he explained that Wheelock and those who witnessed the occurrence misunderstood his actions. He stated that the "true meaning" of this skirmish was "All in Jest," confirmed by Sweetland himself, who "Witnesses to it." Johnson was aware, however, that he must still confess to behaving inappropriately. He went on to say that "In a mean & Sordid Manner, I told him that I would do the Same to him. As he would do to the

dog." Johnson acknowledged his anger toward Sweetland for the latter's treatment of a dog, but continued to affirm that both he and
Sweetland were no more than playing around. If we take this letter in
its social context, we see nothing more than a thirteen-year-old boy
roughhousing with his peers. Wheelock, however, turned this normal
activity into an opportunity to increase his control over Johnson and
the other students by requiring a public and permanent confession.

Wheelock compelled his students to structure their confessions in
the form of a letter, ensuring both the public knowledge of their sins
and, by association, their public humiliation. What does this tell us
about the power relations between Wheelock and the Indian students?
One thing the letters illustrate is Foucault's theory of surveillance as
a form of disciplinary power.

> The exercise of discipline presupposes a mechanism that
> coerces by means of observation; an apparatus in which
> the techniques that make it possible to see induce effects
> of power, and in which, conversely, the means of coercion
> make those on whom they are applied clearly visible.[25]

Confessional letters written by Hezekiah Calvin, David Fowler,
Nathan Clap, Hannah Nonesuch, Mary Secutor, and Jacob Wolley, as
well as Joseph Johnson, are still extant. In addition, some letters were
composed while the writer was still attending at Moor's Charity
School; others, including Johnson's letter quoted below, were written
from the student's assigned missionary post.

Wheelock's control over his Indian students reached much farther
than mere physical proximity, as a letter to Wheelock from Hezekiah
Calvin illustrates. Calvin, who entered Wheelock's school in 1757, left
in 1765 to teach among the Mohawks in Fort Hunter, New York. He
wrote the following letter two years later:

Honored Sir

   With shamefacedness & humbleness of Heart I write you these Lines, owning & *Confessing* my heinous *Crimes*.

   the last evening being the 25th of X[ber] I *Confess* I was Drunk: Swearing & Curseing followed, which I knew not of only as I was infor'd so this Morning, & am Sorry for it—I hear that they say I make mock at your Night Discourses; which I think is false, But But I *promise* never to Drink Liquor again & *Promise* to Attend my Life & Conduct for the future God assisting me *I am willing to Suffer any thing* that might make my Schoolmates know the wickedness of getting Drunk or that *they might not take that example of me.*

Sir I am thy *Disobedient*
& *undutiful Servant*
Hezekiah Calvin[26]

Calvin's statement that his "[s]choolmates . . . not take that example of me" indicates that he was aware of the public nature of the confession as employed by Wheelock. However, even more startling is the need Calvin felt to confess his behavior to Wheelock two years after leaving Moor's Charity School. In this letter one can discern the extent of the power Wheelock had over his students and the students' awareness of his "all-seeing" gaze. Confessing to Wheelock was tantamount to confessing to God. Calvin directed his promise to refrain from liquor not to God, but to Wheelock. In fact, the only mention of God is an appeal for assistance in keeping that promise.

   Three of the confessions cited above were written in Wheelock's handwriting, and at least one is believed to have been dictated by Wheelock. We have no way of knowing whether Wheelock copied these confessions or wrote them himself. Based on Foucault's theory of the confession as a production of truth, I would argue that Wheelock *impelled* his students to produce their own confessions and then copied the confessions for use in his fundraising efforts. For the confession to produce truth, the speaking (or writing) subject must acknowledge his or her behavior. Foucault wrote that the confession is "a ritual that unfolds within a power relationship, for one does not confess without the presence (or virtual presence) of a partner who is not simply the interlocutor but the authority who requires the confession, prescribes and appreciates it, and intervenes in order to judge, punish, forgive, console, and reconcile . . . "[27] As letters such as Calvin's and Johnson's show, Wheelock was always present in the minds of the Indian students.

## The Confession and Reformed Doctrine

Several of the confessional letters began as Mary Secutor's did:

I May [*sic*] Secuter do with shamefacedness acknowledge that on the evening of the 8th Inst I was guilty of going to the tavern & tarrying there with much rude & vain company till a very unreasonable time of night where was dancing & other rude & unseemly conduct, & in particular drinking too much spiritous liquor whereby I was exposed to commit many gross sins, which offence is doubly aggravated in that *it is a direct violation of a late promise I have publickly made before this school*—all which wicked & sinful conduct of mine, I am fully sensable is much to the dishonour of God & ver prejudicial to the design & reputation of this school, and in opposition to the good of my own soul & the souls of my mates—for which I deserve to be turned out of this school & be deprived of all the privileges of it—*I desire to lie low in the dust therefor & do now ask forgiveness of God, the Rev^d Doct^r Wheelock, his family and school, and all others whom I have hereby offended*—and I desire now with my whole heart to renew my former engagement that I will never more drink any spiritous liquor on any occasion where necessity does not require it, and *I do promise that (by the grace of god) I will amend my past life* & never offend by any of the like or any other misconduct. for time to come—*And desire once more to warn all my mates not to take occasion by this or any other instance of my misconduct, to commit the like or any other evil*—and I beg the privilege of continuing still a member of this school & that I may enjoy the privileges of it, for a trial of the sincerity of this my confession & my engagements for an amendment of life

*Lebanon March 11*^th *1768 Present*          Mary Secutor
D^r Wheelock
B. Woodward[28]

Secutor's confession illustrates the views that Wheelock and other colonists held concerning Indian character. Exposure to drinking, dancing, and other "rude & unseemly" conduct was all that was needed to turn the Indian from civilized to savage. Secutor was unable to refrain from sinning because her very character prevented her from making that choice. The fact that she was a young girl who had been removed from a culture steeped in community gatherings was not considered. Mary Secutor and the other Indian students were expected, even obligated, to act as members of an English Protestant community, notwithstanding their upbringing as Indian children prior to their attendance at Moor's Charity School.

The circumstances surrounding Secutor's foray to the tavern provide evidence of yet another shortcoming. Her descent into sin followed a "publickly made" promise before the school not to "drink any spiritous liquor." The fact that Secutor did so after she vowed to refrain from such behavior caused such abjection that the rest of her confession is almost too painful to read. However, what one finds striking in her statement is not the tone, but her *will* to sin. She was "fully sensable" [*sic*] that her conduct was both "wicked & sinful," an action for which she was completely responsible *after* promising to refrain from such behavior. Secutor's will to sin came some three months after an earlier transgression, after which she promised *"by divine Grace* to walk morally and in all Respects circumspectly, for time to come."[29]

Protestant congregationalists strongly held that one could not refuse divine decree, that once justification had occured a person had experienced regeneration and was then a covenanted member of the community—a "visible saint." Secutor's two confessions clearly indicate a person who was not covenanted according to any Protestant definition. Furthermore, she had proactively engaged in committing "many gross sins." Her ability to withstand "divine Grace" placed her squarely in the Arminian camp.

In several ways, Secutor's confession was strikingly similar to that of Hezekiah Calvin. Both individuals stated that with God's help they would rehabilitate themselves and abstain from such behavior in the future. In addition, both Calvin and Secutor warned others not to mimic their behavior, so as to avoid falling into the wickedness that had consumed them.

Like Mary Secutor's confession, all those written within the school proper conclude with some type of attestation, usually by Eleazar Wheelock himself, Bezaleel Woodward, or Ralph Wheelock. As Murray states, writing down one's actions serves as a reminder to "the confessor of the inferiority of his judgement and [causes] him to relive the embarrassment of misconduct reproved."[30]  In addition, the attestation provides evidence of social hierarchy, not only that of Moor's Charity School, but of the European colonizers and their Indian subjects. Wheelock's signature (or that of Woodward or Ralph Wheelock) offered a validation to the confessor. Without the acknowledgment of one in authority, the confession would be ineffectual.

As noted above, Calvin's confession was written after he had left Moor's Charity School. As such, it is not an anomaly, as the correspondence of Johnson and others proves. Several of these letters are confessional in tone; Johnson penned one of them in 1768, two years after he had left Wheelock's school and taken a position among the Oneida Indians as an assistant teacher to Samuel Kirkland. During this, Johnson's final year among the Oneidas, he evidently engaged in behavior that was, by "Christian" standards, opprobrious. He "kept . . . strumpets . . . nigh two months last spring—drank up near three Gall$^n$ of wine . . . & between 6 & 7 Gall$^n$ of Rum." In an even more heinous act, Johnson "turn'd pagan for about a week—painted, sung—danc'd—drank & whor'd it, w$^h$ some of the savage Indians he cou'd find."[31]

Johnson's letter to Wheelock, written in December of 1768, reveals a man deeply ashamed of his behavior, yet oddly defiant. In it, he repeated the word *deceitful*, a direct reference to his perceived treatment by Wheelock himself. It is evident from a previous letter that Johnson was not trusted with any money and was hurt by this slur on his character. As he stated in a letter dated September 27, 1768, "I have not as yet been trusted with one Copper not So much as in sight . . . I have not yet been lavish of any of Christ money, or been found Dishonest. . . . Or ask M$^r$ Kirkland if I Ever proved dishonest to any of the Money He has from time to time trusted me with, or to your Honoured son . . ."[32] Johnson's reference to his mistreatment undermines Scott's theory that the *hidden transcript* takes place away from the gaze of the dominant. Johnson's subtle, but obvious, criticism of Wheelock contrasts sharply with the rest of the December letter, which is filled with deep shame and misery.

> Rev^d and Ever honoured Doct^r.
>
> Forgive me for my Repeated presumtion in Writing to you; But this once more give me leave to acquaint you my Once kind Benefactor, the Case I at present am in; But as I have so Often been found *deceitfull*, I know not as you will have patience to Read over this my pretended Confession, as I said, Seeing I have showed So much Deceitfullness in my pretentions, & Undertakings, Since I have been capable of being Improved in some good way; But for Grant—Which way to Betake myself—I know not, I am at a stand. Hon^d Sir; to return to you whom I have so greatly grieved, I dare not; I am ashamed, & Concience stings me to the Measure the down Cast Spirits of Cain when He received his curse; but no Equal to his; tho my Crimes are more than Equal. The thoughts of your School haunts my Mind dayly, and to turn my face that way I dare not. I see nothing; but my Actions in the deepest dye of Ingratitude stare me in the face which Causes my heart to faint Under the thoughts of Returning; but what Course to take. I know that god is Everywhire, and is Acquainted with Actions past, and will punish without Mercy those that Be DisObedient to his Laws, and Commandments Er long.³³

Johnson's letter serves as both confession and explanation. As much as he felt compelled to confess his sins, he also evinced the need to explain his behavior. In the first paragraph, Johnson asked Wheelock to forgive his presumption in writing, but deemed it necessary to present his "Case" so that Wheelock might hear about his actions firsthand, as it were. Johnson's writing depicts a young man unsure of his position within his world. He had behaved, according to Christian standards, in a most heinous manner. For a young Native American man, however, Johnson's actions were quite normal.

Johnson now stood firmly between two worlds: the world of the white Christian and the world of the Indian: " . . . Which way to Betake myself—I know not, I am at a Stand." This "stand" marked a significant point in Johnson's religious conversion. That God had bestowed his Grace, Johnson had no doubt: "Good God seems to be lengthening out his mercy to me, tho I have so Openly Rebeled against Him, and has graciously guided my Doubtfull steps . . ." Johnson had experienced justification, but was not living the sanctified life. In doing so, he separated elements not separable according to Calvinists, who argued that justification and sanctification are complementary: out of justification came sanctification. Thus, Johnson chose, at various times, to live the unsanctified life, a choice that placed his determination over God's determinism. As evidenced by the above letter, Johnson's understanding of grace could be easily defined: it was necessary for salvation but could be refused.

However, the power that Eleazar Wheelock held over his students cannot be discounted or minimized, as this letter proves. Johnson had an almost overwhelming desire to return to Wheelock's school, but his shame prevented him from doing so: "Hon^d Sir; to return to you whom I have so greatly grieved, I dare not; I am ashamed. . . . The thoughts of your School haunts my Mind dayly, and to turn my face that way I dare not." The powerful presence of Wheelock was constantly felt. Johnson's words illustrate the depth of his pain and despair as well as his confusion. He had been removed from his home, his family, and his way of life. He was expected to become civilized, but never to become white. Wheelock sent Johnson, along with the other Indian students, as missionaries and teachers to other tribes without regard for the diversity of their languages and customs. Nevertheless, as Laura Murray points out, the students of Moor's Charity School were meant to consider themselves as better than those whom they were sent to teach.[34] How could these young men and women reconcile their position between cultures? In so many ways they were not quite Indian and not quite white. It would appear that the tensions inherent in such a reconciliation led to Johnson's fall from Wheelock's grace.

Johnson's desperate attempt to obtain forgiveness from Wheelock is apparent in his rhetoric. His powerful use of anaphora illuminates his mindset and reveals his expertise in the art of writing: "But how, it seems as if there was some probability, some glimpse of hope yet, Some ways of Being Recovered from this Unhappy State . . ." Rhetorical questions indicate Johnson's futile desire to erase his behavior and obtain Wheelock's forgiveness: "But how can I make my sorrow Credible—which none can Believe . . . " "What would I give Even all that I have or all that my care or Industry would gain Could I Recall these fatal hours which I consumed in sensless Vanities . . . " If Johnson had learned anything from his tenure at Moor's Charity School, he had learned the power of the written word. He had been compelled to bare his soul on the page. His progress—as a Christian, as a civilized human being, as a teacher, as a missionary—could only be determined through the written word.

## The Letters of Joseph Johnson

The first extant letter written by Johnson after he left Wheelock's school is from the Oneida country, where he was sent in 1766 as an assistant teacher to David Fowler and Samuel Kirkland. As mentioned previously, Fowler was another Indian student of Wheelock's, described by Murray as "a teacher's pet."[35] Samuel Kirkland was one of the Reverend's white students, considered to be "a key agent of Wheelock's hopes for converting the Iroquois."[36] Wheelock kept up a constant communication with Kirkland, on whom he relied for information about the behavior of the Indian missionaries, and his willingness to respond to Kirkland's letters was a point of contention with the Indians. In a 1767 letter written to Wheelock, Fowler complained that "others have received Folio's after Folio's," while "I have not received one Line."[37] The "others" to whom Fowler referred were, of course, Kirkland and, most likely, Ralph Wheelock.

Johnson's letter opens with a reference to a letter no longer extant. He apologized for its contents, saying, "I have not Acknowledged the kind reception it meet with and *the affectionate messages you have Sent me in your Letters to M*ʳ *Kirkland.*"[38] Although subtle, Johnson made it a point to mention that messages for him were relayed through Kirkland. In communicating with Johnson through Kirkland, Wheelock continued to reestablish the hierarchy of power between himself and Johnson, as well as the hierarchy between the white man and the Indian. In other words, Johnson did not merit a response from Wheelock himself. Johnson was aware of his position within this hierarchy; moreover, he was aware of the Indian's position as it related to white society.

In the same letter, Johnson wrote, "That God may grant you an ample reward in the upper world, for all your Labours of Love towards the poor Indians, and me in perticular. . . . " Although his tone was one of deference and humble gratitude, Johnson's view of himself and his people underlay this statement. He closed the letter, "your most Obedient though unworthy Servent Poor good for nothing Indian Joseph Johnson." Johnson's humility and obsequiousness served a dual purpose. On the one hand, he engaged in proper Christian rhetoric, since it was commonly expected that Christians would humble themselves before God and before their religious superiors. Laura Murray points out that many of Wheelock's white students used similar rhetorical devices in their letters. However, she goes on to point out that Christian rhetoric "takes on particular valences" as it pertains to the subordinate status of Native Americans.[39]

Nevertheless, there is more to Johnson's language than Christian rhetoric. Through it we witness a young man's struggle to establish a place in a world that has attempted to negate his existence. Johnson realized that men such as Wheelock played a large part in determining the fate of Native Americans. At the same time, he was trying to come to terms with his own role in shaping that fate. Neither the Mohegans, nor the Oneidas, nor any other tribe could survive without acknowledging European domination. Yet, with this acknowledgment came the awareness that Wheelock (and the majority of Europeans) viewed Indians as inferior; that even as he attempted to educate and train his Indian students, Wheelock always thought of them as savages.[40]

Johnson's confusion about his place in God's plan and his position as a Christian Indian among the "pagan" Iroquois is evident in a letter he wrote to Wheelock in December of 1767:

> Rev[d] & ever hon[d] Doct[r].
> I would once more attempt to write to you Hon[d] Benefactor: Notwithstanding I find my mind so Discomposed, it is as if their was no Solidness in my mind; Sometimes Encouraged, & at other Time Dishearted; So y[t] I cant be Resolute in what I do. At present things look dark—They all wear a Garment of Discouragement, but I hope that Before long Some will change their present Garments, & Look Encourageing to your poor Labourers in the Wilderness.

As do Puritan writings, the above quotation incorporates an important element of the Christian writings of the time. Recording one's despair and sinfulness offered a purgation of that sinfulness as well as relief from despair. Nevertheless, the language employed sounded not only a note of sorrow, but also of hopefulness, as Johnson's writing illustrates: " . . . but I *hope* that before long Some will change their present Garments, & *Look Encourageing* to your poor Labourers in the Wilderness." Johnson was aware that God would only hear the appeal for salvation from one who was actively seeking that salvation.[41] Therefore, the "Wilderness" of which Johnson spoke was not only the physical space he occupied in Oneida country, but a spiritual space in which all Indians resided.

Johnson's desperate search to create a solid, viable identity among a society that thought of his people as less than human is poignantly displayed in the second paragraph of the letter:

> I Fear that God is about to give up these poor Ignorant heathen to walk after their own hearts, and cut them of Intirely from his Earth; I think at present their is Some concern amongst these Indians I would hope a Real concern. I hope that God is about to carry on his own work amongst us, and bring out Some of our Souls from this darkness into his Marvelous Light. I am yet in the Gall of Bitterness and in the bond of Iniquity. I hope that God will yet Enable me to See the pride of my heart, & the great Sin of Unbelief and the Necessity I stand in of Christ Jesus. I believe that unless God be pleased to Open my Eyes that I may See the wickedness of my heart I greatly fear I Shall never Obtain the One thing needfull.[42]

Johnson's ambiguous position within this society is markedly evident in the above quotation. Murray points out his shifting pronouns, which reveal his confusion, but she fails to analyze the importance of these grammatical changes.[43] To whom should Johnson have related? Did he belong with those "poor Ignorant heathen," or did he belong with those who could see the damnation to which those "poor Ignorant heathen" were condemned?

The above paragraph begins with Johnson distancing himself from the Oneidas as he stated that " . . . God is about to give up *these* poor Ignorant heathen," yet the next sentence brings the fear of damnation closer to himself as his pronouns shift to the first person and the possessive. "I hope that God is about to carry on his own work amongst *us* and bring out Some of *our* Souls from this darkness . . . " However, in the next sentence, Johnson moved completely inward, focusing solely on himself and his fear that he would never receive God's grace: "*I* am yet in the Gall of Bitterness. . . . *I* hope that God will yet Enable *me* to See the pride of *my* heart. . . . *I* believe that unless God be pleased to Open *my* Eyes that *I* may See the wickedness of *my* heart *I* greatly fear *I* Shall never Obtain the One thing needful." This transition illustrates the complexity of Johnson's constant struggle to create an identity that would allow him to function in both the Indian and the white worlds.

Furthermore, Johnson believed that although God had not yet opened his eyes, He still might. Then Johnson would "Obtain the One thing needfull": salvation. That Johnson was still seeking salvation shows his belief in his own determination to achieve grace. In order to create a specific place in this new world order, Johnson would have to step outside of Wheelock's Calvinist theology and refashion a theology that would allow him and other Indians to survive and prosper in Christian America. As he struggled to determine his fate, Johnson's understanding of grace, regeneration, sanctification, and justification illustrated a subtle, but important, difference.

## Conclusion

To all Enquiring friends, or to all Strangers that my Cast their Curious but dying Eyes upon these lines. Disdain not the feble attempt of a Poor Indian, who wishes well, to all mankind, wishes the well being of mortals, in this World; but above all Sincerely desires their well being, in the World to Come. But O! friend would you know more Concerning me. I am, kind friend, an Indian of the Mohegan tribe, known by the Name of *Joseph Johnson*. . . . As for my great Undertaking, I can assure you it was not the Purpose of my heart; till of late. My dear friend, let me freely tell you, that *I was 21 years in this World, before I was born*, and as Soon as I was born, I had my Eyes Opened. . . . But let me tell you, before I let you go, that I am but one year, and three months old properly, and my friend, you Cant expect that in such a short time, I have arrived to manhood. No. I confess, I am but a child in the knowledge of Jesus my Lord, and a babe in Understanding.[44]

Joseph Johnson, along with other students of Moor's Charity School, personified a constant struggle between Euroamerican Christianity and Native American identity. In order to unite these seemingly incompatible parts into a coherent whole, Johnson and his colleagues strove to fashion a Christianity that would allow them freedom to create an identity fundamentally different than that being created for them by Wheelock and others like him.

Calvinistic theology contended that human depravity and, therefore, divine salvation were not a matter of choice: God elected individuals prior to creation and those individuals, because of that election, lived a life of faith. Wheelock's constant demand for confessions of misbehavior and backsliding reinforced the idea that God had not chosen any of Wheelock's Indian students to receive salvation. To accept this interpretation of Christianity would lead to nothing but despair, a despair to which many, even Johnson himself, succumbed for a time.

Nevertheless, Johnson was able to overcome this despair through his own understanding of the Christian God and reinterpretation of the Christian faith. Johnson's understanding of Christianity was much closer to Arminianism than to Calvinism. Arminian theology allowed humans to acknowledge their sinful state, repent and believe. God elected those whom He knew would accept salvation, but it was up to the individual to make that choice. Therefore, one could acknowledge divine grace, but still struggle to accept the gift. According to Calvinistic theology, Johnson's failure to lead a Christian life ensured his damnation. Johnson believed differently. His spiritual struggles, although many, culminated in a life of faith as evidenced by his later writings and the founding of the Brotherton settlement. Those writings show a man secure in his faith and in his belief of God's salvation and mercy.

Although he would die before Brotherton was completed, Johnson, along with Samson Occom, was a driving force behind the creation of the community. Within this community, Native Americans could live together, free from the constant concern that they might lose their land. Brotherton would embrace European agriculture and Christian religion combined with the Indians' sense of community. Brotherton became for Johnson and the others the perfect amalgamation of European and Indian ways.

# Notes

1. Joseph Johnson to Eleazar Wheelock, May 2, 1774, in Laura J. Murray, *To Do Good to My Indian Brethren: The Writings of Joseph Johnson, 1751–1776* (Amherst: University of Massachusetts Press, 1998), 228. I am indebted to Laura Murray for her exemplary edition of Joseph Johnson's writings. Spelling in this quotation, and all subsequent letters, has not been corrected. The term "Wheelock's Indians" is meant to illustrate the mindset of the Euroamerican colonizer. I use the terms *Indian* and *Native American* interchangeably, realizing that each is flawed in a particular way.

2. On this point I differ from other scholars who have focused on Johnson and Wheelock's Indians. Murray argues that Johnson's Christian discourse is the discourse of all Christians in the eighteenth century, as shown by his humility. Johnson's discourse, although a strong example of Christian humility, depicts a man struggling with the issue of will in regeneration and justification, an issue that would be considered heresy by Wheelock or Wheelock's colleagues. See Murray, *To Do Good to My Indian Brethren*, 12.

3. Joseph Johnson to Eleazar Wheelock, May 2, 1774, Eleazar Wheelock Papers, Dartmouth College, 774302 (emphases mine).

4. See Perry Miller, esp. "The Means of Conversion," in Miller, *The New England Mind: The Seventeenth Century* (Cambridge: Harvard University Press, 1954), 280-99.

5. James C. Scott, *Domination and the Arts of Resistance: Hidden Transcripts* (New Haven: Yale University Press, 1990), xii.

6.   Michel Foucault, *The History of Sexuality*, trans. Robert Hurley (New York: Vintage Books, 1980), 58.

7.   The Wheelockian definition of Christianity is firmly embedded in Protestant congregationalism: the community is formed by covenant-ed members of the Church, among them "visible saints" and those whose regeneration had been confirmed by the educated ministry. Arnold Krupat, *The Voice in the Margin: Native American Literature and the Canon* (Berkeley: University of California Press, 1989). Krupat argues that one can determine Indian "authenticity" in autobiographical writings: the true Native American autobiography is dialogic repre-senting both a collective self and a collective society. Autobiographies *by* Native Americans (his distinction) are monologic, representing the singular self in an effort "to accommodate themselves to a reigning authorative discourse" (134). Johnson's writings create a textual self that refuses both the Wheelockian and Krupatian definitions.

8.   Laura Murray writes, "[Wheelock's] ultimate ambition was to gain influence among the Six Nations, who were what he called 'a much better breed.'" Murray, *To Do Good to My Indian Brethren*, 54.

9.   Wheelock wrote to George Whitefield, 1756: "My dear, dear broth-er, I feel in behalf of the poor, savage, perishing creatures like a cov-etous, craving beggar, as though I could not tell them when to ha' done, or how to leave begging for them, till the Great Design of their being brought to Christ be accomplished." In James Dow McCallum, *Eleazar Wheelock, Founder of Dartmouth College* (Hanover, N.H.: Dartmouth College Publications, 1939), 75.

10.   McCallum, *Eleazar Wheelock, Founder of Dartmouth College*, 76.

11.   Eleazar Wheelock, *A plain and faithful Narrative of the Original Design, Rise, Progress and present State of the Indian Charity-School at Lebanon, in Connecticut.* (Boston: Richard & Samuel Draper, 1763), 36.

12.  Michel Foucault, *Discipline & Punish: The Birth of the Prison*, trans. Alan Sheridan (New York: Vintage Books, 1995), 138, 136.

13.  Foucault, *Discipline & Punish*, 157.

14.  Murray, *To Do Good to My Indian Brethren*, 50-51.

15.  Edward Deake to Eleazar Wheelock, June 21, 1768, Wheelock Papers, 768371.2.

16.  Eleazar Wheelock, *A Continuation of the Narrative of the State, &c., of the Indian Charity School at Lebanon, in Connecticut.* (Hartford: Ebenezer Watson, 1775).

17.  James Dow McCallum, *The Letters of Eleazar Wheelock's Indians* (Hanover, N.H.: Dartmouth College Publications), 91.

18.  Joseph Johnson to Eleazar Wheelock, May 2, 1768, Wheelock Papers, 768302.

19.  Scott, *Domination and the Arts of Resistance*, 2, 4.

20.  David Fowler to Eleazar Wheelock, June 24, 1765, McCallum, *Letters of Eleazar Wheelock's Indians*, 97.

21.  Joseph Johnson to Eleazar Wheelock, November, 10, 1767, Wheelock Papers, 767610.

22.  Murray, *To Do Good to My Indian Brethren*, 17. Although I agree with her statement, Murray does not address the complexity of doctrinal differences that lie between Wheelock and his students. As I have stated earlier, Wheelock's understanding of grace is that of the Congregationalist, while Johnson's understanding—like that of several other of Wheelock's students—is closer to the Arminian definition of will and the role human reasoning plays in one's acceptance of grace.

23.  Scott, *Domination and the Arts of Resistance*, 4.

24. Joseph Johnson to Eleazar Wheelock, September 6, 1764, Ayer Collection, MS 453, Newberry Library. Eleazar Sweetland went on to become a minister after graduating from Dartmouth College in 1774. Gourdain may be the nephew of Samson Occom Gourdain Wyyougs (Murray, *To Do Good to My Indian Brethren*, 60).

25. Foucault, *Discipline & Punish*, 170-71.

26. McCallum, *Letters of Eleazar Wheelock's Indians*, 60 (emphases mine).

27. Foucault, *History of Sexuality*, 61.

28. McCallum, *Letters of Eleazar Wheelock's Indians*, 237 (emphasis mine). Bezaleel Woodward was Preceptor in Moor's Charity School.

29. McCallum, *Letters of Eleazar Wheelock's Indians*, 236 (emphasis mine).

30. Laura J. Murray, "'Pray Sir, Consider a Little': Rituals of Subordination and Strategies of Resistance in the Letters of Hezekiah Calvin and David Fowler to Eleazar Wheelock," in *Early Native American Writing: New Critical Essays*, ed. Helen Jaskoski (New York: Cambridge University Press, 1996), 26-27.

31. Samuel Kirkland to Eleazar Wheelock, December 29, 1768, in McCallum, *Letters of Eleazar Wheelock's Indians*, 140-41.

32. Joseph Johnson to Eleazar Wheelock, September 27, 1768, Wheelock Papers, 768527.

33. Joseph Johnson to Eleazar Wheelock, December 28, 1768, Wheelock Papers, 768678.2

34. Murray, *To Do Good to My Indian Brethren*, 34.

35. Murray, "'Pray Sir, Consider a Little,'" 24. Murray presents a masterful reading of resistance in the letters of David Fowler and Hezekiah Calvin, another student of Wheelock's. Although a teacher's pet, several of Fowler's letters show a disenchantment with Wheelock, espe-

cially Wheelock's refusal to communicate with Fowler and his obvious preference for Samuel Kirkland.

36. Samuel Kirkland entered Moor's Charity School in 1760, where he remained for two years before attending the College of New Jersey (Princeton). From 1764 through 1766, Kirkland served as missionary to the Oneidas and the Senecas before returning to Lebanon, Connecticut, to be ordained. He returned to the Oneidas with whom he worked for more than forty years. Kirkland severed relations with Wheelock in 1770, in a dispute over the use of funds for Dartmouth College. See Samuel K. Lothrop, *Life of Samuel Kirkland: Missionary to the Indians* (Boston: Little Brown, 1848).

37. McCallum, *Letters of Eleazar Wheelock's Indians*, 108.

38. Joseph Johnson to Eleazar Wheelock, December 1, 1766, Wheelock Papers, 766651.3, emphasis mine.

39. Murray, *To Do Good to My Indian Brethren*, 294, n. 12.

40. Eleazar Wheelock to George Whitefield, July 4, 1761, in McCallum, *Eleazar Wheelock*, 84: "None know, nor can any, without experience, well conceive of, the difficulty of educating an Indian. They would soon kill themselves with eating and sloth, if constant care were not exercised upon them at least the first year. They are used to set upon the ground, and it is as natural for them as a seat to our children. They are not wont to have any cloaths but what they wear, or will without much pains be brot to take care of any. They are used to a sordid manner of dress, and love it as well as our children to be clean."

41. Again, a specifically Arminian view where the sinner chooses Christ. This contrasts with the Calvinist idea of God choosing the sinner.

42. Joseph Johnson to Eleazar Wheelock, December 29, 1767, Wheelock Papers, 767679.2.

43. Murray, *To Do Good to My Indian Brethren*, 58.

44. Wheelock Papers, 772900.2.

# The Church in
# New England Indian
# Community Life:

## A View from the Islands and Cape Cod

DAVID J. SILVERMAN

I
N SEPTEMBER OF 1767 a great meeting took place at the
Wampanoag village of Mashpee on Cape Cod, drawing together "the Indians of Martha's Vineyard, and the neighbouring
Indians on the Continent," as well as some English committeemen
from Boston. On the first morning, everyone filed into Mashpee's
one-room public building, seated themselves on the benches, and
assumed a posture of "gravity" appropriate to the serious matters at
hand. The natives' leaders went before the assembly and then launched
into a time-honored ceremony marked by ritualistic, metaphorical
sayings in the Wampanoag language and symbols of the Indians' connection to one another and to the spirits. Only after this rite was
completed did a buzz of less formal activity begin, as small groups of
Indians and Englishmen met to talk business, discuss politics, catch
up with old friends and relatives, and of course, negotiate the terms
of land deals.

On the surface, this Mashpee meeting resembled the great eighteenth-century treaty conferences associated with imperial crossroads such as Johnson Hall or Detroit, but appearances can be deceiving. The Wampanoags' stately language and ritual were not about native politics; they were an annual celebration of what missionary Gideon Hawley called the "Great Sacrament," or Lord's Supper. The building in which the people gathered was not a council house, but a large square-framed church, and the delegates were not sachems, but congregants, led by Mashpee's pastor, Solomon Briant, and the minister of Aquinnah (or Gay Head) on Martha's Vineyard, Zachariah Hossueit. This was indeed a Christian event, and yet much more. The sideline discussions allowed Indians from throughout southeastern Massachusetts to renew their ties to one another, and to match stories and strategies about their endless grievances against the colonists. The presence of colonial ambassadors from the natives' missionary sponsor, the New England Company, encouraged Wampanoags to petition for much-needed resources: several villages lacked ministers; Briant needed religious books and debt relief; the natives of Yarmouth and Herring Pond thought different men should distribute their annual allotment of company supplies. Other requests were more overtly political. Hossueit wanted the Company men to tell their superiors, members of the Massachusetts elite, that the Vineyard Indians' colony-appointed guardian was illegally leasing out Indian land. Native islanders, Hossueit made clear, "desired ... that they might have no more guardians."[1]

As this account suggests, the Church played a multivalent and principal role in offshore Wampanoag community life, reinforcing the Indians' village, tribal, and colonial ties, and providing an institutional framework in which to address issues often unrelated to religion. Moreover, its centrality extended beyond what might be called the "golden age" of New England Indian missions before King Philip's

War, well into the eighteenth and nineteenth centuries. By performing so many critical functions over such a long period, the Church
helped communities such as Mashpee on Cape Cod and Aquinnah,
Christiantown, and Chappaquiddick on Martha's Vineyard to remain
Indian places long after natives were supposed to have disappeared
from southeastern New England.

This telling both complements and contrasts with recent scholarship. Current histories emphasize that Indians were pushed into
Christian missions by English coercion, as well as pulled towards
them, first by colonial promises of sheltered land and military protection, and second by Christianity's explanation of a world upturned
by epidemic disease and Machiavellian politics. Historians also agree
that these enticements were illusory. After King Philip's War,
Englishmen steadily chipped away at the boundaries of mainland
praying towns such as Natick, Punkapoag, and Hassanamisco, economically exploited the Indians, and eventually drove most of the
dispirited natives west or into the company of the wandering poor. In
the end, conversion postponed Indian dispossession but it could not
halt it. [2] Kathleen Bragdon's and James Ronda's analyses of Christian
Indian communities on Martha's Vineyard somewhat temper this
interpretation. These scholars found that for centuries Christianity
gave the island Wampanoags' leading families skills and structures
that upheld their authority, and offered the broader native population
a safe forum in which to maintain selected traditions.[3] This essay
builds upon Bragdon and Ronda's larger point—that in important
ways Christianity promoted native identity—by arguing that the
Church's role in colonial diplomacy, local society, and inter-village
networking facilitated the survival of the longest-lasting, most geo-
graphically-distinct native communities on the Cape and islands, and
even of the Wampanoag tribe itself. Furthermore, in contrast to current histories emphasizing the declension of Indian churches, this

essay submits that, in Wampanoag country, their importance expanded over time. Such an assertion should not be read as a challenge to the idea that the mission was a constituent part of colonial expansion and led to the weakening of native self-determination. Rather, it serves as an addendum: the multifunctionality of native churches gave Indians their best chance of remaining peacefully on some of their lands while maintaining a sense of local and tribal identity, despite living in a region increasingly dominated by whites.

* * *

The Church's rise to prominence in offshore Wampanoag community life began in the earliest days of English settlement. Thomas Mayhew Jr., launched missionary work on the Vineyard in 1643, and with a dedicated core of native assistants, spread the Word across the island with remarkable speed. By the mid-1660s, Christian services took place in every native community on the island, and by 1674, all but one of the Vineyard's three hundred or so Indian families called themselves Christian.[4] They were led by fifty Indian visible saints, divided into six meetings, and served by ten Indian preachers. And they were not alone in the region. In 1669, Cape Cod missionary Richard Bourne reported that the Indians of Mashpee "and other places neere adjoyning they are Generally Praying Indians," while on the outer Cape "there is some praying Indians & App[e]areth great inclination to receive the knowledge of God & forsake their former wayes."[5] By 1673, missionary visits to Nantucket by Mayhew and his Indian converts had convinced ninety of three hundred Indian families to adopt the Christian faith and gather together in a recognized church.[6] In all, approximately 3,400 Indians from the Cape and islands had entered the fold by the mid-1670s.[7]

The Church made one of its earliest and most important contributions to the long-term survival of offshore Wampanoag communities by brokering peace with the English during King Philip's War. It was able to assume such a role because the praying Indians had adopted several Christian community institutions and were enforcing a Christian standard of behavior that advertised their intention to live peacefully alongside the colonists under a single faith. As early as the 1650s, Indian ministers, ruling elders, and teachers on Martha's Vineyard began actively discouraging sins such as drunkenness, theft, Sabbath breaking, and falling out with one's neighbors, which they knew offended not only Jehovah, but the English too. Yet eventually Indian converts reached the same conclusion as their fellow English Congregationalists, that without the support of civil officers, church authorities could not produce a godly society. Accordingly, beginning in 1671, each native village held elections for three magistrates to enforce Christian law, with appeals passing from the Indians' own courts to colonial justices. Cape Cod natives launched a similar initiative in 1675. The native courts were an integral part of the Christianizing program, since magistrates enforced biblical law and demanded that transgressors recognize and confess their sinfulness. Whether from the pulpit or the bench, Wampanoag officials with titles recognized by native and newcomer alike were enforcing a moral code to which both communities aspired.[8]

Aside from the Indians' religious interest in suppressing sin, what made this new order successful was that most of the new moral police hailed from the natives' elite families and thus were entitled to deference. As the Chappaquiddick sachem Seeknout explained to colonial authorities, "we have desired that your Order should come to us, rather than your Officer."[9] In Experience Mayhew's 1727 collection of biographical sketches, *Indian Converts*, at least six of nine Indian magistrates were members of a sachem's family or served as a sachem's counselor, while a minimum of sixteen out of thirty church officials claimed elite genealogy.[10] At the same time, church figures dominated the Wampanoags' political ranks. Not only were Vineyard sachems

Mittark, Wobamog, and Tawanquatuck leading Christians, but in 1675 nine of Mittark's ten counselors held church positions such as preacher, deacon, or magistrate.[11] Indian political leadership and church leadership had become all but indistinguishable, meaning that Wampanoags who made decisions affecting war and peace were unlikely enemies of the English.

Church leaders governed the islands through the tense days of King Philip's War. The most important native figure in wartime was Japheth Hannit, reputed among the Indians to be blessed by God. Before Japheth's birth around 1638, some four years before Englishmen moved to the Vineyard, his mother, Wuttunuohkomkooh, had lost six infants to death. She attributed Japheth's life to an anonymous spirit's offer of mercy, and once Mayhew Jr., began preaching the Gospel, she was convinced that Jehovah was the source of this miracle. Subsequently, she and her husband were among the earliest converts. When the Mayhews opened an Indian school in 1651, the parents immediately enrolled thirteen-year-old Japheth, and by adulthood he had learned to read and write both Wampanoag and English. At age thirty, Hannit gave a public narrative of his conversion that allowed him to become a full member of the Indian church; afterward he was elected Chief Indian Magistrate in the natives' new court system. Later in life he entered the ministry and won acclaim for proselytizing to mainland Indians, including the Narragansetts and Mohegans. His widely recognized accomplishments and upstanding character made Hannit an obvious choice to serve during King Philip's War as "captain" of the newly formed native militia with the added responsibility "to observe and report how things went among the Indians." To "his Faithfulness in the Discharge of this Trust," wrote Matthew Mayhew, "the Preservation of the Peace of our Island was very much owing, when the People on the Main were all in War and Blood."[12]

English missionaries such as Thomas Mayhew Sr., were equally valuable to the peace.[13] Since 1642, Mayhew had been a force in native affairs as the island's sole proprietor and the colonists' chief magistrate, but his influence reached its peak when he took over the island mission in 1657 following the death of his son. The Indians showed respect for his work and status by asking him in 1670 to become one of their pastors, an offer he declined. After the Indians created formal courts, Mayhew enlarged his already substantial power base by consulting with the natives on their choice of magistrates and ruling on their appeals. "The Governor," as he was known, demonstrated a light touch in all of these capacities. He tolerated native customs within the boundaries of Christianity and showed rare sensitivity towards native understanding of the sins that brought them before his bench. He determined that peace on an island where Indians vastly outnumbered colonists depended upon inter-cultural relations based on persuasion rather than force, and that Christianity was essential to that influence. "The temporall sword is good," Mayhew wrote to John Winthrop Jr., "the spirituall is longer & more sharpe."[14] When war broke out on the mainland and Vineyard Englishmen clamored to disarm the local Indians, Mayhew boldly accepted his Indian converts' counterproposal that they be employed in the island militia. He even extended this offer to the praying Indians of Nantucket. His confidence showed foresight, since island Wampanoags steadfastly turned in Philip's men who sought refuge with them, and both Martha's Vineyard and Nantucket escaped the mainland's carnage.[15]

Information relating to the war years on Cape Cod is sparser than that for the Vineyard, but extant evidence makes it abundantly clear that the Cape Wampanoags' Christianity was equally vital to their peace with the colonists. Upon receiving word of Philip's uprising, Cape Indians immediately procured men to fight alongside English forces and renewed their 1671 submission to the New Plymouth colony. Their pledge envisioned "that wee noe more be strangers and forraigners, but by the grace of Christ revealed in the gospell wee hope to be of the household of God."[16] Lest the colonists question the Indians' sincerity, before their campaigns during King Philip's War, Wampanoag militiamen gathered at the house of missionary John Cotton Jr., and insisted that he preach to them.[17] They knew that, aside from risking their lives in battle against Philip, there was no greater proof of their commitment to the English.

The importance of Christianity to peaceful cross-cultural relations was not lost on mainland Wampanoag war refugees, who initially supported Philip, but later turned on him in exchange for Plymouth's quarter.[18] Fresh memories of the conflict's horrors convinced these battered survivors to remodel themselves on the praying Indians of the Cape and islands. To that end, mainland Wampanoags hosted missionary visits from native islanders Japheth Hannit and Thomas Sissetom, recruited a handful of Vineyard religious figures to join their communities, and entered the shelter of the Church.[19] As early as 1689, Increase Mather described Saconet as "a great Congregation."[20] Nine years later, mainland Wampanoags had organized into four meetings with at least 240 attendees, an array of Indian and English preachers and teachers, and schools that were producing a remarkably literate population.[21] What the colonists found especially striking was that these natives had been "under none, in a manner, but Indian-Instruction."[22]

The mainlanders' conversion reintegrated them into a greater Wampanoag community that was increasingly based upon church networks rather than sachem marriage alliances. By the early eighteenth century, Wampanoags boasted approximately thirty congregations with "some thousand of souls."[23] Experience Mayhew observed Cape Cod Indians moving to Martha's Vineyard expressly to join island congregations.[24] At the same time, Wampanoags from the shores of Buzzard's Bay and the inner Cape gathered to hear the preaching of missionaries John Cotton Jr, and Richard Bourne; even larger crowds attended major church events such as ordinations and the Lord's Supper.[25] The Church was more than a protective cocoon against colonial expansion or a mediating institution between natives and newcomers. For the first time since the beginning of the Mayhew mission in the 1640s, both mainland and offshore Wampanoags had a ritual basis for gathering together, a common faith, and a shared leadership structure.

Like John Eliot's mainland missionary charges, offshore natives gathered into Christian reserves to protect their land; on the Cape and islands, however, this movement was as much an effort to limit the sachems' territory as it was a response to English demand.[26] In 1669, Keteanummin, sachem of Takemmy (today's Tisbury and West Tisbury), alienated a huge swath of land to four island colonists, evoking such protest from his followers that "Mr. Mayhew had hard work to quiet the matter." Ultimately, the common Indians consented to the sale, but only after the sachem guaranteed them a permanent square mile of ground, contingent upon their upholding "god his wayes." Thirty years later Keteanummin tried to renege on his promise, but a group of natives led by minister Isaac Ompany, assisted by missionary Thomas Mayhew Jr.'s son, Matthew, battled him on the ground and in the courts until he acknowledged his earlier grant. In both crises, the Church provided Christiantown with alternative leaders to the sachem and links to English power brokers in law and government who could raise the "paper barriers" Indians needed to lay collective claim to the land. The Christiantown grants contributed to the natives' retention of their village in Tisbury until the late nineteenth century.[27]

Mashpee became an Indian reserve through similar means. In 1665, missionary Richard Bourne convinced inner-Cape sachems Weepquish and Tookonchasm to cordon off land for the praying

Indians and agree that none of it was to be alienated without the converts' unanimous consent. Plymouth confirmed this agreement in 1680, adding for emphasis that the Mashpee Indians' land "was to be perpetually to them and their Children." It is no coincidence that throughout the eighteenth century, Mashpee, despite its own struggles to fend off the English, served as a place of refuge for Indians whose communities lacked such protective agreements. Nor is it a coincidence that Mashpee remains an Indian place to this day. As the Mashpees themselves noted in 1752, they alone were supposed to enjoy their reserve "as long as Christian Indians live."[28]

Unlike Christiantown and Mashpee, where common Indians used the Church to battle local sachems for control of the land, in Aquinnah on Martha's Vineyard, the local leader, Mittark, used it to resist incursions by a more powerful sachem. During the 1660s, Wamsutta (or Alexander), successor to Massasoit as the paramount Wampanoag sachem, began to issue one land deed after another in communities that paid him tribute, including Aquinnah. Just after these deeds began to appear, Mittark and then his people suddenly became enthusiastic converts, despite having previously refused to allow Vineyard missionaries to preach in their jurisdiction. Mittark was fully aware that the purchasers would have to secure the approval of proprietor Thomas Mayhew for their deeds to take effect. From a practical standpoint, Mittark's resistance to the mission only made sense as long as Wamsutta offered protection from outsiders and contained his own wrath. Once Wamsutta became the threat, it was time for Mittark to find a new protector. Mayhew was that man, and conversion was the best way to secure his favor. After Mittark's conversion, neither Wamsutta nor his successor, Philip, issued another deed for Aquinnah land.[29]

Aquinnah's adoption of Christianity did not make it immune to the troubles that plagued neighboring Indian communities. Soon after Mittark's death in 1683, his son and successor, Josiah Mittark, created a land sale crisis of such proportions that a takeover of his sachemship by the missionary New England Company became necessary.[30] In 1687, Josiah Mittark sold his title to the Governor of New York, Thomas Dongan, who, after fending off an innovative Indian attempt to discredit the purchase, moved to divide Aquinnah into a series of plots for sale and lease. The New England Company's fear that its showcase converts were about to be "scattered up and down the Continent, and returning to the barbarous Customes of their Ancestors," led it to purchase Dongan's title for a hefty £550. The Company's intention, asserted its commissioner Samuel Sewall, was to refuse "to part with one foot of [the land] to Englishmen upon any term" in order to "preserve it Entire for an Indian Plantation; which may become numerous and well ordered."[31] The Aquinnahs were uncertain about these developments. History had taught them to see a Trojan horse in the Company's plans to lease out some Indian territory to fund Indian schools and poor relief.

Despite such concerns, Company management ultimately strengthened the native community. The Company's consolidation of Aquinnah's title eliminated the risk of individual Indians' selling the land. When Englishmen encroached on the Indians' lands, the Company hired able lawyers to contest such violations in court. The Company introduced Indians to the practice of charging colonists to graze their livestock at Aquinnah with native, rather than English, shepherds watching over the animals. This enterprise allowed the Aquinnahs to raise money from their territory without selling it or leasing it out. The Company also encouraged the Indians to form a governing body to distribute shares of grazing land, and this group became the foundation for an Aquinnah town meeting that exists to this day. Although the Indians resented the Company, it did prevent the sale of Aquinnah land for almost a century, and introduced the

Wampanoags to the institutions and land management techniques that they would need to survive as a distinct entity in New England.[32]

As land-sale crises afflicted one native community after another, Indians began to unseat their sachems and, in the best-documented cases, replace them with assemblies synonymous with the church congregation. Christiantown made governing so difficult for Keteanummin's successor, Josiah, that in 1702 he stepped down and deeded the praying Indians all of his claims, whereupon the natives formed what they called a "Legall Town meeting" and ordered that all land sales receive the unanimous consent of its members. In essence, their meeting was a politicized church congregation, with ministers, ruling elders, and teachers acting as spokespersons, moderators, and clerks, the laity forming the representatives, and the organization gathering together in the Congregational meetinghouse.[33] Similar changes appear to have occurred in other communities, although the information is less abundant. The people of Chappaquiddick broke with their sachem, Jacob Seeknout, in the 1730s, and afterwards fell under the leadership of Samuel and Hepzibath Cogenhew. Samuel was the Baptist minister, Hepzibah was Seeknout's daughter, and their house was the site of community worship.[34]

Ives Goddard and Kathleen Bragdon's careful analysis of a 1749 Wampanoag language petition from Aquinnah to Boston provides further evidence that the Church had become a central Wampanoag political institution. They believe that the document was drawn up in Sunday meeting because its author was the pastor Zachariah Hossueit, and the signatories' names were clustered by sex, like the gendered seating in church. It is not surprising, given the aforementioned developments in Christiantown and Chappaquiddick, that this same pattern marks at least six other petitions issued during the mid- to late eighteenth century, two from Aquinnah and four from Chappaquiddick.[35] Only Sunday worship regularly gathered everyone together where they could discuss common problems under the guidance of church leaders, members of the traditional political elite who were best equipped to draw up petitions because of their facility with written English and acquaintance with English authorities. The Church was a natural political body.

After church leaders oversaw public debate and drew up the Indians' petitions, they were the figures most likely to bring those documents directly to the attention of colonial officials. In 1763, Mashpee selected its schoolteacher (a position designed to promote religion), Reuben Cogenhew, to travel to London to present the community's grievances to the King.[36] Most years, however, native petitioners trekked only as far as Boston, as in 1763, when two of Mashpee's three complainants before the Massachusetts Legislature were Cogenhew and minister Solomon Briant.[37] The tradition of churchmen's engaging outside authorities continued well into the nineteenth century. Deacon Isaac Coombs and preacher William Apess led Mashpee's 1833 movement for self-rule, and Deacon Simon Johnson of Aquinnah was said to have left Martha's Vineyard only three times in his lifetime between 1794 and 1875, including two journeys to Boston to deliver anti-liquor petitions to the General Court.[38]

The churchmen's messages consistently referred to the common faith of all New Englanders and charged that whites failed to live up to what they preached.[39] In 1700, Simon Popmonet's remonstrance against debt peonage chided Boston that the "inhabitants of Mashpee" were "a people that do own the Great Jehovah and His Son our Lord, Jesus Christ."[40] In the mid-eighteenth century, Aquinnah contested Boston's appointment of an Indian pyromaniac and land swindler as one of their magistrates by citing Job 34:30, confident that Massachusetts authorities would know that it warned, "Let not the hypocrite rule."[41] Judah Coquit charged that, whereas the Chappaquiddicks were a praying people, the guardian Boston provided for them, Benjamin Hawes, was hopelessly corrupt and "in a League with the Devil."[42] Nantucket's natives complained that their English creditors made them chase whales on Sunday, prompting the question, "how can we any ways be like christians when we should be praying to God on the Sabbath day morning when we must be Rowing after whal[e] . . . we should be at rest on that day and do no worldly labor only to do sum holy duties to draw near to god." It was enough to make them conclude "these English . . . are no ways like christons."[43] In an era of hardening racial attitudes and almost nonexistent Indian economic and military leverage, the Indians had few means other than the language of Christianity to remind the state of its obligations to them.

The influence of Indian church officers extended not only from their ancestry, facility with the written word, and ability to manipulate Christian themes, but from their access to the New England Company's treasury. Preachers, ruling elders, deacons, and semi-Christian officials such as schoolmasters, magistrates, and town clerks drew annual salaries from the organization, a rare source of steady income. Such compensation was seldom high, but when an individual held multiple offices, he could earn a comfortable allowance.[44] For example, throughout his long eighteenth-century career, Zachariah Hossueit worked as a preacher, schoolmaster, town clerk, and magistrate of Aquinnah and Christiantown, earning a salary that reached as high as £100 Massachusetts currency in 1771.[45] Unlike his neighbors, whose English creditors forced them to work on colonial ships and farms or in English kitchens, Hossueit was a constant presence at Aquinnah by virtue of his liquidity, and, even if he were to fall behind, he could count on the New England Company for assistance.[46] Aquinnahs knew that day in and day out Hossueit would be there to help them build community coalitions and monitor the Indians' deeds, leases, and lawsuits.[47]

The fixity, equity, education, and connectedness of New England Company employees made them jacks-of-all trades who managed their communities' financial, legal, and political affairs, in addition to performing their day jobs. Stable finances made them good credit risks for colonial storeowners, thereby allowing them to purchase goods for the community, as, for example, when Hossueit and magistrate Josiah Ponit bought two thousand nails and shingles for the Gay Head church.[48] They loaned money to neighbors in temporary straits, and put up bail for congregants in trouble with the law.[49] They served as point men for the distribution of New England Company supplies, such as corn to relieve the effects of a drought, and dividends from rents the Company collected on Indian lands.[50] Literacy, steady incomes, and the ability to drum up Company support enabled them aggressively to pursue the Indians' antagonists through the courts or, in some cases, the halls of government. Hossueit became the undisputed leader of Aquinnah in the 1740s after he defeated Indian Israel Amos's lawsuit to seize one-quarter of the community's land. Following the lengthy court battle, Aquinnah extended to Hossueit the right to graze one hundred sheep on the commons in appreciation of how he "stood by us and bore the big[g]est part of the Charge" in the Amos affair.[51] In short, Company ties gave church leaders opportunities to make themselves valuable to their neighbors in a variety of capacities.

Throughout the colonial period, the Indians' ability to adapt their church to meet multiple needs made it the central institution for handling village, tribal, and state affairs. Perhaps the greatest test of the Church's capacity for mediating interpersonal relations came during the late eighteenth and early nineteenth centuries, when scores of outsiders married into Wampanoag communities.[52] By the end of the American Revolution, New England Indian villages suffered a serious gender imbalance due to the number of men lost to military casualties and seafaring accidents. Native women had little choice but to consider outsiders as potential spouses, and since legal and cultural barriers made whites off-limits, and low-wage employment in port cities put native women in frequent contact with other "people of color," a disproportionate number of the resulting relationships were with African-Americans. At the turn of the eighteenth century, exogamous unions made up at least one-third of marriages at places such as Aquinnah, and one-half or more in other native communities.

The task of acclimatizing non-natives to community life was charged with tension. Many Indians held racial prejudices against blacks, to which were added the deep and legitimate concerns that whites would deny that the children of exogamous marriages and the communities in which they lived were Indian at all. Furthermore, the newcomers threatened to erode several cherished traditions that served as pillars of Indian identity. Outsiders could not speak native languages, nor would the majority of their children. African-American men, particularly those who had recently won their freedom, were determined to assert their manhood according to dominant American values, which included owning land, participating as free agents in the market, and receiving public recognition as heads-of-household. Their aspirations received little encouragement in native villages where people held land communally and could not sell it without town meeting and state permission, and where the affluent were expected to share their wealth with others, not hoard it. Moreover, Indian women frequently were unwilling to leave public affairs to their husbands, particularly if they were non-native. In 1777, such clashes led Aquinnah's Tobish Pomit to complain that he was "very much Greefed by one of the new comers the strangers."[53] Seven years later, Aquinnah decided to choose a committee to determine just who the "Proper Proprietors" were.[54] Around 1788, the Mashpees declared that they "fear the coming of Negroes and

English who have happily planted themselves here . . . that they and their children unless they are removed will get away our Lands & all our Privileges in a short time."[55] In 1823, a lawyer defending African-American Richard Johnson against the charge of murdering an Indian woman countered that Johnson's Indian accusers were "a peculiar set of people" because "land and rights which they enjoy as a tribe" made "a stranger who comes among them . . . an object of suspicion."[56]

The Church did not solve the problem of acculturating outsiders to Wampanoag norms, but Indians did use the meeting as a space where they could be brethren rather than adversaries of the newcomers and their children.[57] During the period marked by the Indians' highest rates of exogamous marriage, one community after another shifted from the Congregationalist to the Baptist church for reasons directly related to the presence of African-Americans. In Aquinnah, one of the factors in this shift was that the Congregationalist pastor, Zachariah Howwoswee Jr., refused to preach in any language but Wampanaog, whereas Baptist preacher Thomas Jeffers conducted services in English.[58] The Wampanoag tongue had been in steady decline for decades, but only with the arrival of non-natives and the birth of their children, most of whom spoke English, did the community shift *en masse* to the Baptist church where the Word was accessible to all.[59] The last blow to the native language and the Congregationalist church was the growing number of children raised in English-only homes, particularly the homes of newcomers. However much the Indians cherished their ancestors' tongue, they went to church to receive the Word and were unwilling to have themselves or their loved ones endure week after week of unintelligible sermons. By 1808, Elisha Cape accurately predicted that Howwoswee's "Congregational order would soon become extinct. Only a few aged Indians, who do not understand English, attend his meeting, as he preaches in the native language solely."[60]

The religious preferences of Aquinnah newcomers also promoted the Baptist schism. During the 1740s Great Awakening, the Baptist church, with its egalitarian themes, plain language, and ecstatic reception of the Holy Spirit, drew in scores of New England blacks and mainland natives such as the Narragansetts and Mohegans who had previously remained outside of orthodox Congregationalism.[61] After the Revolution, evangelical churches exploded in popularity among all segments of the population, but especially non-whites. Whaling centers such as Nantucket and New Bedford, where Wampanoags worked and met non-Indian mates, contained a rich array of evangelical Baptist and Methodist meetings plus Quaker and Congregationalist assemblies.[62] Baptists and Methodists began actively proselytizing free and enslaved blacks throughout the United States, North and South, winning scores of converts with their accessible language, their radical claim that blacks were the spiritual equals of whites, and in some cases, the charge that slavery was sinful. "Respectable" whites eventually entered the fold and put an end to such leveling rhetoric, but the ironic consequence of their reforms was that blacks broke away to create their own churches where they could highlight the evils of slavery and racial discrimination, and proclaim that justice, including revenge, awaited blacks in the afterlife.[63]

When African-Americans or their offspring moved into native communities, they brought with them a commitment to evangelical faiths that soon spread to their Wampanoag family members. In 1793, a nonplussed Gideon Hawley reported that the Indians of Herring Creek followed "a Negroe man fanatick, who can neither read nor write, Scolds at a few, who are his attendants every Lord's day," and by 1798 Mashpee's Baptists had ordained as their pastor John Freeman, a man described by Isaac Backus as "a mulatto of about 23 years old."[64] Furious that almost nobody attended his own Congregationalist services, Hawley spewed forth bile against the

Baptists, including the charge that they were "principally mongrels."[65] Reportedly, the father-in-law of Aquinnah preacher Thomas Jeffers was half black and "brought up with the Dunkers, in the Baptist way."[66] Jeffers's contemporary, William Apess, a man of Pequot and African-American ancestry, traveled his own preaching circuit, which ultimately led him to the Mashpee pulpit. His message was consistent with that of other non-white preachers, and appealed to natives, blacks, and their children searching for a voice to protest discrimination and exploitation at white hands. Apess preached that whites, through a process of "murder by inches," were primarily responsible for Indian landlessness, melancholy, poverty, and alcohol abuse. "Assemble all nations together in your imagination," wrote Apess, "and then let the whites be seated among them. . . . Now suppose these skins were put together, and each skin had its national crimes written upon it—which skin do you think would have the greatest?"[67] *All* the people of Mashpee, regardless of race, knew the answer, and it strengthened their sense of belonging to the same faith.

Bringing African-Americans and their children into the community church exposed them to a long and living native Christian tradition, inexorably tied to the maintenance of the people in their ancestral territory, and to other Indian communities. For instance, outsiders who married into Aquinnah attended funerals in Christian cemeteries where they saw headstones covered with Wampanoag language epitaphs. They heard stories about the old "Church of the Standing Order" led by ancient Indian ministers who challenged both sachems and Englishmen who tried to rob the people of their natal ground.[68] Along the road to Edgartown, a pile of rocks indicated the spot where, in 1657, Thomas Mayhew Jr., last addressed the Indians before he was lost at sea, prompting grander stories about the history of the mission. And contemporary church services made it clear that Christianity linked the Wampanoags to their past and to one another. Mashpee's Blind Joe Amos made regular appearances at Aquinnah, preaching and presiding over baptisms at the foot of the community's glistening clay cliffs, where the Indians' ancient culture hero, Moshup, was said to reside.[69] The ancient spirits of place and the Holy Spirit were intimate acquaintances in native homelands.

Given the argument that the Church offered so many benefits, the question naturally arises of why more of the seventeenth-century Christian Indian communities on the Cape and islands failed to survive the colonial period. There is both positive and negative evidence linking the decline of certain native communities, in part, to the woeful states of their churches. The Church, through its dealings with Massachusetts and the New England Company, was the greatest generator of historical documentation for offshore Indian communities. It seems no coincidence that data is woefully scarce for communities on the outer Cape, where distinct native villages ceased to exist by the turn of the eighteenth century.[70] Yet there is more than silence on which to hang one's interpretive hat. Take, for example, the Vineyard's east-end communities of Nunnepog and Sengekontacket. In 1690, a "sore fever" blasted these communities. Three-quarters of the fever's more than one hundred adult victims ranked among the most pious Indians, prompting a "Great Decay of Religion." Moreover, the Nunnepogs' meetinghouse burned down and the pastorate went unfilled for many years, thus giving disaffected Christians additional reasons to miss the Sunday service with all its concomitant political functions.[71] Lacking adequate church leadership, Nunnepog and Sengekontacket addressed their land-sale problems not by unseating their respective sachems and replacing them with church or town meeting government, but by demanding fee simple title to individual plots, the same strategy followed by mainland communities such as Natick. It was a tragic choice. Once native communities divided their ground into individually owned tracts, it was only a matter of time before the English took possession. Like the Indians of Natick, whose church experienced a precipitous decline in the early eighteenth century and whose church leaders played a limited role in civic government, the Nunnepog and Sengekontacket communities had all but disintegrated by the time of the Revolution.[72] Of course, the Church's demise was symptomatic, the byproduct of an uncontrollable disease. And the east-end communities' proximity to Edgartown, the center of the Vineyard's English population, meant that they faced greater pressure from creditors and potential land purchasers to part with their territory. Nonetheless, the Church's weakness closed off the options that helped natives in places such as Mashpee, Aquinnah, and even nearby Chappaquiddick cope with similar dilemmas.

No Indian community halted English encroachment on its territory, jurisdiction, or social and cultural practices, but those who had stable churches, whose officers dominated village government, and who successfully lobbied the New England Company for fiscal and legal support, were the best at damage control. This story has been overlooked because the decline of the Natick church in the late seventeenth and early eighteenth centuries, followed by the Indians' rampant land loss, exposure to disease, and demoralization, has become symbolic of church history for all of native New England.[73] To a degree, such neglect is warranted since, indeed, most praying communities collapsed during the eighteenth century, not only those on the mainland but those on the Cape and islands as well.[74] Yet some did not. In the late nineteenth century, Aquinnah, Christiantown, Chappaquiddick, Mashpee, and Herring Pond were still distinct Indian places, and Aquinnah and Mashpee remain alive and well today. Their persistence derives in no small part from their historic commitment to the Church, which mediated between them and a dangerous world in which they exercised little strength. Early missionaries to the Indians declared that they wanted the Church "to be all things to all men," and in certain communities on Cape Cod and the islands it certainly became that, but mostly because the Indians adapted it successfully in unanticipated and multiple ways to their ever-pressing needs. The Indians transformed the Church from a colonial imposition to a Wampanoag institution that served as a vigorous bulwark for Indian interests and culture.

# Notes

1. All quotes and the majority of data for this account are from "Report of a Committee on the State of the Indians in Mashpee and Part Adjacent," Massachusetts Historical Society, *Collections*, 2d ser., 3 (1815): 12-17 (hereafter *MHS Collections*). The "Great Sacrament" quote is from Gideon Hawley, Diary, 1757–1767, entry for September 11, 1757, Massachusetts Historical Society (hereafter MHS).

2. For an earlier literature skeptical of missionaries' intentions and results, see Francis Jennings, "Goals and Functions of Puritan Missions to the Indians," *Ethnohistory* 18 (1971): 197-212; Neal Salisbury, "Red Puritans: The 'Praying Indians' of Massachusetts Bay and John Eliot," *William and Mary Quarterly*, 3d ser., 31 (1974): 27-54 (hereafter *WMQ*); Kenneth M. Morrison, "'That Art of Coyning Christians': John Eliot and the Praying Indians of Massachusetts," *Ethnohistory* 21 (1974): 77-92. Salisbury revisits and revises his earlier work in, "'I Loved the Place of my Dwelling': Puritan Missionaries and Native Americans in Seventeenth-Century New England," in Carla Gardina Prestana and Sharon V. Salinger, eds., *Inequality in Early America* (Hanover, N.H.: University Press of New England, 1999), 111-33. For the new emphasis on missions as *temporary* cloisters, see James Axtell, *The Invasion Within: The Contest of Cultures in Colonial North America* (New York: Oxford University Press, 1985); Robert James Naeher, "Dialogue in the Wilderness: John Eliot and the Indian Exploration of Puritanism as a Source of Meaning, Comfort, and Ethnic Survival," *New England Quarterly* 62 (1989): 346-68 (hereafter *NEQ*); Harold W. Van Lonkhuyzen, "A Reappraisal of the Praying Indians: Acculturation, Conversion, and Identity at Natick, Massachusetts,

1646–1730," *NEQ* 63 (1990): 396-428; Daniel Mandell, "'To Live More Like My Christian English Neighbors': Natick Indians in the Eighteenth Century," *WMQ* 48 (1991): 552-79; Dane Morrison, *A Praying People: Massachusett Acculturation and the Failure of the Puritan Mission, 1600–1690* (New York: Peter Land, 1995); Mandell, *Behind the Frontier: Indians in Eighteenth-Century Eastern Massachusetts* (Lincoln: University of Nebraska Press, 1996); Jean M. O'Brien, *Dispossession by Degrees: Indian Land and Identity in Natick, Massachusetts, 1650–1790* (New York: Cambridge University Press, 1997); and Richard W. Cogley, *John Eliot's Mission to the Indians Before King Philip's War* (Cambridge, Mass.: Harvard University Press, 1999). More compatible with the themes emphasized here is John Webster Grant, *Moon of Wintertime, Missionaries and the Indians of Canada in Encounter since 1534* (Toronto: University of Toronto Press, 1984).

3.   Kathleen Bragdon, "Native Christianity in 18th Century Massachusetts: Ritual as Cultural Reaffirmation," in Barry Gough and Christie Laird, eds., *New Dimensions in Ethnohistory: Papers of the Second Laurier Conference on Ethnohistory and Ethnology* (Hull, Quebec: Canadian Museum of Civilization, 1991), 119-26; Bragdon, "Language, Folk History, and Indian Identity on Martha's Vineyard," in Anne Elizabeth Yentsch and Mary C. Beaudry, eds., *The Art and Mystery of Historical Archaeology: Essays in Honor of James Deetz* (Boca Raton, Fla.: CRC Press, 1992), 331-42; James Ronda, "Generations of Faith: The Christian Indians of Martha's Vineyard," *WMQ* 38 (1981): 369-94.

4.   Daniel Gookin, "Historical Collections of the Indians in New England," *MHS Collections*, 1st ser., 1 (1792): 205; "Thomas Mayhew, Sr., to the Commissioners of the United Colonies, August 23, 1671," in John W. Ford, ed., *Some Correspondence between the Governors and Treasurers of the New England Company in London and the Commissioners of the United Colonies* (London: Spottiswoode and Co., 1896), 40.

5.   Richard Bourne to the Commissioners of the New England Company, September 1, 1669, New England Company Manuscripts,

No. 7957, p. 1, Guildhall Library, Corporation of London, U.K. (hereafter cited NE Co. MS).

6. John Eliot, *A Brief Narrative of the Progress of the Gospel Among the Indians of New England* [1670], ed. W. T. R. Marvin (Boston, 1868), 20-21; Eliot, "Account of the Indian Churches in New England (1673)," *MHS Collections*, 1st ser., 10 (1809): 124-29; Matthew Mayhew, *The Conquests and Triumphs of Grace: Being a Brief Narrative of the Success which the Gospel hath had among the Indians of Martha's Vineyard (and the Places adjacent) in New-England* (London, 1695), 37.

7. Gookin, "Historical Collections," 180-201, 205. For a general discussion of the Mayhew mission, see David J. Silverman, "Conditions for Coexistence, Climates for Collapse: The Challenges of Indian Life on Martha's Vineyard, 1524–1871" (Ph.D. diss., Princeton University, 2000), chaps. 2-3.

8. Silverman, "Conditions for Coexistence, Climates for Collapse," 163-65.

9. M. Mayhew, *Conquests and Triumphs of Grace*, 42-43.

10. The magistrates were Mittark (Aquinnah sachem), Japheth Hannit (son of "petty sachem" Pammehannit), Tawanquatuck (Nunnepog sachem), Abel Wauwompuhque Sr. (brother of Mittark), Ekoochuck (son-in-law of Mittark), and William Lay (son of "a noted Indian called Panunnut"). The church officials were Momanaquem (preacher; son of Aquinnah sachem Annawantoohque), John Nahosoo (ruling elder; son-in-law of Cheeschamog, a "petty sachem" of Martha's Vineyard), Wunnanuahkomun (preacher; son-in-law of Cheeschamog), Jannawanit (minister; brother of Pammehannit), Jonathan Amos (deacon and preacher; son-in-law of sachem Myoxeo), Elisha Paanout (preacher; nephew of Mittark), Joash Panu (pastor; grandson of Mittark), Abel Wauwompuhque Jr. (deacon; nephew of Mittark), John Amanhut, (preacher; grandson of a mainland sachem), Wobamog (preacher; Sengekontacket sachem), and Panuppaqua (preacher; brother of William Lay and son of the

"noted" Panunnut). All of the above information is contained within Experience Mayhew, *Indian Converts: Or, Some Account of the Lives and Dying Speeches of a considerable Number of the Christianized INDIANS of Martha's Vineyard, in New-England* (London, 1727). However, the high status of several church officials only becomes clear by cross-checking *Indian Converts* against other records. Kequish, who was paid as a teacher and schoolmaster in 1662, and Sam Mackakunit, who preached at Nunnepog, were both related to Towtoowee, sachem of the Kophiggon area of Nashuakemuck (modern Chilmark). See Nathaniel B. Shurtleff and David Pulsifer, eds., *Records of the Colony of New Plymouth in New England*, 12 vols. (Boston: Press of W. White, 1855–1861), 10:277; Dukes County Deeds, 1:93-94, Dukes County Registry of Deeds, Dukes County Courthouse, Edgartown, Mass. (hereafter DCD); Farm Neck Proprietors Records, 1:320, 322, Dukes County Registry of Deeds; and Charles E. Banks, *History of Martha's Vineyard, Dukes County, Massachusetts*, 3 vols. (Boston: George H. Dean, 1911), 2:Chilmark:14-15. Nanosco, brother of Momanaquem and grandson of Annowantooque, was paid as a teacher by the New England Company in 1662. See *Records of New Plymouth*, 10:277; DCD, 1:257; E. Mayhew, *Indian Converts*, 12, 284. Christiantown preacher Joel Sims was the son of Pockqsimme, or Poxim, a Christiantown founder and one of seven Indians who approved the paramount Wampanoag sachem Wamsutta's 1661 sale of Nashaquitsa land. See *Indian Converts*, 73; DCD, 1:357, 3:12. And Christiantown pastor Hosea Manhut was son of Wannamanhut, the Massachusett-born Takemmy sachem. See *Indian Converts*, 207; Ives Goddard and Kathleen J. Bragdon, eds. *Native Writings in Massachusett*, 2 vols. (Philadelphia: American Philosophical Society, 1988), 1:159-61; Suffolk Files #12248, Massachusetts State Archives, Boston, Mass.

11. DCD, 6:369-73; Goddard and Bragdon, eds., *Native Writings*, 1:82-89. The counselors, their offices, and pertinent relatives were as follows: Yonohummuh—no supporting data; Samuel Coomes—magistrate and son of Hiacoomes (E. Mayhew, *Indian Converts*, 91-93); Abel Wauwompuhque—magistrate and brother of Mittark (*Indian Converts*, 67, 98); Wompamog (or Wobamog), alias Mr. Sam—

Sengekontacket sachem and preacher (*Indian Converts*, 74); Akoochuck—magistrate and Mittark's son-in-law (*Indian Converts*, 101-2); John Momonaquem—east-end preacher and son of Nashuakemuck minister Momonaquem (*Indian Converts*, 12, 140); Wuttinomanomin—magistrate and Nashuakemuck deacon (*Indian Converts*, 31-33); Nashcompait—no office, but one of Aquinnah's first converts (*Indian Converts*, 100); Elisha—on New England Company dole in 1710–1711 for unspecified service (New England Company Ledger, p. 25, MHS); Wuttahhonnompisin—early Aquinnah convert (*Indian Converts*, 131-32).

12. Cotton Mather, *Magnalia Christi Americana, or, The Ecclesiastical History of New England, From Its First Planting, in the Year 1620, Unto the Year of Our Lord 1698*, 2 vols. (1702; repr. Boston, 1853), 2:440-42; E. Mayhew, *Indian Converts*, 44-45, 129, 135-36; M. Mayhew, *Conquests and Triumphs of Grace*, 46 (quote).

13. On Mayhew's career, see Banks, *The History of Martha's Vineyard*, vol. 1, chaps. 5-14, and 19; Lloyd C. M. Hare, *Thomas Mayhew: Patriarch to the Indians, 1593–1682* (New York, 1932); Margery Ruth Johnson, "The Mayhew Mission to the Indians, 1643–1806" (Ph.D. diss., Clark University, 1966); Neal Salisbury, "Missionary as Colonist," in William Cowan, ed., *Papers of the 6th Algonquian Conference* (Ottawa: Carleton University Press, 1974), 253-73.

14. "Thomas Mayhew, Sr., to John Winthrop, Jr., 7 December 1675," *MHS Collections*, 4th ser., 7 (1865): 43.

15. More generally on the islands during the war years, see Silverman, "Conditions for Coexistence, Climates for Collapse," chap. 4.

16. *Records of the Colony of New Plymouth*, 5:66-67, 70-72 (quote), 177-78.

17.. Len Travers, ed., "The Missionary Journal of John Cotton, Jr., 1666–1678," *Proceedings of the Massachusetts Historical Society* 109 (1998): 97.

18. *Records of the Colony of New Plymouth,* 5:201, 202, 224-25.

19. M. Mayhew, *Conquests and Triumphs of Grace,* 37; John Cotton Jr., to Increase Mather, March 23, 1693, Mugar Library of Boston University Special Collections (transcription courtesy of Sheila McIntyre and Len Travers), and typescript at the New York Historical Society, New York City; Travers, ed., "Missionary Journal of John Cotton, Jr.," post-1676 entries; Cotton Mather, *A Brief Account of the Evangelical Work among the Christianized Indians of New England,* appended to his *Just Commemorations. The Death of Good Men, Considered* (Boston, 1715), 53; E. Mayhew, *Indian Converts,* 161; E. Mayhew, "A Brief Journal of my visitation of the Pequot & Mohegin Indians," in Ford, ed., *Some Correspondence,* 110; NE Co. MS, No. 7953, p. 12.

20. Increase Mather, *A Brief Relation of the State of New England* (London, 1689), in William H. Whitmore, ed., *The Andros Tracts: Being a Collection of Pamphlets and Official Papers,* 3 vols. (Boston: The Prince Society, 1868–1874), 2:165-66, 168.

21. M. Mayhew, *Conquests and Triumphs of Grace,* 37; John Cotton Jr., to Increase Mather, March 23, 1693, Mugar Library; Grindal Rawson and Samuel Danforth, "Account of an Indian Visitation, A.D. 1698," *MHS Collections,* 1st ser., 10 (1809): 129-30; Cotton Mather, "Concerning the Essays that are made, for the Propagation of Religion among the Indians, in the Massachuset Province of New England," appendix to his *Bonifacius: An Essay upon the Good, that is to be Devised and Designed, by Those Who Desire to Answer the Great End of Life, and to do Good While They Live* (Boston, 1710), 195-96.

22. "A Conference with an Indian of New England, December, 1708," NE Co. MS, No. 7957, p. 3 (quote); John Cotton to Increase Mather, March 23, 1693, Mugar Library. For more on the refugee communities, see Thomas Weston, *History of the Town of Middleboro, Massachusetts* (Boston: Houghton, Mifflin, and Co., 1906), 13, 18, 582 (map), 583; Hugo A. Dubuque, *Fall River Indian Reservation* (Fall River, Mass., privately printed, 1907), 3-4, 10, 61; Frank G. Speck, *Territorial Subdivisions*

of the Wampanoag, Massachusett, and Nauset Indians, Indian Notes and Monographs No. 44 (New York: Heye Foundation, 1928), 180; Laurie Weinstein, "'We're Still Living on Our Traditional Homeland': The Wampanoag Legacy in New England," in Frank W. Porter III, ed., *Strategies for Survival: American Indians in the Eastern United States, Contributions in Ethnic Studies* 15 (Westport, Conn.: Bergin and Garvey, 1986), 94-95; Goddard and Bragdon, eds., *Native Writings*, 1:13.

23. Cotton Mather, *A Brief Account of the Evangelical Work among the Christianized Indians of New England*, appended to his *Just Commemorations*, 49.

24. Experience Mayhew to Roland Cotton, July 1699, Misc. Bound Manuscripts, MHS.

25. Gookin, "Historical Collections," 99; John Cotton Jr., to Increase Mather, March 23, 1693, Mugar Library; Rawson and Danforth, "Account of an Indian Visitation," 129-34.

26. The content of the following two pages is developed in Silverman, "Deposing the Sachem to Defend the Sachemship: Land Sales and Native Political Structure on Martha's Vineyard, 1680–1740," *Explorations in Early American Culture* 5 (2001): 9-44.

27. On the Takemmy Indians' contests with Keteanummin, see Silverman, "Conditions for Coexistence, Climates for Collapse," 105-8, 231-36. The above quotes are from "Testimony of Joseph Merry, 3 March 1688/89," Misc. Bound Manuscripts, MHS; and DCD, 1:378.

28. Jack Campisi, *The Mashpee Indians: Tribe on Trial* (Syracuse, N.Y.: Syracuse University Press, 1991), 78, 80; Francis G. Hutchins, *Mashpee: The Story of Cape Cod's Indian Town* (West Franklin, N.H.: Amarta Press, 1979), 46-51, 60-61; *Records of the Colony of New Plymouth*, 6:159-60 ("perpetually . . ."); Goddard and Bragdon, eds. *Native Writings*, 1:372-73 ("as long . . ."). Mashpee's troubles can be traced in Mandell, *Behind the Frontier*.

29. Silverman, "Conditions for Coexistence, Climates for Collapse," 99-101.

30. E. Mayhew, *Indian Converts*, 21.

31. "New England Company Governor Sir William Ashust to Governor Nicholson, 15 January 1712," in Ford, ed., *Some Correspondence*, 94 ("scattered . . . "); NE Co. MS, No. 7955/1, p. 38 ("to part . . . ").

32. More generally on the contest for Aquinnah, see Silverman, "Conditions for Coexistence, Climates for Collapse," 246-59. On the evolution of Aquinnah government, see Gloria Levitas, "No Boundary is a Boundary: Conflict and Change in a New England Indian Community" (Ph.D. diss., Rutgers University, 1980).

33. Silverman, "Conditions for Coexistence, Climates for Collapse," 220-21, 237-39.

34. Silverman, "Conditions for Coexistence, Climates for Collapse," 241-48.

35. Goddard and Bragdon, eds., *Native Writings*, 1:22; Massachusetts Archives Series, 31:551, 32:356, 33:470, 33:488, 33:444-46, 33:470-71, Massachusetts State Archives.

36. Hutchins, *Mashpee*, 73; Mandell, *Behind the Frontier*, 157.

37. Hawley Journal and Letters, entry for June 23, 1763, Congregational Library, Boston, Mass.

38. *Vineyard Gazette*, April 22, 1847, p. 2. Microfilm available at Edgartown Public Library, Edgartown, Mass.; *Harper's New Monthly Magazine* 124 (September 1860): 453.

39. For excellent studies illustrating how Indians used Christian themes to charge whites with hypocrisy, see Barry O'Connell's introduction to *On Our Own Ground, The Complete Writings of William Apess, a Pequot*

(Amherst: University of Massachusetts Press, 1992), xiii-lxxvii; Bernd C. Peyer, *The Tutor'd Mind: Indian Missionary-Writers in Antebellum America* (Amherst: University of Massachusetts Press, 1997); Laura K. Arnold, "Crossing Cultures: Algonquian Indians and the Invention of New England" (Ph.D. diss., University of California, Los Angeles, 1995), chaps. 4-5; and David Murray, *Forked Tongues: Speech, Writing, and Representation in North American Indian Texts* (Bloomington, Ind.: Indiana University Press, 1991), chap. 4.

40. Quoted in Hutchins, *Mashpee*, 63.

41. Goddard and Bragdon, eds., *Native Writings*, 1:224-25.

42. Dukes County Inferior Court of Common Pleas, March 28, 1727, Miscellaneous Bound Manuscripts, MHS (quote); Dukes County Court of Common Pleas, Records, 1722-367, p. 662, Dukes County Superior Court, Dukes County Courthouse (hereafter DCCCP); Suffolk Files #29178, Massachusetts State Archives.

43. Quoted in Alexander Starbuck, *The History of Nantucket, County, Island and Town, Including the Genealogies of the First Settlers* (Boston: C. E. Goodspeed and Co., 1924), 154.

44. In 1771, Indian ministers earned between £69 and £95 Massachusetts currency, teachers between £12 and £24, justices about £2, and those hosting worship in their houses between £2 and £4. See Corporation for the Propagation of the Gospel in New England, Records, Box 1, New England Historic and Genealogical Society, (hereafter CPGNE).

45. CPGNE, Box 1, December entries, Box 2, October 8, 1757; Memorial of Zachariah Mayhew, October 1, 1759, Miscellaneous Bound Manuscripts, MHS; Indian Accounts at Martha's Vineyard for the year 1771, Miscellaneous Bound Manuscripts, MHS.

46. In 1727 the Company granted Nantucket Indian minister Zachariah Hoit £10 to keep him from "being forced to go afishing." See NE Co. MS, No. 7953, p. 79 (verso).

47. On Hossueit's career, see Silverman, "Conditions for Coexistence, Climates for Collapse," chap. 6.

48. John Allen Account Book, 1780–1820 [the actual dates are 1730–1759], p. 21, Martha's Vineyard Historical Society, Edgartown, Mass. Ponit (also spelled Pomit) is listed as a Company employee in the December entries for 1733–1738 and 1740, Box 1, CPGNE. See also Goddard and Bragdon, eds., *Native Writings*, 1:66-69. When Martha's Vineyard store owner Robert Cathcart died in 1718, his seven non-desperate debtors with New England Company salaries carried balances averaging £4 6s. 4d., while his 49 non-desperate debtors carried debts averaging 17s. 15d. Yet New England Company employees made up only 3 of 73 desperate debtors. See Dukes County Probate, Records, 1:102, Dukes County Court of Probate, Dukes County Courthouse.

49. DCCCP, 1730–1755, pp. 811, 835.

50. October 9, 1762, Box 2, CPGNE.

51. Zachariah Hossueit Papers, 1763, Mr 24=N28, #3306-8, John Carter Brown Library, Providence, R.I. (hereafter ZHP). My thanks to Michael Fickes for drawing my attention to this source.

52. The following discussion draws largely from Silverman, "Conditions for Coexistence, Climates for Collapse," chap. 8. See also Mandell, *Behind the Frontier*, chaps. 5-6; Mandell, "Shifting Boundaries of Race and Ethnicity: Indian-Black Intermarriage in Southern New England, 1760–1880," *Journal of American History* 85 (1998–1999): 468-69; Russell Lawrence Barsh, "'Colored' Seamen in the New England Whaling Industry: An Afro-Indian Consortium," in James F. Brooks, ed., *Confounding the Color Line: The Indian-Black Experience in North America* (Lincoln: University of Nebraska Press, 2002), 76-107; O'Brien, *Dispossession by Degrees*, chap. 5; Thomas L. Doughton, "Unseen Neighbors: Native Americans of Central Massachusetts, a People Who Had Vanished," in Colin G. Calloway, ed., *After King Philip's War:*

*Presence and Persistence in Indian New England* (Hanover: University Press of New England, 1997), 207-30; Doughton, "Red Men, Women, and Children in Chains: Enslaved Indians in Eighteenth-Century New England," paper presented at the Fourth Annual Meeting of the Omohundro Institute for Early American History and Culture, Worcester, Mass., June 1998 (my thanks to Professor Doughton for permitting me to cite his unpublished work); John Wood Sweet, "Bodies Politic: Colonialism, Race, and the Emergence of the American North. Rhode Island, 1730–1830" (Ph.D. diss., Princeton University, 1995); Ruth Wallis Herndon and Ella Wilcox Sekatau, "The Right to a Name: The Narragansett People and Rhode Island Officials in the Revolutionary Era," *Ethnohistory* 44 (1997), 433-62; Herndon, "Racialization and Feminization of Poverty in Early America: Indian Women as 'the poor of the town' in Eighteenth-Century Rhode Island," in Martin Daunton and Rick Halpern, eds., *Empire and Others: British Encounters with Indigenous Peoples* (London: UCL Press, 1999), 186-203.

53. File 1777, May 12-August 28, ZHP.

54. File 1784, April 16-22, ZHP.

55. Petition and Address of the Indians of Mashpee, Hawley Journal and Letters, Congregational Library.

56. Cited in Levitas, "No Boundary is a Boundary," 184.

57. On persisting disputes, see Ann Marie Plane and Gregory Button, "The Massachusetts Indian Enfranchisement Act: Ethnic Contest in Historical Context, 1849–1869," *Ethnohistory* 40 (1993).

58. Silverman, "Conditions for Coexistence, Climates for Collapse," 315-16, 398-99.

59. Silverman, "Losing the Language: The Decline of Algonquian Tongues and the Challenge of Indian Identity in Southern New

England," in John Nicholls, ed., *Papers of the Thirty-First Algonquian Conference* (Winnipeg: University of Manitoba Press, 2000), 346-66.

60. Elisha Cape to Jedidah Morse, July 22, 1808, Miscellaneous Bound Manuscripts, MHS.

61. William Dillon Pierson, *Black Yankees: The Development of an Afro-American Subculture in Eighteenth-Century New England* (Amherst: University of Massachusetts Press, 1988), chap. 6; William S. Simmons, "Red Yankees: Narragansett Conversion in the Great Awakening," *American Ethnologist* 10 (1983): 253-71; Simmons, "The Great Awakening and Indian Conversion in Southern New England," in William Cowan, ed., *Papers of the Tenth Algonquian Conference* (Ottawa: Carleton University, 1979), 25-36; Erik R. Seeman, "'Justice Must Take Plase': Three African Americans Speak of Religion in Eighteenth-Century New England," *WMQ* 56 (1999): 393-414.

62. Edward Byers, *The Nation of Nantucket: Society and Politics in an Early American Commercial Center, 1660–1820* (Boston: Northeastern University Press, 1987), chap. 5; Thomas Walcut Papers, Folder 5, Item 12, MHS.

63. Sylvia R. Frey, *Water from the Rock: Black Resistance in a Revolutionary Age* (Princeton, N.J.: Princeton University Press, 1991), chaps. 8-9; Nathan O. Hatch, *The Democratization of American Christianity* (New Haven, Conn.: Yale University Press, 1989), 102-13.

64. Hawley, Account of the Number of Indian Houses, July 1, 1793, Houghton Library, Harvard University ("fanatick"); Isaac Backus, *The Diary of Isaac Backus, 1741–1806*, ed. William G. McLoughlin, 3 vols. (Providence, R.I.: Brown University Press, 1979), 1431 ("mulatto"). Thanks to Brian Carroll for calling my attention to the latter entry. For more on Freeman, see Hutchins, *Mashpee*, 98-99, 102.

65. Hawley to James Freeman, March 1803, Hawley Letters, MHS.

66. Frederick Baylies, "The Names & Ages of the Indians on Martha's Vineyard taken about the 1st of Jan, 1823," MSSA/S53/Folder 1HA, p. 9, NEHGS; Hawley to Jedidah Morse, Undated, Hawley Journal and Letters, Congregational Library (quote).

67. Apess, *On Our Own Ground*, 157.

68. On the role of historic storytelling in native communities, see William S. Simmons, *Spirit of the New England Tribes: Indian History and Folklore, 1620–1984* (Hanover: University Press of New England, 1986); and Bragdon, "Language, Folk History, and Indian Identity."

69. Francis Parkman, Report of a Visit of Enquiry at Nantucket, Martha's Vineyard & to the Narragansett Indians, October 29, 1835, Andrews-Eliot Collection, MHS; Dr. Albert C. Koch, *Journey Through a Part of the United States*, trans. and ed. Ernst A. Stadler (Carbondale and Edwardsville, Ill.: Southern Illinois Press, 1972), 20.

70. Nantucket is an exception. The comparative lack of documentation about its Indians' Congregationalist churches stems from the predominantly Baptist and, later, Quaker faiths of the island's colonists and the subsequent lack of regular New England Company-sponsored missionary activity. Moreover, the decline of distinct Indian communities on Nantucket clearly stemmed from a 1763–1764 yellow fever epidemic that carried away two-thirds of the native population, especially adults.

71. E. Mayhew, *Indian Converts*, 116-17, 119.

72. Mandell, "To Live More Like My Christian English Neighbors," 571.

73. O'Brien, *Dispossession by Degrees*; Van Lunkhuyzen, "Reappraisal"; Mandell, "To Live More Like My Christian English Neighbors."

74. Mandell, *Behind the Frontier*.

# "We, as a tribe, will rule ourselves":

## Mashpee's Struggle for Autonomy, 1746–1840

### Daniel R. Mandell

O N MAY 21, 1833, the Mashpees agreed to tell Massachusetts Governor Levi Lincoln that "we, as a tribe, will rule ourselves, and have a right to do so; for all men are born free and equal."[1] This was the opening salvo in the Mashpee revolt of 1833, launched by the tribe to regain political and religious autonomy at a time when most white New Englanders believed that Indians had vanished from the region. The revolt generated intense public interest for several months, was settled peaceably between the state and the Mashpees, and was then generally forgotten. Over the past two decades, various books and articles have reminded us of this important event, and of the key role played by the Pequot Methodist minister William Apess.[2] Accounts rarely note, however, that the revolt was not a singular incident arising from immediate, unique grievances. Instead, it was the final push in a long series of Mashpee efforts to regain control of their community, and it reflected the growing tendency of surviving southern New England Indian groups to seek more autonomy.

When in 1746 Massachusetts appointed white guardians to manage each Indian reservation in the province, the Mashpees protested. They ultimately took their objections to the King in London and won a large measure of self-government in 1763. Twenty-five years later, Rev. Gideon Hawley persuaded the state legislature to reimpose the guardianship, giving him daily management of the Indian community. A decade-long struggle ensued, in which the Mashpees increasingly targeted Hawley's ecclesiastical and legal rule as the nucleus of their subordination to non-Indian gentry. Their campaign drew on long-standing concerns about communal control and became particularly heated with the meteoric rise of a Baptist church in Mashpee headed by an Indian minister, Thomas Jeffers. Unsuccessful in their efforts against the elderly Hawley, after his death the Mashpees tried again to regain their autonomy in 1807 and 1817, still with little success. The Indians finally regained their right to "rule ourselves" with the revolt of 1833, which joined political, economic, and religious concerns within the community, and successfully meshed with the political and intellectual climate of southern New England.

✳ ✳ ✳

Mashpee, established by Plymouth colony authorities in 1665 for Christian Wampanoags, gradually attracted Natives of the Cape from neighboring areas as the Anglo-American population there increased. The reserve boasted outstanding hunting, fishing, and clamming, abundant timber, and salt marsh hay for cattle, and was sufficiently isolated so that Anglo-Americans rarely intruded. By the mid-eighteenth century, many men worked in the growing whaling trade and women made and sold crafts to neighboring whites. Their minister was Solomon Briant, who led the community and kept the Wampanoag language alive even though he was occasionally forced onto long whaling voyages to support his family. Briant also helped to lead Mashpee's effort to regain its autonomy.[3]

The Massachusetts General Court had, in 1746, extended to all Indian communities the guardianships that had gradually been created for particular Native groups in the province. Guardians were Anglo-American gentry, usually lawyers or businessmen, who were appointed by the Governor and Council. They were given the power to handle all legal and financial matters on behalf of the community, including the allotment of lands and other resources to Indians and their families, leasing "excess" land to white farmers, and selling timber and other resources to support the poor and elderly of the community.[4] Provincial leaders took this measure because, after decades of dealing with fraud and trespass, they believed that Indians, like orphans and other minors, were incapable of dealing with the dominant legal system. But the Mashpees found that these imposed officials "do [us] more hurt than good." The community's own rules were increasingly flouted as "our wicked neighbors have advised young men & others not to submit to our Rules & orders because we had no power to make them." Until 1746, the Mashpees had managed to maintain a relatively high level of cohesion and autonomy that allowed them to keep their own language, leadership, and communal rules, while incorporating Christianity, English dress and speech (and for a few, reading and writing), and many other elements of the dominant culture. But the imposition of the guardians' rule presented a new threat to the community's culture, identity, and stability.[5]

Mashpee and the other surviving Indian villages had based their hard-won stability and autonomy on their ability to retain sufficient communal resources—fish, wood, fields, and pasture—to provide subsistence and a little surplus for market. The guardians were a fundamental threat to this system. Most felt that they needed to "optimize" a community's resources in order to gain the most capital for the community's account. In Mashpee that meant renting the best planting fields and meadows to white farmers, selling the right to fish from the Mashpee River to whites, and barring the Indians from taking more than a minimal amount of timber or fish from the commons. The Mashpees feared that their fields and rivers would be ruined and noticed that their young men were leaving to go whaling because the guardians had left them insufficient land. Practicing their traditional way of caring for the elderly and the poor, in which the able-bodied donated labor and supplies to keep the assisted within their own homes—a very different system than that practiced by Anglo-Americans—would also become more difficult if not impossible. The Mashpees therefore embarked on a campaign to regain their autonomy. In midst of this struggle, they were visited by the Rev. Gideon Hawley.

Hawley, a 1749 Yale graduate, had taught at an Indian boarding school in Stockbridge, Massachusetts, and then became a missionary to the Oneida village of Oquaga until the Seven Years' War forced him to flee to Boston.[6] In 1756, the Society for the Propagation of the Gospel, an English missionary society administered by Boston elites, sent Hawley to visit Mashpee for six weeks. Hawley later wrote that he was "disinterested" when the Indians asked him to stay and that their appearance "struck me with a gloom," but when SPG offered him an extremely high salary if he would remain for a decade, he agreed to stay and help Briant.[7] He also remembered that the Indians were "very uneasy" under their guardianship, but that he "did not much intermeddle" at the time.[8] As time went on, however, he would increasingly "intermeddle" in Mashpee affairs until, as an elderly man in the late 1780s, *he* became the focus of their anger and frustration. Much of the resulting controversy would stem in large part from his conservative belief in hierarchy and deference, his racial attitudes, and his curmudgeonly personality.

When the Mashpees' petitions to the General Court brought no relief, they decided to take their complaints to a higher authority, the King of England. In the early spring of 1760, Reuben Cogenhew, Mashpee's schoolmaster, embarked on what turned out to be a long and epic journey. He traveled to Rhode Island and boarded a vessel destined for London, but the captain instead took the Mashpee emissary to the West Indies, intending to sell him into slavery. Although the plan failed when the ship wrecked on Hispaniola, Cognehew and the others were picked up by a British man-of-war, whose captain was quite happy to impress the entire lot. When the ship put in at Jamaica, Cogenhew somehow managed to talk his way into an audience with the British Admiral. He not only persuaded the Admiral to free him, but also to give him passage on a ship to England. By the end of June, just a few months after leaving home, the Mashpee ambassador was pressing his case to George III. Given the British government's increasing desire to tighten control of the North American empire it had just won, it is not terribly surprising that Cogenhew's complaints that the Massachusetts legislature and its agents were acting improperly received a sympathetic hearing. The Board of Trade ordered Massachusetts Governor Francis Bernard and the provincial legislature to look into measures of relief for the Mashpees.[9]

The Board's orders arrived in Massachusetts that fall, around the time that Cogenhew returned to the colony. In response, Governor Bernard asked the legislature to modify the law—not to grant Mashpee autonomy, but to institute measures that would prevent debts, such as imposing corporal punishment instead of fines in civil court cases.[10] The legislature responded by sending a delegation to Mashpee to make an inquiry. At this point, Hawley supported the Indians' call for autonomy, and the committee upon its return to Boston reported favorably on the change.[11] But the resolution that actually passed the General Court instead supported the prevailing system, noting that "such of the Indians as are sober and virtuous are convinced of [its] necessity." Cogenhew immediately left to plead the Indians' case to Bernard, but without success, as the gentry in the towns surrounding Mashpee threw their weight against any additional autonomy for the Indians.[12]

Finally, in June 1763, the Mashpees persuaded the legislature to allow them considerable self-rule. They were permitted to manage their resources as other towns and to hold annual meetings to elect officers, although instead of selectmen they were to choose five overseers—two of whom had to be whites—who held considerable power over legal matters such as land allotments and leases, fishing and timber regulation, indentures, seamen's contracts, and the ejection of vagrants or trespassers. The Indians were also required to choose Englishmen for the offices of district clerk and treasurer. In an effort to regulate the influence of immigrants to Mashpee—a matter that would become increasingly significant in the 1780s—the right to vote was restricted to proprietors, who were defined as the children of a Mashpee mother or father, and only proprietors could gain access to the community's commons. As one of the two overseers, Hawley praised the new government: he noted that the Mashpees settled disputes peacefully instead of suing in court, that a growing number were staying home to farm, and that more were attending services.[13]

But the Mashpees who had fought so doggedly for self-rule found the overseers, including Hawley, annoyingly authoritarian and expensive. The first note of contention appeared in April 1766, when some Mashpees complained about the "exorbitant fees" charged by the officials.[14] Relations steadily worsened, and a year later Hawley asked the legislature for "further regulating" of the Indians, while Cognehew called a community meeting to choose delegates to Boston—probably to lobby against the minister's request.[15] This emerging controversy occurred, of course, in the wake of the Stamp Act crisis, which also involved suspicions about the nature and cost of governmental "fees." But in April 1771, Hawley told a friend on the Governor's Council that good relations had been restored with the Mashpees, and that his "difficulty with them" was "owing to the spirit of the times."[16]

Only a month after the battles of Lexington and Concord, Solomon Briant died, and Hawley perceived another opportunity to increase his influence in the community. While Hawley sought to claim what he saw as his rightful, unrivaled authority, the Mashpees never embraced him as Briant's successor. The minister never recognized, let alone explained that failure, but no doubt it was in large part because he was a "foreigner," had already generated conflict within the community, and was quite open about his desire to "Anglicize" the Indians. Considering the timing and subsequent events in Mashpee, another reason may have been Hawley's opposition to the war. In December 1776, he told a missionary official that "it is not for me to justify one party or the other: both are to blame," and "shewed as much displeasure against [Patriot recruiters] as I could with propriety but was menaced for it."[17] But while the missionary confidently claimed that his Indians "have not a disposition to take up arms," Mashpee men showed an eagerness to help the Revolution (or perhaps a desire to fulfill warrior traditions, or their need of a salary) and flocked to enlist.[18] No wonder that the number attending Hawley's sermons shrank, although when he asked for a reason members of the congregation politely replied that they lacked decent clothing.[19] Although the military records are incomplete, they indicate that 25 to 50 Mashpee men died in the war; considering that Hawley recorded just 39 male heads of house-holds in June 1776, this represented a devastating loss. No Mashpees wrote during the war to explain their support for independence, although their 1795 petition—written by a white lawyer but express-ing Mashpee views (see below)—trumpeted that they had hoped to win their rights by joining the "early martyrs to the Cause of this Country" on "the crimsoned fields of battle."[20]

While the Mashpees fought alongside their white neighbors for liberty and independence, the upheaval of the Revolution hardened Hawley's belief in the need for hierarchy and laid the groundwork for further conflict between the Indians and their minister. Before the war, noticeable numbers of Mohegans, Narragansetts, Naticks, and Wampanoags from the Cape Cod area had moved to Mashpee; this never bothered Hawley. But at the end of the war, he com-plained to friends that that growing numbers of poor whites and blacks "have encroached upon this territory."[21] In part, Hawley's concerns were racist, for he (like other Anglo-Americans) suspect-ed that an increase in this population would have harmful moral and behavioral effects—although he had also had some very posi-tive things to say about the children of black-Indian marriages.[22] More significant in the minister's mind was the challenge to order, religion, and his authority that newcomers both within and outside of Mashpee represented.[23] In addition, non-Indian residents of neighboring towns were buying or stealing land, wood, and fish from the Indians. Perhaps as a result, new conflicts emerged within the community. In early 1783, eighteen Mashpees signed a letter protesting that the elected Indian overseers—not the white offi-cials—were giving away or selling wood to outsiders. In response, Hawley and another white official tried yet failed to obtain special powers to eject non-Indians and prevent the illegal cutting of wood on the reserve.[24]

The clash between Mashpee autonomy and Hawley's desire for order became increasingly acute following the eruption of populist politics and religion in Massachusetts after 1785. This crisis had its foundation in New England's troubled economy and in the political system that kept the Boston-centered merchants and lawyers entrenched in power, and continued to maintain public funding for churches and Harvard College. In 1786, the agrarian revolt known as Shays's Rebellion evoked the spirit of 1775 for some, but drove conservatives like Hawley into a frenzy of fear. The movement for reform was, moreover, wider and deeper. The number of Baptists increased, as did their influence, and they were joined by many "orthodox" believers in their push for democratizing measures and a wider divide between church and state.[25] The townspeople of Sandwich, Mashpee's neighbor, strongly supported the more radical aspects of the Revolution, continuing a long history of dissident religious and political activity that horrified Hawley.[26] It was in this tumultuous, fearful atmosphere that the minister asked the legislature, in May 1788, to pass new laws that would give him tighter control of Mashpee. He told the General Court that, while the 1763 body of regulations worked well for awhile, "it no longer continues to answer any good to my Indians; it being too popular & ineffectuous—It has lost its power—and the Indians will never elect the most suitable men."[27] In response, the state repealed the 1763 law and reimposed a system of rule by three appointed guardians, including Hawley and two men from Barnstable, Rueben Fish and Captain John Percival.[28]

The Mashpees' reaction to the new regime was mixed, pointing to conflicts within the community and in nearby towns. In July 1788, twenty-four Mashpee men signed a petition submitted by Hawley, echoing the minister's fear of immigrants while calling the new law "a very disagreeable constitution" and saying that it was "mortifying to be under Guardianship and considered minors." Yet they did not seem angry at their minister, asking that, if they must have guardians, they be "men of the first characters for religion and learning, abilities integrity & honor"—i.e., like Hawley.[29] The issue of "character" arose in response to a nasty conflict among whites in the area, for Percival, a Baptist, had challenged Hawley's honor and authority, and the minister in turn tried to get the captain thrown off the board of guardians.[30] Gentry from nearby towns supported Hawley and expressed their fear that "men of no religious principles who make it their business to ridicule the Scriptures & the Christian religion" might govern the Indian community.[31] Percival was backed by other whites from the same towns—and by a large group of Mashpees who asked him to represent them before the legislature.[32] Shortly thereafter, the minister submitted another Mashpee petition warning of "pretended petitions" from "Negro trespassers" who backed Percival. No "real Proprietors" were dissatisfied with the guardianship, Hawley's supporters told the assembly, "but those who are deceivd with false stories from our enemies."[33] Among those who signed this petition, most would stand by the minister in subsequent conflicts. Factions were forming in Mashpee, with Hawley representing and fueling the dissension that grew from indigenous concerns but also reflected outside issues. Indeed, the language in their petitions hints at the manipulation of Mashpee proprietors by various white factions.

In early 1789, the legislature agreed to change the law, replacing the three guardians with a five-member board of overseers having extensive authority. The board was empowered to appoint one or more persons as guardians, who would carry out their policies and act as their legal agents.[34] Hawley was one of the five appointed overseers (Percival was not), and at their first meeting the board selected two guardians and chose Hawley to be their treasurer.[35]

Hawley's religious and political authority would make him the target of Mashpees trying to regain their autonomy. Although the new system caused the minister to feel more secure, opposition to him swelled over the next decade, as his dogmatic insistence on secular and religious hierarchy increasingly clashed with emerging "doctrines of liberty and equality" in Mashpee and the surrounding region.[36]

In November 1789, a group of Mashpees protested to the overseers that they were poor and needed help that Hawley would not provide.[37] The complaints had little effect, so a year and a half later, twenty-one Indians complained to the legislature about Hawley's overbearing behavior and demanded "the old Constitution and our Liberty." Their protest pointed to the connections between social, political, and religious concerns: "[W]e do not want his Conduct in our affairs we wants nothing at all that is his own he has Conducted in such manner that we have left his meeting entirely and never want to hear him preach nor even to see his face in our place any more." Hawley "discourages us" in "spiritual and temporal" affairs, which included their ability to "injoy our property." The Mashpees wanted political and economic liberty, including the right to hold and sell resources.[38] Levi Mie, for example, testified that in 1786 he had obtained the rights to a large wood lot, cut, split, and shipped five cords to Nantucket, and found the venture so profitable that he decided to stop cutting and hold the rest "for my children." But that future was destroyed when Hawley sold 120 cords from the lot and kept the funds for the Mashpee treasury.[39] Hawley fought back with a series of letters that blamed the protests on a few "designing men" from Mashpee and neighboring towns and emphasized that his authority as overseer was critical to keeping order.[40]

Their initial efforts rejected, in May 1792 Mashpee protesters again petitioned the legislature "to set us free By restoring to us our good Liberty and that we may injoy our o[w]n property again." They were angered by Hawley's violation of social and land management traditions, for "if any our near kindred dies [Hawley] takes their interest and hires it out and the Nearest relation Cannot have it." In addition, these Mashpees linked the expense of the overseers' administration to their oppression and begged the legislature "to restore us our Liberty" to choose their own people as officers and therefore reduce expenses.[41] The Mashpees' protests could be read alternately as individual (concerning *his* right to hold and pass on resources to *his* children) and as communal (concerning *their* rights as Indians against the arbitrary authority of an outsider, Hawley).[42] Mashpees and other Indian groups in the region had, by the mid-eighteenth century, developed a land management system that combined aboriginal and Anglo-American traditions. In July 1788, they had told the legislature that "we are tenants in common, all our lands being undivided, but our improvements are in allotments." They could not legally *sell* land to outsiders without the permission of the legislature. But the sale of resources or lease of land was quite legal and did not require the approval of a cranky Gideon Hawley.[43]

When their 1792 effort also failed, the Mashpee activists hired a prominent young attorney, Nathaniel Freeman Jr., to draw up a petition seeking the restoration of their autonomy and to represent them before the legislature in any subsequent hearings.[44] The resulting document connected Mashpee's complaints with America's Revolutionary ideals and the Indians' sacrifices during that conflict:[45]

> At the Commencement of the late Revolution, when a high sense of civil liberty, and the oppressive policy of an arbitrary Court roused the Citizens of America to

noble and patriotic exertions in defence of their freedom, we anticipated the time when a liberal and enlightened spirit of philanthropy should extend its views and
its influence to the increase of liberty and social happiness among all ranks and classes of mankind. We supposed a just estimate of the rights of man would teach
them the value of those privileges of which we were
deprived, and that their own sufferings would naturally
lead them to respect and relieve ours. Impressed with
these sentiments, and animated by a portion of that
ardent sense of freedom and love of independence,
which characterized our Ancestors, we voluntarily
entered the crimsoned fields of battle, & freely mingled
our blood with that of the early martyrs to the Cause of
this Country.

The petition termed the current regime "an infringement of
that freedom to which as men they were justly entitled." As in previous protests, this petition focused on two Mashpee grievances:
that they were not allowed "the miserable privilege of choosing our
own Masters," and that they "cannot alienate a single inch of our
Land, nor indeed enjoy it, as the Government have undertaken to
modify, & apportion it as they think proper." This last concern was
particularly prominent: they charged "those who forge our shack-
les" with removing all "incentives to industry or improvement." As
in the past, Hawley tried to discredit the petitioners as "ignorant
Indians" who "will never arrive to the knowledge of their true interests" and in any case "know not the purpose of petitions or
papers."[46] But the legislature took the petition seriously and, on
June 11, 1795, appointed an investigating committee to hold extensive
hearings at Mashpee.

In the time between the Freeman petition and the committee hearings, religion joined politics and economics as a source of conflict. Thomas Jeffers, an ordained Baptist minister of Wampanoag or Massachusett ancestry, moved to Mashpee and quickly mounted a significant challenge to Hawley. This religious conflict became an extension of the more secular Mashpee concerns. In his testimony to the committee, Hawley blamed the growing opposition on a Barnstable white man who was "preaching up the doctrines of liberty and equality" among the Indians "to bring them to his side in Politicks and to the Baptist side in religion." The weary minister concluded by emphasizing that his authority was a dam against anarchy: "They need an umpire or Superintendent."[47] But in fact, Jeffers, not a Barnstable white, had become an important rallying point for Mashpee efforts to regain religious as well as political autonomy. In January 1796, the Indians submitted another petition, emphasizing that they rejected Hawley: "we not chusing his ways of Worship, we do not hear him, we Rather chusing to Worship the devine being in the Bapptist Order." Many more Mashpees signed this petition than had approved previous complaints: fifty-five, compared to the second-highest count of twenty-nine in July 1788. Particularly remarkable was the sudden involvement of Mashpee women in the struggle, for among the signatories were twenty-two women, compared to only three in the 1792 petition. Clearly, Hawley's religious and political rule had become quite unpopular in Mashpee, perhaps even temporarily overcoming the community divisions hinted at in the 1788 petitions.[48]

But again Hawley and his allies managed to persuade the legislators that the Mashpees were incompetent and would be easy prey for manipulative newcomers, although the committee did note that the minister "was inadequate" and was not a teacher "on whose preaching they can consciously attend." The committee recom-

mended few substantive changes except to remove the treasury from
Hawley's control and saw no need to reduce the overseers' powers.[49]
Hawley viewed this as a vindication of his rule. Six months later, at
his request, the legislature passed a law that gave the overseers the
power to eject "vagrant poor" who lacked proper residency.[50] By
midsummer, Hawley felt certain that all but a few Mashpees had
deserted Jeffers, but he was either boasting or willfully blind.[51] In
1798, Jeffers would leave to revive the Baptist congregation at Gay
Head, and another part-Indian minister, James Freeman, would take
his place.[52] Until the end of his life, on October 3, 1807, Hawley
would regularly write letters that confidently described his unchal-
lenged authority over his flock and reported that the Baptist congregation was "coming to nothing." Yet in 1799 Freeman led
another campaign to overturn the guardianship, complaining "that
[the Mashpees'] property is placed in the hands of certain commissioners and guardians and praying for relief in their civil and
religious concerns."[53] But that effort also failed, as the power and
connections held by Hawley were sufficient to bar any change.

Mashpees waited until two months after Hawley died to mount
another effort against the 1789 regulations. Their petition, signed by
about fifty men and women, began by echoing previous declarations
of their sacrifices fighting for the Revolution and their disappointed expectations that they would be given their rights after the war:
"At the commencement of the late revolution, when a high sense of
civil liberty and the oppressive policy of an arbitrary Court, roused
the citizens of America, to noble and patriotic exertions in defence
of their freedom; we anticipated the time, when a liberal and
enlightened philanthropy, would extend its vie[w] and its influence
to the increase of Liberty & social happiness among all races and
classes." Moved by "these sensations," many Mashpees fought for
the Revolution; half of the men "fell victim in the cause of their

Country and of Liberty," including many of the signatories who "can exhibit the traces of wounds." But they were bitterly disappointed that the promises of the Revolution were still unfulfilled. "How could we conceive it possible that a people who were exhibiting such illustrious proofs of their attachment to freedom & so enlarged ideas of civil Liberty and of the orig[ins] and design of Government, that they should not respect those rights in others which they contended for themselves?" 54

The petitioners, as in past campaigns, compared the 1763 regulations granting self-rule with the 1788 and 1789 laws, noting that "By the former we had the privileges in part of choosing our Masters, By the latter even this small portion of Liberty is taken away." Unlike previous efforts, however, this petition was careful not to impugn or assail their guardians. "We do not mean to object to the personal character, integrity, or conduct of any of the present board of overseers"—which of course no longer included the deceased Hawley. Instead, the Mashpees focused on the high costs of the system (fees for five overseers, two guardians, a treasurer, secretary, constable, and timber agent) and the difficulties that members of the tribe often suffered because several of the overseers lived at great distances in other counties. Religion was not even mentioned in the petition. The prickly, authoritarian Hawley was dead, and his passing seemed to temper much of the bitterness that the Mashpees felt towards the guardianship system and to cause the Mashpees to adopt a more practical and less confrontational approach in their efforts to regain autonomy.55

Once again, neighboring whites were actively involved in the Indians' efforts. James Freeman, the state senator for Sandwich (not the part-Indian minister who confronted Hawley), became the Mashpees' patron: he may actually have written the petition (considering its flowery and erudite language), presented it to the legislature, and arranged for several other men from Sandwich to witness the Indians' signatures and make depositions testifying to the Mashpees' situation and concerns. Freeman also may have helped organize or lead the Sandwich town meeting of December 9, 1807, which urged the legislature to heed the Mashpee petition and reduce the number and expense of the Indians' overseers.[56] In response, the Mashpee overseers, including Hawley's son, Gideon Hawley Jr., quickly maneuvered to forestall any changes. In January, they collected seventy-eight Mashpee signatures (of both men and women) on a petition supporting the current system. The document accused conniving whites from neighboring towns of collecting signatures, such that "some of our brethren have been influenced by promises of reward and other improper motives, to subscribe their names to said petition." It emphasized the absence of debt in Mashpee, as well as the availability of schools, decent medical care, and other benefits of the current regime and noted that most of the community was "contented and happy." Not only was the current regime relatively inexpensive, the petitioners countered, since most of the offices were actually shared among the overseers, but it contained checks on fraud that would not exist in a more streamlined system. The nearby Herring Pond community also sent a petition, signed by thirty-eight men and women, which opposed changes in the guardianship system, noting that fewer guardians would lessen their confidence in the system and diminish safeguards against fraud and trespass.[57]

While the opposing petition highlighted conflict among the Indians—perhaps because Hawley could no longer serve as a lightning rod—it was apparently riddled with fraud. Zaccheus Pognit, a Mashpee proprietor, testified that the overseers, aided by several Mashpees, had used pressure and deceit to obtain the signatures. John Fish and Lemuel Ewer of Sandwich, the two men who had witnessed the signatures of those asking for reforms, echoed

Pognit's charges. Benjamin Burgess of Barnstable lodged similar complaints about the Herring Pond petition. Fish also emphasized that the Indians "have always appeared to be disatisfied [sic] with the act of 30 Jan. 1789 and complained of their deplorable situation. . . . their wood was very much diminished & cut off and that the great sums raised thereby were in a great measure consumed by the expensiveness of their government."[58] Such evidence, the support of prominent whites, and the relatively modest nature of the Mashpees' request were persuasive. For the first time since 1763, the Indians' plea for reforms was successful. In March 1808, the legislature reduced the number of overseers from five to three and granted them the power to appoint one guardian.[59]

While those asking for reforms passed over the issue of religion, the controversy did retain a religious component that, as in the past, echoed the Mashpees' social and political concerns. Those who had bitterly opposed Hawley were prominent in the renewed campaign, while the petition against changes included the comment that, when Hawley died, "we not only lost our religious teacher, but our father and friend, who preached to us by his example as powerfully, as by his exhortation." At their request, the overseers now sought "to supply his loss, by providing for us an exemplary teacher in the principles of Piety, Religion & Morality."[60] That summer, the SPG sent a Congregationalist minister, Elisha Clapp, to preach in Mashpee for several months. After he left, four Mashpees wrote to ask the organization for another, permanent orthodox minister, "lest the Itinerant Preachers of different denominations, who are traveling about in this part of the Country, should distroy our harmony & bring us to nothing." The initial signatory on this petition, Solomon Francis, had been identified by Pognit, Fish, and Ewer as a leader of the effort to garner support for the overseers.[61]

Mashpee's struggles to regain autonomy ushered in a period of renewed confidence among Indians in southern New England. After 1800, and particularly between 1815 and 1835, Indian communities increasingly demanded an end to guardianships or became quite willing to ask the legislature to replace particular individuals. Their protests became sharper, more insistent, and demanding of self-rule. Gay Head, Chappequiddick, and Christiantown, all on Martha's Vineyard and connected to Mashpee by kinship networks, sought autonomy or the replacement of incompetent guardians.[62] In 1819 and 1820, the Mohegans in Connecticut sought the right to nominate their guardians or at least the authority to determine who truly belonged to their community.[63] During this period, the Mashantucket Pequots protested their overseers' actions in ways that demonstrated that they considered the officials, at least to some degree, to be their agents rather than the state's.[64] Despite the Indians' initiatives, state officials continued to believe the Indians incapable of acting in a properly virtuous, responsible manner.

As might be expected, the Mashpees did not rest with their partial victory but continued their campaign for self-determination. In June 1817, nine men, including Levi Mie and others who had opposed the late Reverend Hawley, asked that the tribe be allowed to choose their own overseers and that the number be reduced to two—essentially a return to the 1763 regulations. While they asked for these deeper changes, their complaints echoed the more modest 1807 petition. They emphasized the increasing amount of meadow leased and wood cut by the three guardians, their rising debt, the officials' refusal to show their accounts, and the resulting moral harm to the Mashpees and costs to the state: "We formerly had our Children schoolled When we Chused our Overseers ourselves, but now we cannot have a school for them, We wish to know what becomes of all our money, that we cant have now privelege of that, that is really or own. We are informed that there is money drawn out of your treasury to repair our

Meetinghouse, but we are asured that if we could have the same Regulations we formerly had when we had but two Overseers and that of our own chusing wee should be able to build our own Meeting house without going to your States treasury for it."[65]

The legislature again dispatched an investigating committee to Mashpee, which returned a report that stressed the "diversity of opinion" among the Indians:

> a very small part claiming the entire right of self gov-
> ernment,—a much more considerable portion wishing
> to share it with the authority of the Commonwealth, by
> choosing overseers to be joined with those appointed by
> the governor and Council; while others not less intelli-
> gent, believed no share in selecting their overseers could
> not safely be rested in the Indians & that the present
> mode of government ought to be continued.

The investigators agreed with the last view, arguing that "To give the Right of choosing their own overseers" would "place them in the hands of the worst of all of the community's men, whose objects would be entirely selfish." They also rejected Indian complaints that the overseers were too expensive and told the legislature that the guardians' only failure was that "the administration of the government had been always too lax."[66] Yet the legislature did replace the three with two others, meeting one of the complainants' demands. On the other hand, the overseers were also granted the power to bind out anyone who, in their judgment, was a "habitual drunkard and idle" for up to three years' service, and to give the income to his family. In addition, the officials were also put in charge of regulating how Indians could cut timber, even for their own uses.[67] Apparently little had changed in the perceptions and attitudes of Anglo-American elites—or in the lack of consensus among Indians about the degree to which they could manage complete autonomy while protecting their lands.

New pressures developed in Mashpee in the 1820s as the children of those who had opposed Hawley returned from whaling to settle down and raise families. They found the guardians' repressive control irritating and harmful to the community. Daniel Amos told the committee investigating the 1833 revolt that dissatisfaction had grown during the previous decade as the guardians refused to account for their actions, provide any additional powers to those who wished to help their community, or allow enterprising individuals to claim additional resources.[68] Mashpee's minister, Phineas Fish, whom Harvard had appointed as Hawley's successor in 1811, was also infuriating. Fish was not only white, but was a liberal, intellectual Unitarian, whereas the Mashpees had embraced the evangelical antinomian Baptist faith in the 1790s. Avoiding Fish, the Indians instead went to Daniel's brother Joseph, who began preaching there and at Chappequiddick and Gay Head around 1825 and received Baptist ordination in 1830. "Blind Joe" Amos fit into Mashpee's tradition of Indian Baptist ministers. By 1833, Fish's congregation consisted almost entirely of white families living in or near Mashpee, and Amos's congregants grew increasingly angry that the white minister refused to let them use the meetinghouse and that his salary was paid by Harvard College's Williams fund for Indian ministers.[69]

Open revolt began with the arrival in Mashpee of the itinerant Pequot Methodist preacher William Apess.[70] Apess attended services at the Indian meetinghouse and, as he later wrote, was shocked to find only whites in the congregation. Apess became angry when he found Fish not only unconcerned with the lack of Indian participation in the church, but also utterly unsympathetic to the notion of granting the Mashpees more political and economic autonomy. Apess was probably not really surprised by Fish's attitude, however, considering his own longstanding struggles with white racism. He preached a few days later to his Indian brethren on "the soul harrowing theme of Indian degradation"—arising out of white oppression and racism—and triggered a series of community meetings in which the Indians discussed their problems and considered solutions.[71]

On May 21, a large body of Mashpees agreed to adopt Apess in order to give him the authority to press their case, to petition the governor for redress of their grievances, and to petition Harvard to discharge Fish and instead support the Methodist minister. The appeal to Gov. Levi Lincoln not only declared that the Mashpees would "rule ourselves," but informed him that on July 1 they would flout the authority of their guardians by preventing white men from cutting or taking wood from Mashpee. The petition to Harvard emphasized their alienation from Fish and that minister's ineffectiveness, and ended with the resolution that "we will rule our own tribe and make choice of whom we please for our preacher." Ten days later, two Mashpees traveled to Boston and left the governor's petition with his office. On June 25, after waiting in vain for a reply, they convened a meeting, elected officers including Daniel Amos as president, and agreed to post their May resolves in the surrounding towns. They also sent notices of dismissal to their guardians, insisting that they surrender all Mashpee funds and accounts, and to Fish, demanding that he abandon his home in Mashpee and surrender the key to the meetinghouse.[72]

At this point, Governor Lincoln sent Josiah Fiske to investigate. Fiske arrived on July 1 to find the Indians "in a state of open rebellion against the laws of the Commonwealth" and the surrounding inhabitants on edge over the Indians. The Mashpees had, as promised, stopped a group of whites from removing timber that the guardians had previously sold. They had also entered the meeting-house by climbing through a window and changed the locks, taking possession of the building. Fiske called a meeting on July 4 that drew nearly a hundred Mashpees, many carrying muskets. With Daniel Amos presiding, the Indians reiterated their grievances and Apess pressed the commissioner to end the guardianship immediately. Fiske later told the governor that the Methodist minister's apparent purpose was "to establish in the minds of the natives a belief that each generation had a right to act for itself"—suggesting a link between Apess and the ideas espoused by Thomas Jefferson.[73] Over the next few days, tempers began to cool as Fiske toured the reserve, met many Mashpees, and gained their trust on behalf of the governor. On July 6, the Mashpee council agreed to table their measures until the forthcoming legislative session would allow them to press their demands before the General Court.[74] This last, ultimately successful Mashpee campaign to gain independence exhibited similarities to other social reform movements of the 1830s, and like those efforts was driven by a rising generation. But the Mashpee revolt shows continuity rather than change, for its proponents were the children and grandchildren of those who had fought against Hawley and the guardianship, and their goals remained the same.[75]

Apess and the Mashpees skillfully managed the subsequent phase of their campaign. In August, they contacted William Hallett, lawyer, editor of the *Boston Advocate,* then a leader of the Massachusetts anti-Masonic Party and later of the region's Democratic Party; Hallett provided the Mashpees with essential publicity and other assistance.[76] In mid-January 1834, the young President Daniel Amos, the elderly Deacon Isaac Coombs, and William Apess traveled to Boston to press their case. The city was primed for the Indians, having just celebrated the visit of a group of Penobscots and Edwin Forrest's renowned performance in

*Metamora*, the play that mourned the death of King Philip, disparaged the Puritans who drove him to war, and romanticized the supposed extinction of the Indian.[77] The Mashpees heard their petition discussed in the House and on January 21 spoke to a special evening assembly attended by many of the legislators, during which they emphasized that the guardianship was "retarding their improvement, and oppressing their spirits" by discouraging industry, entrepreneurship, and moral reforms including temperance.[78] Four days later, William Lloyd Garrison published an account of the Mashpee complaints and condemned the Indians' special legal status, which included limits on land sales to whites, as "the chains of a servile dependence" that removed "all motives for superior exertions."[79] The Mashpees and Hallett further displayed their political savvy by publishing articles and letters that accused New Englanders of hypocrisy in fighting for Cherokee rights while denying the same to the Mashpees.[80] Their opponents were few and subdued, and tended to blame the Indians' unrest on Apess.[81] The Mashpees' tactics and the justice of their request, the absence of a strong opposition, and the shift in politics and culture in the region made the Indians' final victory seem easy. In March 1834, the legislature abolished the guardianship and made Mashpee a district with the power to elect selectmen and other town officials. The new law did set up a white commissioner and treasurer to advise the Mashpees and manage their financial affairs, but there was little doubt that the Indians had won their political and economic autonomy.[82]

The battle to oust Fish lasted longer. The Mashpees viewed the church as their historic community center, resented that non-Indians now dominated worship there, and saw little difference between their rights to political and religious autonomy. Already alienated from Fish, they were angered by his condescending, racist petitions against their effort to gain independence. In 1836, the Mashpees asked Harvard to give them half of Fish's salary to pay a minister of their choice; Harvard agreed, and the Indians chose E. G. Perry, an ordained Baptist minister, as their missionary and schoolmaster. Joseph Amos continued to minister to the Indian groups on Martha's Vineyard as well as at Mashpee. One year later, a Mashpee meeting unanimously voted to dismiss Fish but he still refused to leave or to share the meetinghouse with Perry.[83] Finally, in July 1840, after the legislature made Mashpee an independent parish, the Baptists went into the church and forced Fish out.[84]

Between 1746 and 1840, the Mashpees struggled to regain their autonomy from unwanted, arrogant, interfering Anglo-American officials in order to protect their resources and reinforce or rebuild community institutions. Their effort drew from two sources: the Indians' desire to maintain their community against the destructive forces of colonialism, and the intellectual and cultural ferment of the early Republic, with the decline of deference, the emergence of democratic politics and culture, and the widening separation of church and state. After fighting and dying for the Revolution, the Mashpees found the period's political rhetoric meaningful and useful in their efforts to regain their own liberty. Just as significant to those efforts was the growing evangelical movement that swept New England at the end of the century with a new egalitarian message for all believers, for the Mashpees' primary targets were their white ministers.[85] The community's efforts can be viewed as part of, if not partial inspiration for, the growing demand by other southern New England Indian groups to reclaim a measure of sovereignty. But the most significant lesson is that the Mashpee Revolt of 1833–34 was not an isolated or unique incident. Instead, it must be seen as the culmination of a century-long effort by the Indians to regain control of their own community.

# Notes

1. William Apess, "Indian Nullification," in *On Our Own Ground: The Complete Writings of William Apess, a Pequot*, ed. Barry O'Connell, (Amherst: University of Massachusetts Press, 1992): 173-77; Josiah Fiske, report to Gov. Levi Lincoln, undated but probably July 6, 1832, Box 2, File 1, Indian Guardian Accounts and Correspondence, Massachusetts Archives. Apess's and Fiske's descriptions of the meeting are strikingly similar.

2. O'Connell, ed., *On Our Own Ground*; Karim Tiro, "Denominated 'SAVAGE': Methodism, Writing, and Identity in the Works of William Apess, A Pequot," *American Quarterly* 48 (1996): 653-79; Kim McQuaid, "William Apes, Pequot: An Indian Reformer in the Jackson Era," *New England Quarterly* 50 (1977): 605-25; Donald M. Nielsen, "The Mashpee Indian Revolt of 1833," *New England Quarterly* 58 (1985): 400-20; Anne Marie Dannenberg, "'Where, Then, Shall We Place the Hero of the Wilderness?', William Apess's *Eulogy on King Philip* and Doctrines of Racial Destiny," in *Early Native American Writing: New Critical Essays*, ed. Helen Vaskowski (New York: Cambridge University Press, 1996).

3. Jack Campisi, *The Mashpee Indians: Tribe on Trial* (New York: Syracuse University Press, 1993); Francis G. Hutchins, *Mashpee, the Story of Cape Cod's Indian Town* (West Franklin, N.H.: Amarta Press, 1979); Russell M. Peters, *The Wampanoags of Mashpee* (Mashpee, Mass.: Indian Spiritual and Cultural Training Council, 1987); Daniel Mandell, *Behind the Frontier: Indians in Eighteenth-Century Eastern Massachusetts* (Lincoln: University of Nebraska Press, 1996): 108-9. Briant began his ecclesi-

astical career as the minister for the Indian community in Falmouth, but moved to Mashpee in 1742 after Joseph Bourne was stripped of the pulpit for giving some rum to Indians. One of Solomon's brothers, Joseph Briant, ministered to various Cape Cod Indian communities during the 1750s; in September 1758 he was ordained minister for Potawaumacut, on outer Cape Cod, but he died just two years later. Gideon Hawley, A Journal Beginning 29 July 1758 Ending 12 November 1758, Hawley, diary, 1757–69, Massachusetts Historical Society (hereafter MHS); Hawley, Mashpee, to Andrew Oliver, Boston, October 15, 1760, Gideon Hawley Letters, 1754-1807, MHS.

4.  On Massachusetts Indian guardians during the colonial period see Mandell, *Behind the Frontier*, esp. 117-63. On actions by guardians between 1780 and 1880 see records kept by Indian guardians in the Earle Papers, American Antiquarian Society, Worcester, Massachusetts

5.  Mashpees to the Massachusetts General Court, September 8, 1753, Massachusetts Colonial Records, Massachusetts Archives (hereafter MA) 32, 415-16; Mashpees to the General Court, August 4, 1757, Hawley Letters, MHS ("do more hurt than good"). Additional Mashpee petitions against the guardianship were sent to the General Court on December 19, 1753 (MA 32, 424-26), and were answered by the guardians (MA 32, 449-52).

6.  "Gideon Hawley," in Clifford Shipton, ed., *Biographical Sketches of Those Who Attended Harvard College*, vol. 12, 1746–50 (Cambridge, Mass.: Harvard University Press, 1962): 392-411.

7.  Hawley to Peter Thatcher, January 1, 1794 ("to be shown only to friends"), in Hawley Letters, MHS; Boston Commissioners of the Society for the Propagation of the Gospel, Meeting, September 29, 1757, vol. 2, Gideon Hawley Papers, 1753–1806, Congregational Library, Boston. The Mashpees had many reasons for asking Hawley to stay: traditional politeness; his experience among the Oneidas; the aging Briant's need for an assistant and perhaps successor; the desire

of "some others who do not understand our dialect"—i.e., newcomers from other tribes—for a minister who preached in English; and perhaps their perception that he would intervene with his Boston friends to support their fight to regain autonomy. Mashpees to the Massachusetts General Court, August 4, 1757, Hawley Letters, MHS.

8. Hawley to Reverend Lincoln of Falmouth, April 4, 1792, Samuel P. Savage Papers, 1703–48, vol. 2, no. 210, MHS.

9. Referral of Mashpee petition to Lords Commission for Trade and Plantation, July 10, 1760, Public Records Office (hereafter PRO), Colonial Office Records, Class 5, America and the West Indies (hereafter CO5), /890, 30; Reuben Cognehew to Board of Trade, undated but late June 1760, PRO, CO5/890, 31-32; Gov. Francis Bernard to Lords of Trade, April 28, 1761, PRO, CO5/891, 27-28.

10. Gov. Francis Bernard to the Massachusetts General Court, December 19, 1760, MA 33, 151. Bernard suggested four measures: 1) to prevent them contracting large and unnecessary debts that they could pay only by selling themselves; 2) "to prevent parents from selling their children or making them subject to their debts"; 3) to subject Indian offenders to corporal punishment only and not to fines, which they seldom were able to pay "but with loss of their liberty;" 4) "to exempt them from Law charges, which in little Squabbles that ought to have been made up without Expence have sometimes brought ruin, and in consequence Slavery upon a whole Family."

11. Hawley to Reverend Lincoln of Falmouth, April 4, 1792, Savage Papers, vol. 2, no. 210.

12. Hawley to Andrew Oliver, Boston, April 13, 1761, Hawley Letters, MHS. Decades later, Hawley told a friend that the opposition of "the Gentlemen at Court in the adjacent towns" delayed any changes for two years; Hawley to Reverend Lincoln of Falmouth, April 4, 1792, Savage Papers.

13. Massachusetts Acts and Resolves of 1763–1764, Chapter 3, June 17, 1763; Hawley, Mashpee, to Andrew Oliver, Boston, April 3, 1764, May 20, 1765, April 7, 1766, Hawley Letters, MHS. Unfortunately, Hawley's point about a decline in lawsuits cannot be verified, as the Barnstable County court records were destroyed by a courthouse fire in the nineteenth century.

14. Hawley, Boston, to Oliver, Boston, April 7, 1766, Hawley Letters, MHS.

15. Hawley, Mashpee, to James Otis, Barnstable, March 2, 1767, Hawley Letters, MHS.

16. Hawley to William Brattle, April 20, 1771, MA 33, 537. Hawley noted in this letter that "my Indians are much better under their constitution, which might in some things be amended, than under guardianship. As far as appears I am as popular & have as great a share in the confidence of my people as ever I had. They love and respect me." This contradicts his later contentions that he never accepted the 1763 regulation.

17. Hawley to William Phillips, December 26, 1776, Box 3, Folder 59, Mss. B C40, Society for the Propagation of the Gospel (hereafter SPG) Records, New England Historical and Genealogical Society (hereafter NEHGS). His opposition must have been quite muted, however, since the state (Revolutionary) legislature voted in December 1777 to "abate and remit" the taxes of Hawley (and his fellow missionary, Zechariah Mayhew of Martha's Vineyard), "they having heretofore been exempted from public Taxes by Virtue of their sacred Office in which they still continue to be faithful Servants." Massachusetts Acts and Resolves 1777–1778, Chapter 509, December 1, 1777.

18. Hawley to Phillips, Norwich, Conn., via the Reverend Hopkins, Newport, June 15, 1775, and Hawley to Phillips, December 26, 1776, Box 3, Folder 37, SPG Records, NEHGS.

19. Hawley to Phillips, Boston, July 15, 1776, Box 3, Folder 54, SPG Records, NEHGS.

20. Hawley recorded only 12 who died in the army or war, but James Axtell found that 25 out of 26 Indians in Barnstable's regiment died and estimated Mashpee's total loss at 50 men. Mashpee vital records in Hawley Papers, Congregational Library; Axtell testimony at Mashpee trial quoted in Campisi, *Mashpee Indians,* 88. For the 1776 census see Hawley to Phillips, Boston, June 24, 1776, Box 3, Folder 52, SPG Records, NEHGS.

21. Hawley to Phillips, Boston, June 24, 1776, Box 3, Folder 52, SPG Records, NEHGS; Hawley to Isaac Smith, Boston, December 14, 1784, Savage Papers, vol. 3. See also Mashpees to the Massachusetts General Court, October 31, 1788, in Acts of 1788, Chapter 38, approved January 30, 1789, documents relating to passed legislation, Massachusetts Archives. In 1793, Hawley made a census of Mashpee, the first since 1776, which included the "race" and place of origin of many (but not all) of the adults in the community. These included 7 English or German, 1 "Halfblood" (Hawley's term), 27 Indian/Indian unmixed, 3 Indian-African, 1 Indian-white, 4 mixed blood, 14 negro (mostly from Rhode Island, Taunton, and the Vineyard) 1 white-negro (from South Carolina), and 1 partly white. This census was made after Hawley and other white elites gained control of Mashpee, and after he boasted of expelling trespassers and others illegally residing there. Others in Massachusetts were worried about intermarriage, and in 1786 the state passed a law banning the marriage of whites to Indians or blacks. Hawley did not ask for this law, nor was he involved in its passage. Hawley, Mashpee census, July 1, 1793, in Hawley manuscripts, Houghton Library, Harvard University. I wish to thank Andrew Pierce for finding and bringing this census to my attention.

22. Comments in Hawley, Mashpee census, July 1, 1793, in Hawley Manuscripts, Houghton Library.

23. Hawley to Isaac Smith, Boston, December 14, 1784, Savage Papers,

vol. 3. Hawley's disappointment in Mashpee's government, and his opposition to white "encroachment" on the district, apparently did not apply to the valuable land grant made to him by that government in April 1779; Massachusetts Acts and Resolves 1778–1779, Chapter 207, June 26, 1779.

24. Lot Nye, Barnstable, to the Massachusetts General Court, February 3, 1783, in documents relating to Unpassed Senate Legislation (hereafter Unpassed Senate), no. 25d, 1783, Massachusetts Archives.

25. Nathan Hatch, *The Democratization of American Christianity* (New Haven, Conn.: Yale University Press, 1989), 6-11 and *passim*; Peter S. Field, *The Crisis of the Standing Order: Clerical Intellectuals and Cultural Authority in Massachusetts, 1780–1833* (Amherst: University of Massachusetts Press, 1998). Most historians of New England Baptists stress the growing acceptance and respectability of Baptists after the Revolution; the Mashpees' experience, on the other hand, supports the notion, emphasized by Hatch and Field, that Baptists remained a sect that had suspiciously radical implications. Compare John L. Brooke, "A Deacon's Orthodoxy: Religion, Class, and the Moral Economy of Shays's Rebellion" and Stephen A. Marini, "The Religious World of Daniel Shays," in *In Debt to Shays*, ed. Robert A. Gross (Charlottesville: University Press of Virginia, 1993), 205-80; also Susan Juster, *Disorderly Women, Sexual Politics and Evangelism in Revolutionary New England* (Ithaca, N.Y.: Cornell University Press, 1994), 108-44. On the attraction of Baptists and Methodists to "people of color" see William S. Simmons and Cheryl L. Simmons, *Old Light on Separate Ways: The Narragansett Diary of Joseph Fish, 1765–1776* (Hanover, N.H.: University Press of New England, 1982), xix-xxxvii; O'Connell, *On Our Own Ground*, lviii; James Oliver Horton and Lois E. Horton, *In Hope of Liberty: Culture, Community, and Protest Among Northern Free Blacks, 1700–1860* (New York: Oxford University Press, 1997), 133-36.

26. When the two towns passed resolutions in May 1787 demanding far-reaching changes, including an end to the clergy's tax-exempt status, Hawley exclaimed that "[s]uch men ought to be laid under Church

Censure and suspended from the Communion"! "Miscellany," *The Massachusetts Centinel,* June 2, 1798, p. 83; Hawley to Rev. Oaks Shaw, Barnstable, June 9, 1787, Savage Papers, vol. 2, no. 204. The towns, like others during this period, also sought to move the legislature away from Boston, to reduce government salaries, to end speculation in government bonds, to tax luxury goods heavily, to regulate the prices that country merchants charged for goods, and to end state support for Harvard College.

27. Hawley to Cushing, Boston, May 8, 1788, William Cushing Papers, 1664–1814, MHS. Strangely, no one discussed the legislature's appointment of three guardians for Mashpee in April 1778: Daniel Davis, Esq., Simon Fish, and Thomas Smith—a close friend of Hawley. This act may have been a wartime emergency measure that was temporary and largely ineffective. Massachusetts Acts and Resolves of 1777–1778, Chapter 1068, April 30, 1778. The legislature also received a petition from several whites complaining that only nineteen proprietors attended the last district meeting; that they were plied with liquor by corrupt overseers; and that the overseers had become dictators who forced young men on whaling voyages. Petition in documents relating to Massachusetts Acts and Resolves of 1788, May Session, Chapter 2, approved May 1788, quoted in Campisi, *Mashpee Indians,* 88.

28. Massachusetts Acts and Resolves of 1788, Chapter 2, May 1788.

29. They told the legislature that they opposed "the coming of Negroes & English, who, unhappily, have planted themselves here, hath managed us, and it is to be feared, that they and their Children, unless they are removed, will get away our Lands & all our Privileges in a short time." Petition of Mashpee proprietors, July 1788, in documents relating to Acts of 1788, Chapter 38, approved January 30, 1789, Massachusetts Archives.

30. Hawley to the Massachusetts General Court, November 5, 1788, and Fish to the General Court, December 23, 1788, in documents relating to Acts of 1788, Chapter 38.

31. Letter from justices of peace, selectmen, and other inhabitants of Barnstable, Sandwich, and Falmouth, adjoining Mashpee, December 22, 1788, in documents relating to Acts of 1788, Chapter 38.

32. John Percival, Barnstable, to the Massachusetts General Court, November 19, 1788, in documents relating to Acts of 1788, Chapter 38.

33. Mashpees to the Massachusetts General Court, October 31, 1788, in documents relating to Acts of 1788, Chapter 38.

34. The board consisted of two men from Barnstable County and one from each of the adjoining counties: Bristol, Plymouth, and Dukes (Martha's Vineyard). The overseers had the power to establish rules and regulations for the community; control land and other resources; care for the poor (by leasing land and distributing food and other assistance); bind out children to white families and review seamen's contracts; and hold and manage Mashpee funds. Documents relating to Acts of 1788, Chapter 38.

35. Hawley's recollection of a letter to Governor Hancock written July 8, 1791; at the bottom of the ms., he noted that he was not sure if it was an exact copy, because he had also written to Hancock in August and October. He served as treasurer until he was forced to resign in 1795, due to advanced age and apparent incompetence; however, he continued to sit on the board of overseers until 1804, just three years before his death, when he engineered the appointment of his son to take his place; Hawley to James Freeman, Boston, December 24, 1805, Hawley Letters, MHS.

36. A few months after the implementation of the new rules, Hawley reported that the new regime was generally "very acceptable to these Indians"; Hawley to the Massachusetts General Court, May 12, 1789, in documents relating to Unpassed Senate, no. 1036.

37. Mashpee Indians to Mashpee Overseers, November 24, 1789, Savage Papers, vol. 2, no. 209. Only a corner of the petition remains, so little of the text can be reconstructed.

38. Mashpees to the Massachusetts General Court, June 13, 1791, in documents relating to Unpassed Senate, no. 1419a.

39. Deposition by Levi Mie, June 13, 1791, Unpassed Senate, no. 1419a.

40. Hawley to Governor Hancock, probably July 8, 1791; Hawley to Robert Treat Paine, Boston, November 25, 1791, Robert Treat Paine Papers, vol. 28. (reel 5 of 19), MHS; Hawley to Peter Thacher, December 12, 1791, Hawley Letters, MHS.

41. Mashpees to the Massachusetts General Court, May 28, 1792, no. 1643/2, in documents relating to Unpassed Senate, no. 1643.

42. This connection that at least some Mashpees made between their political liberty and their unfettered use of resources, and the rejoinder by Hawley that this was a vocal minority, point to a possible division in Mashpee between those who embraced newer notions of liberty and private property and those who held to older values—who may or may not have supported the guardianship. Studies of other Indian communities in the midst of similar cultural and political earthquakes—particularly the Cherokees and Creeks at the end of the eighteenth century, and the White Earth Anishinaabe a century later—find similar divisions and conflicts erupting. Theda Perdue, "The Conflict Within: Cherokees and Removal," in *Cherokee Removal, Before and After,* ed. William L. Anderson (Athens: University of Georgia Press, 1991), 55-74; Claudio Saunt, *A New Order of Things: Property, Power, and the Transformation of the Creek Indians, 1733–1816* (New York: Cambridge University Press, 1999); Melissa L. Meyer, *The White Earth Tragedy: Ethnicity and Dispossession at a Minnesota Anishinaabe Reservation* (Lincoln: University of Nebraska Press, 1994). Among the Creek and White Earth Anishinaabe, in fact, "mixed" or metis family backgrounds often indicated those who supported the shift to private landholding and Anglo-American political paradigms of representative democracy. Hawley's letters, while often vile, describe the large-scale immigration of Indians from other places before the Revolution, and of non-Indians who married into Mashpee families

or were "adopted" by the community during the Revolution—and reveal that these individuals and their children were among the leaders of those pushing for more liberty.

43. Mashpee to the Massachusetts General Court, July 1788, in documents relating to Acts of 1788, Chapter 38, Passed Legislation.

44. Depositions by Levi Mie and Ebenezer Crocker, June 1795, in Hawley Papers, vol. 2, Congregational Library, Boston. Freeman was an inspired choice: he was a recent Harvard graduate, and had become prominent in part because he was the son of a famous Revolutionary general. Nathaniel Freeman Sr., had also served as head of the Sandwich Committee of Correspondence, in which capacity he had probably encountered Hawley and his muted loyalism. Nathaniel Jr., graduated from Harvard in 1787; he was twice elected to Congress before he died of tuberculosis in 1800; RA Lovell, Jr., *Sandwich: A Cape Cod Town* (Sandwich: Town of Sandwich, 1996), 244.

45. Mashpees to the Massachusetts General Court, undated but probably before December 1794, since this is the first document in the file, and the second is Hawley's letter to the legislature of December 15, 1794, which attests to the popularity of his rule and the efforts by a small minority to regain their power in Mashpee. In documents relating to Passed Legislation, Acts of 1795, Chapter 48, approved February 22, 1796, Massachusetts Archives. I have assumed that this petition was Freeman's work because its language is vastly different from that of earlier and later petitions. Also, the testimony about Freeman's participation in the Mashpee's cause was recorded in late June and July 1795, after the legislative committee was created and began its inquiry; Hawley Papers, vol. 2, Congregational Library. Interestingly, few of the signatories of this petition signed any other petition; in fact, Levi Mie, who was among those who commissioned Freeman and whom Hawley named as one of his greatest opponents, did not sign the document.

46. Hawley to the Massachusetts General Court, May 1, 1795, Hawley Letters, MHS.

47. Hawley to the Massachusetts General Court committee, September 2, 1795, vol. 2, Savage Papers.

48. Mashpees to the Massachusetts General Court, January 8, 1796, documents relating to Unpassed Senate, no. 2194.

49. Committee report, January 16, 1796, in Acts of 1795, Chapter 48, Massachusetts Archives.

50. "An Act especially providing for the Removal of poor Persons from the District of Marshpee, who have no legal Settlement there," Acts of 1796, Chapter 23.

51. Hawley to Belknap, July 27 and August 30, 1796, J. Belknap Papers, P-380, reel 6 of 11, no. 161, B. 157, B. 160-61, MHS.

52. John Tripp, "Native Church at Gay Head," *Zion's Advocate*, September 1831, reprinted *Magazine of New England History* 3 (1893): 250-53; William G. McLoughlin, ed., *The Diary of Isaac Backus*, vol. 3, 1786–1806 (Providence, R.I.: Brown University Press, 1979), 1431-32. Hawley referred to Freeman as a "half-blooded Indian"; Hawley, Mashpee, to Rev. Dr. Jedidah Morse, Boston, May 1804, Papers of the Society for the Propagation of the Gospel (hereafter SPG Papers), Peabody Essex Museum.

53. Mashpees to the Massachusetts General Court, n.d., in documents relating to Unpassed Senate, no. 2525, February 1799. In October 1801, Hawley referred to a petition carried to Boston by party from Mashpee "in the year 1799 with the baptist minister at their head." Hawley to "Gentlemen" (SPG?), October 6, 1801, Savage Papers, vol. 2, no. 220.

54. Mashpees to the Massachusetts General Court, December 1807, in documents relating to Chapter 109, Acts of 1807, Passed Legislation.

55. Mashpees to the Massachusetts General Court, December 1807, in documents relating to Chapter 109, Acts of 1807, Passed Legislation.

56. Mashpees to the Massachusetts General Court, December 1807, and Sandwich town meeting to the Massachusetts General Court, December 9, 1807, in documents relating to Chapter 109, Acts of 1807, Passed Legislation. The Sandwich letter was also signed by the Barnstable selectmen. James Freeman served as state representative and senator and as Barnstable County High Sheriff before drowning in January 1816 during a trip to Martha's Vineyard; Lovell, *Sandwich*, 265.

57. Mashpees to the Massachusetts General Court, January 1808, and Herring Pond and Black Ground Tribe to the Massachusetts General Court, January 1808, in documents relating to Chapter 109, Acts of 1807.

58. Zaccheus Pognit deposition, January 2, 1808; John Fish, Sandwich, deposition, January 2, 1808; Lemuel Ewer, Sandwich, deposition, January 2, 1808; Benjamin Burgess, deposition, January 7, 1808, all in documents relating to Chapter 109, Acts of 1807.

59. Committee report, draft act, and final act, all in documents relating to Chapter 109, Acts of 1807.

60. Mashpees to the Massachusetts General Court, undated, in documents relating to Chapter 109, Acts of 1807.

61. Solomon Francis et al. to John Davis, Boston, August 15, 1808, Miscellaneous Bound Documents, MHS. See Fish and Ewer depositions, above. Both Fish and Ewer called Francis a "lazy, idle, mischief-making, lying fellow"—a mantra that seems suspicious because both men used precisely the same words in their separate dispositions.

62. Gay Head to the Massachusetts Governor, July 23, 1811, Box 19, February-December 1811, Massachusetts Council Files, Massachusetts Archives; Christiantown petition to the Massachusetts General Court, April 24, 1817, in documents relating to Chapter 20, Resolves of 1817; documents relating to Chapter 99, approved February 12, 1818, Acts of 1817; documents relating to Chapter 123, approved February 16, 1818, Resolves of 1817; Chappequiddicks to

Massachusetts General Court, June 1, 1805, in Box 14, Massachusetts Council Files, Massachusetts Archives; report of committee, June 7, 1809, in Box 17, June 1808–July 1809, Massachusetts Council Files; Chappequiddick petition to the Massachusetts governor, October 28, 1811, Box 3, Folder 15, Indian Guardian Accounts.

63. Mohegans to the Connecticut General Assembly, April 30, 1819, doc. 86a-c, Indian Archives, 2d ser., vol. 1, Connecticut Archives, Hartford; petition of John Uncas and other Mohegans to the Connecticut General Assembly, April 24, 1820, Box 5 (1820–1824), Folder 1 (Rejected bills, 1820), Rejected Bills, Connecticut Archives; Connecticut General Assembly committee on Mohegan petition, May 25, 1820, doc. 87, Indian Archives, 2d ser., vol. 1, Connecticut Archives.

64. Jack Campisi, "Emergence of the Mashantucket Pequot Tribe, 1637–1975," in *The Pequots in Southern New England: The Rise and Fall of an American Indian Nation*, eds. Laurence M. Hauptman and James D. Wherry (Norman: University of Oklahoma Press, 1990), 126.

65. Mashpees to the Massachusetts General Court, June 13, 1817, in documents relating to Chapter 89, Resolves of 1817, Passed Legislation.

66. Massachusetts legislative report, June 18, 1818, Box 2, Folder 10, Guardian accounts and correspondence. Lemuel Ewers, for a time a Mashpee overseer and treasurer, testified in 1834 that this committee never actually visited Mashpee. They spent two days in the area: one day meeting over five miles from the village, and the next day meeting at the Crocker residence or tavern in Cotuit, on Mashpee's southwest border—and the home of a man disliked and perhaps feared by many Mashpees. Ewer testimony, "Minutes of the Legislative Committee Appointed to Inquire into the Complaints of the Mashpee Indians," February 5–March 8, 1834, Box 1, Folder 1, Ira Moore Barton Papers, American Antiquarian Society.

67. Chapter 105, passed February 18, 1819, in Benjamin Hallett, *Rights of the Marshpee Indians* (Boston: J. Howe, March 1834), 14-15.

68. Testimony by Matthias Amos in E. B. Chace, letter to the editor of the *Providence Journal,* date unknown but probably 1870, in Narragansett Collection, Rhode Island State Archives, Providence; testimony by Daniel Amos in "Minutes of the Legislative Committee."

69. Testimony by Joseph Amos in "Minutes of the Legislative Committee." Matthias Amos also noted that Fish "took no interest in them, beyond preaching to them on Sunday, never visited them, and did them no good. He was a Unitarian, and most of those who cared for religion at all, wanted to be Baptists." E. B. Chace, letter to the editor of the *Providence Journal.* On the Methodists' appeal and following see Tiro, "Denominated 'SAVAGE,'" 661-62.

70. Apess visited Mashpee as part of his work among Indians and other communities in the region. He had been ordained by a group of dissident Methodists in 1829, and in that year violated older norms of authority by publishing his memoirs. On the "privileged" nature of public discourse, even in the early nineteenth century, see Christopher Grasso, *A Speaking Aristocracy: Transforming Public Discourse in Eighteenth-Century Connecticut* (Chapel Hill: University of North Carolina Press, 1999), 2, 4.

71. Apess, "Indian Nullification," in *On Our Own Ground, 169-72.* For Apess's life through 1829, see generally Apess, "A Son of the Forest," in *On Our Own Ground,* 3-52.

72. Apess, "Indian Nullification," 173-86; Josiah Fiske, report to Gov. Levi Lincoln, undated but probably July 6, 1832, Box 2, File 1, Indian Guardian Accounts and Correspondence; Mashpees to Fish, June 26, 1833, Box 1, File 1, Indian Guardian Accounts and Correspondence. Apess's and Fiske's descriptions of the meeting are strikingly similar.

73. Fiske to the Governor, July 4, 1832, and Fiske, report, Box 1, File 1, Indian Guardian Accounts and Correspondence.

74. Fiske, report, Box 1, File 1, Indian Guardian Accounts and Correspondence.

75. Elders did play an important role in the Mashpee uprising: the two men who signed the initial petition and headed the May 21 meeting, Ebenezer Attaquin and Israel Amos, were born in 1782 and 1786, respectively. But the three men who clearly spearheaded the revolt and then led the community were all born between 1795 and 1810: William Apess (1798), Daniel Amos (ca. 1804), and Joseph Amos (1806). This was also the generation that, among African Americans, became increasingly unwilling to accept political and social subordination. Anglo-Americans such as Charles Finney (1792), Henry David Thoreau (b. 1817) and William Lloyd Garrison (1805), would drive the reform ferment in the North. "Minutes of the Legislative Committee Appointed to Inquire into the Complaints of the Mashpee Indians" (Daniel Amos and Isaac Combs); list of Mashpee proprietors taken November 1832 (Matthias Amos, Ebenezer Attaquin, Israel Amos), by Charles Marston and the Mashpee overseers, Box 2, Folder 15, Indian Guardians Accounts and Correspondence; 1860 Federal census, Mashpee schedule (Joseph Amos).

76. Apess, "Indian Nullification," 196-98. On Hallett as a supporter of radical politics and labor movements in 1834 see Alfred Young, *The Shoemaker and the Tea Party* (Boston: Beacon Press, 2000), 143-44. On Hallett as head of the Barnstable County Antimasonic Party see the *Barnstable Patriot*, September 11, 1833, p. 2, col. 4; for Hallett's obituary see the *Narragansett Weekly*, October 9, 1862, p. 3 col. 8.

77. Jill Lepore, *The Name of War: King Philip's War and the Origins of American Identity* (New York: Alfred A. Knopf, 1998), 210-16.

78. William Apess, Daniel B. Amos, and Isaac Coombs to the Speaker of the Massachusetts House of Representatives, January 21, 1834, in doc-

uments relating to Unpassed House legislation, no. 12843, Massachusetts Archives.

79. *The Liberator,* January 25, 1834, reprinted in Apess, "Indian Nullification," 220-23.

80. Apess, "Indian Nullification," 177.

81. Apess, "Indian Nullification," 205-42; "Minutes of the Legislative Committee Appointed to Inquire into the Complaints of the Mashpee Indians."

82. In 1833, Massachusetts had ratified a constitutional amendment that ended tax support for the Congregational Church, finally separating church and state and symbolically severing an important link to the Puritan past. That same year, the General Court organized a Legislative Temperance Society, and during the first year 160 members signed up. No doubt the members of that Society were quite impressed by the Mashpee Temperance Society organized by Apess rather than Fish, and heavily publicized by the Indians and their allies. They were also moved by the Indians' emphasis that, given more autonomy, they could improve their schools. One year later, Massachusetts established the first state fund for public education, designed to raise the level of primary education in every town. Cornelius Dalton, et al., *Leading the Way: A History of the Massachusetts General Court, 1629–1980* (Boston: Commonwealth of Massachusetts, 1984): 126, 135. For a description of the first district meeting, on May 5, 1834, see documents relating to Unpassed House legislation, no. 13838, December 15, 1834.

83. See petition of 1838 in Unpassed Senate legislation, no. 10417. "[T]he Indians would more punctually attend public worship, feeling that they had rights which they might exercise without obtrusion by the white inhabitants, who they stated took the lead of singing, and, as one Indian observed, put the Indian singers back, and the Indian wanted to take the lead in his own meeting." Legislative

Commissioners' Report on Mashpee Meetinghouse, *1839 Reports of the Massachusetts House of Representatives*, no. 72 (Boston, 1839), 7.

84. See various documents in Unpassed Senate, no. 111612, 1842, including petitions from the Mashpees and from Fish describing these events. Fish protested to the state and to Harvard, but finally accepted the construction of a new meetinghouse in Cotuit, at Mashpee's southeast corner, where he ministered to the few white families and a few still-loyal Mashpees. He continued to preach on alternate Sundays at Herring Pond. Fish also retained his racist sensibilities. In 1853, one year before his death, he wrote to an SPG official that the Indians held "a considerable degree of false ambition of equality with Whites, without proper fitness for it—and it threatens to impair that docile spirit by which alone they can reasonably hope to increase their true respectability." Fish, Cotuit, to L. K. Lathrop, October 13, 1853, Box 2, Folder 8, MS 48, SPG Papers, Peabody Essex Museum. Fish was actually buried in the Mashpee church burial ground.

85. With the exception of Karim Tiro's article on William Apess and Methodism, publications on the Mashpee uprising have barely noticed how the revolt took place within these larger contexts. But Tiro focused entirely on Apess, with very little attention to Mashpee, ironically confirming those who, in 1833 and 1834, tried to discredit the Indians' uprising by blaming their unrest on Apess. Tiro, "Denominated 'SAVAGE.'"

# "A Precarious Living":

## Basket Making and Related Crafts Among New England Indians

NAN WOLVERTON

HEN JOSEPH MCKINSTRY OF STURBRIDGE, Massachusetts, died in 1804 at the young age of thirty-seven, he had among his belongings some thirteen baskets. The appraisers of McKinstry's estate valued most of them at roughly five cents apiece.[1] The number of baskets listed among the pounds of wool and flax and bushels or half bushels of beans, malt, rye, and corn suggests how important they were for the work of Yankee farmers like McKinstry, who used them for storing and transporting a wide variety of products.[2] But the low values assigned to these vessels, which were labor-intensive to produce, reflect on another group of workers that operated within the same web of social and economic relations as McKinstry's farm. The makers of baskets like those owned by McKinstry were often marginalized craftspeople, many of whom were Native American. This essay considers the shared experiences of Indian and non-Indian basket makers, in an attempt to understand how Indian artisans fit into an economy that demanded cheap labor from marginalized workers producing inexpensive, necessary goods. In addition to crafting baskets, these same individuals often practiced trades such as chair bottoming, broom making, and mat making to eke out livings. Recognizing the significance of these crafts alongside basket making helps us to gain a better understanding of how, in eighteenth- and nineteenth-century New England, many Native Americans utilized local, natural materials to earn livelihoods that in turn helped sustain their identity as Indians.

What do we know about itinerant basketmakers in early New England? In most cases they were craftspeople who were politically, socially, and/or economically marginalized. Many, especially Indians, were literally living on the edge of white New England society—some lived within swamps, some in shacks—but they were nonetheless participants in an economic network. They traded their handmade goods as a necessary means of eking out what might easily be described as a "precarious" existence. Many who took up basket making and related crafts did so as the only available means of making a living. The plight of Yankee basket makers in early nineteenth-century York, Maine, is clear from a footnote to the manufacturing census of 1832: "The basket makers are indigent persons, living in the back part of the town, on rocky sterile land, who employ themselves in making baskets, as the only means of affording a living."[3]

A common trait among most of those who made baskets was the ability to practice more than one craft—chair bottoming, broom making, and mat making were among these other activities. The Nedson family of Southbridge, Massachusetts, for instance, were Indians who lived near Hatchet Pond, where they existed by "swingling flax, chopping wood, weaving baskets and chair-bottoms."[4] Simon Gigger and Bets Hendricks were remembered in antiquarian Harriette Merrifield Forbes's history of Westborough, Masssachusetts, as Nipmucs who made baskets and "often found work in rebottoming the chairs."[5] Peter Salem, who served as a soldier during the Revolutionary War, was a former black slave who earned "a precarious livelihood by making and mending baskets, bottoming chairs, and the like."[6] Yankee Judah Wright of Holden, Massachusetts, born in 1774, was blind from the time he was an infant. From age twelve, following the death of his father, Judah supported himself and his mother by making baskets and bottoming chairs.[7] Nathan Hunt from Boscawen, New Hampshire, was a Yankee noted for his strong and evenly woven baskets. He reportedly earned "a precarious living by making baskets and bottoming chairs."[8] Sylvester Judd, author of the *History of Hadley*, noted that "Indians and squaws peddled brooms and baskets" in Hadley, Massachusetts, and other towns [*Figure 1*].[9] In her account of the characters of South

*Figure 1: Three Maliseet women peddling basket and brooms, c. 1840, watercolor by John Stanton. Photo courtesy of The New Brunswick Museum, Webster Canadiana Pictorial Collection, #6712.*

County, Rhode Island, *South-County Neighbors,* Esther Bernon Carpenter introduces Ailse Congdon, whose dooryard was always "guiltless of litter" since its short grass was fiercely swept with the birch brooms brought to the door by "the sullen lords of the Charlestown squaws, who, at other seasons, tramped with baskets."[10] In his 1895 reminiscence of his native Williamstown, Massachusetts, Judge Keyes Danforth recalled that among the town inhabitants was the "Ballou" family, who lived in a shanty and "eked out a miserable existence by making door mats of corn husks and coarse baskets."[11] Danforth describes the Ballous as a "poor white family" who "for many generations annoyed the people of the village with their begging."[12] The local Williamstown history describes the Ballou family of mat and basket makers as "whitish mulattoes" or as "very dark whites" and "extremely dirty in either case."[13] Both writers considered this family a nuisance because of their begging and abject poverty and perhaps because of their uncertain racial identity.[14]

It is clear from references to both Indian and Yankee itinerant basket makers and bottomers in nineteenth-century century local histories that, although members of both groups shared a common social class, poverty, and to some extent ridicule as peculiar local "characters," in other ways they were nevertheless distinct from one another in the eyes of nineteenth-century town historians. The Yankees were often remembered as local geniuses who made up for their lack of education with wit or natural ability, as harmless individuals who practiced a craft to get by. John Davis of Gilsum, New Hampshire, was, according to the town history, "quite a remarkable man." He was a mechanical genius who had made a stringed instrument that resembled a piano. Yet in 1815, he reportedly walked to Keene barefoot to seat chairs to earn enough money to pay his taxes. Yankee Stephen Messer, of Gorham, New Hampshire, was remembered for his natural mechanical and artistic skills: "no one could make a handsomer basket, snow-shoe or moose-sled, or bottom chairs with more artistic skill."[15]

Indian makers were more often noted for their itinerant lifestyle and fondness for rum and cider than for their craft skills. "Like all the Indians," Forbes generalized as she wrote of Andrew Brown and other Indians who lived in Westborough in the nineteenth century, "he and his family spent their time making baskets and drinking up the profits from them."[16] Forbes's racism and condescension are representative of most descriptions of Indian basket makers in local histories and memoirs. In 1897, *The Warren Herald* published the recollections of Emily Allen Woods, who, as a child in Brimfield, Massachusetts, remembered that the Dorus family "made a few baskets which they traded mostly for rum."[17] Certainly Yankee basket makers indulged in alcohol as well. Yankee Nathan Hunt, for instance, was a basket maker known among his customers for his procrastination and drinking habits. It was, however, Indian makers, at once marginalized because of their race, who were stereotypically associated with alcohol in local history descriptions.

The above-mentioned itinerant makers are just some of the many artisans in nineteenth-century New England who made baskets and related crafts. Many makers were part-time producers, while others devoted most of their time to their craft. Some had no choice but to turn out these products.[18] Early nineteenth-century institutions forced juvenile delinquents and prisoners to make baskets, bottom chairs, and practice other trades in an attempt to teach them skills but also to provide some income for the facilities that housed them. These children provided cheap labor that helped such institutions support themselves. The Juvenile Institution of South Boston reported that there were fifteen boys employed at basket making as of January 14, 1829 and that after they had worked forty-two days the institution garnered $4.20 for the baskets they produced.[19]

Prisons employed inmates in a similar fashion to reform schools and houses of correction. In the 1830s and 40s the inmates of the Connecticut State Prison in Wethersfield were employed at making chair bottoms and at other activities such as shoe and nail making, all of which helped maintain the institution. In the 1840s, female inmates at the Wethersfield prison were also weaving chair bottoms. Contractors worked with the agents of such institutions to receive and sell the products, and the market determined what was produced.[20]

Women and girls also routinely performed chair bottoming as outwork for chair factories in northern Worcester County throughout the nineteenth century.[21] Covering glass bottles with willow or wood splint to protect them from breaking was another, related activity that women took on as outwork for some glass factories, and juvenile delinquents also performed this task at Houses of Refuge.[22] It has also been suggested that Indians were sometimes employed by glass factories to weave basket-covered bottles, perhaps as outwork.[23]

What was it about crafts such as basket making and chair bottoming that relegated these activities to poor, marginalized artisans and even prisoners? These products took time to make, but brought in low returns. Prices varied depending upon the size of the product and when and where it was sold, but usually ranged from two cents to seventy-five cents per object. Paugusett Molly Hatchett, for instance, is said to have received four cents for one of her baskets around 1800. In 1733 Mohegan Sarah Cooper received from sixteen to forty-eight cents for her baskets, depending upon their size.[24] Peter Salem received twenty cents for bottoming a chair in 1806.[25] Jonas Clapp, a Yankee basket maker from Oakham, Massachusetts, received fifty cents for a bushel basket and seventy-five cents for a two-bushel basket in 1834. For his smaller, handled baskets he received twenty-five cents and for a cheese basket thirty-three cents in 1835.[26] A uniform price for making splint brooms for country stores throughout Vermont in the late 1820s was six cents. Indian women peddled such brooms for nine pence apiece.[27]

These trades were not hard to learn (hence they could easily be taught to juvenile delinquents), but it took time to learn to practice them well. The work was tedious, and for those who gathered raw materials or peddled their own wares, it was also strenuous. Baskets and brooms were both crafted at home or while traveling, and then peddled to households near and far [*Figure 2*].[28] John Johnson, who grew up making and peddling baskets as an Indian captive in Maine, recalled in his narrative published in 1861 that peddling baskets was "a

*Figure 2: Indian woman peddling baskets, watercolor by Cornelius Krieghoff. Photo courtesy of National Archives of Canada, Ottawa.*

hard life, and although a person might be very tough, yet this kind of life followed up pretty closely, would wear upon him."[29]

Trades like basket making, chair bottoming, and broom making involved minimal or no expenditure for materials, which could usually be gathered locally at no cost. The wood splint used for baskets—usually brown ash, white ash, or white oak—was the same material used for splint chair seats or bottoms. The checker weave of splints woven in an "over one, under one" pattern used on baskets was related to that used on many splint chair bottoms. In some cases inventories even make reference to the similarity. The probate inventory of Nathan Fiske of Sturbridge, Massachusetts, for instance, indicates that he had two dozen "basket bottom chairs" in his household when he died in 1829.[30] The most common weave used on chair bottoms was a twill weave—splints woven "over two, under two" (or "over three, under three") to create a twill design. This type of weave was sometimes used on baskets as well.

While making flag seating does not resemble wood splint basketry or bottoming in its technique, it is similar in its economy of materials. The technique for flag, or rush, seating involves twisting wet rush and pulling it around seat rails to create the woven seat. Making flag-bottomed chairs, commented one nineteenth-century observer, was a "common trick of economy."[31] The materials for flag chairs—sweet flag, cattail, rush, or corn husk—could be gathered locally and could also be used for making mats. Lydia Howard Sigourney reminds readers in her *Sketch of Connecticut, Forty Years Since* that neat farmhouses in New England had white sanded floors and broad mats made of the husks of Indian corn at each door.[32]

Brooms were made from ash or birch. What had come to be known as "Indian," "peeled," or "splinter" brooms were made from sticks of birch or ash long enough to include the broom and the handle. The brooms were made by slivering thin splints from both ends of the base stick, with one set turned down upon the others until a thick, round broom was formed—all this from a single stick of wood. When Yankee Levi Dickinson began a broom business in 1797 in Hadley, Massachusetts, he was scoffed at and told that only Indians made brooms.[33] What Dickinson set out to do, however, was to make brooms from broom corn rather than from ash or birch. Dickinson was attempting to develop a business in brooms that required that he *grow* his materials rather than gather them from the wild—an altogether different enterprise.

It was the demand for such everyday, utilitarian products as baskets and brooms that helped keep their makers in business. These products were among the most common objects in New England households. Chairs, the most numerous pieces of furniture in the home, often were bottomed with flag seats that wore out with use and had to be replaced, sometimes several times during the life of a chair. Having a chair rebottomed was much cheaper than purchasing a new one. Brooms and mats, too, were common, everyday items used in New England households, and because they wore out they had to be replaced with some regularity. Repeat customers, therefore, were common. Some makers followed familiar circuits in order to deliver their goods to the same customers on a regular basis. Molly Hatchett of Derby, Connecticut, well known for her little fancy stained baskets, visited one hundred or more families once or twice a year. She came to know the families well and would routinely deliver a basket rattle [*Figure 3*] containing six kernels of corn when any one of them welcomed a new baby.[34]

Baskets had many functions and were used in every part of a household, from the woodshed to the parlor. [35] Probate inventories from the eighteenth and nineteenth centuries indicate not only how common baskets were, but also the variety of their uses. Examples include "basket of feathers," "basket of knives and forks," "two bas-

*Figure 3: Wood splint rattle attributed to Molly Hatchett. Photo courtesy of Old Sturbridge Village.*

kets and wool," "basket, clothespins & line," "basket & old clothes," "basket and tools," and even "a basket of powder, files, awls, borer, etc."[36] Households could easily have had ten or more baskets on hand. Clothes baskets and bushel baskets were among the most common. Other types included cheese, fruit, knife, corn, and sewing or workbaskets, hat and bonnet baskets, and eel pots.[37]

Rarely do we find baskets described as "Indian" in probate inventories, although occasional examples exist. Some entries only suggest Indian makers: a "colored basket and contents," for instance, worth ten cents in the 1837 inventory for Prudence Clark of Sturbridge, Massachusetts, may refer to a paint-decorated Indian basket.[38] Because they were so common, Indian baskets may not have warranted special mention in probate listings. We do, however, see them included in period paintings such as the watercolor of "Charity," showing a Connecticut interior, c. 1810 [*Figure 4*] or the girl with a stamped splint basket of fruit and corn, c. 1830-35 [*Figure 5*].

*Figure 4: "Charity," c. 1810, artist unidentified, watercolor with crystalline decoration. Photo courtesy of New York State Historical Association.*

*Figure 5: "Girl with Painted Splint Basket of Fruit and Corn," c. 1830-1835. Private collection.*

*Figure 6: Cover of wood splint basket showing painted vase design. Photo courtesy of Old Sturbridge Village.*

As commodity goods, Indian baskets were often specifically designed to cater to the Euro-American market in ways that set them apart and were intended to increase sales.[39] Makers sometimes employed design motifs that were commonly found on other forms of decorative arts within Yankee households. Baskets with hand-painted designs of vases with flowers, for instance, have been attributed to the Arnold family that lived at Hassanimisco, near Grafton, Massachusetts [*Figure 6* ].[40] Fireboards painted with vases of flowers may have been among those objects that inspired such designs [*Figure 7*].

Some baskets combined traditional Native American with European inspired designs. A geometrical rosette or compass pinwheel inscribed on a basket [*Figure 8*] may have been inspired by the use of the motif in other common contexts such as on a Bible box

*Figure 7: Painted fireboard with vase painted design. Photo courtesy of Old Sturbridge Village.*

*Figure 8: Basket detail showing inscribed geometrical rosette. Photo courtesy of Old Sturbridge Village.*

*Figure 9: Bible box dated 1744 with carved geometrical rosettes. Photo courtesy of Old Sturbridge Village.*

*Figure 10: Wood splint basket showing traditional Native American and European motifs. Photo courtesy of Old Sturbridge Village.*

*Figure 11: Chest-like storage basket with painted and stamped decoration.*
*Photo courtesy of Old Sturbridge Village.*

[*Figure 9*]. The stockade design on the same basket is a traditional Indian motif whose symbolism varied from one group to the next. The juxtaposition of both designs on the same basket is a good example of how Indian basket makers combined motifs from two traditions [*Figure 10*].

While many baskets had freehand decoration (applied with a brush or a chewed twig), there were also many with stamped decoration—a technique that speeded up the decorating process and, hence, the number of baskets that one could produce. Forms also occasionally reflected market demand. Storage baskets with legs imitating chests were made in both decorated and undecorated styles [*Figure 11*].

*Figure 12: Detail of "View of Quebec," 1844. Photo courtesy of National Archives of Canada C2643.*

In addition, "fancy" souvenir baskets were developed and sold to the growing tourist industry by the mid-nineteenth century [*Figure 12*].[41]

Not all Indian-made baskets were decorated, so baskets of Indian manufacture are not always obvious. John Avery noted in the *History of the Town of Ledyard* that the Indians made baskets of all shapes and sizes, "from tiny ornamental ones holding only a pint or even less up to strong oaken baskets for farm use, holding one or two bushels apiece."[42] A painting depicting two young Indian girls peddling a variety of basket types includes both decorated and undecorated baskets [*Figure 13*]. The knife inserted in the front of the large basket suggests that the girls were making or refining baskets as they traveled.

Like basket makers, chair bottomers traveled to the homes of their customers, and there they performed their craft, often telling stories simultaneously. By spending many hours within the family circles,

*Figure 13: Two young girl basket peddlers, first half of the nineteenth century. Private collection.*

these artisans often earned the respect and friendship of their customers through their work and their stories. Chair bottomer Peter Salem's trade gave him admittance to everyone's home, where "his good nature rendered him a universal favorite, especially with the children."[43] While Peter was engaged in mending household chairs, children gathered around him to listen to stories of his service as a soldier during the Revolutionary War.

Rarely are the makers of particular chair seats known today, since their work was unmarked. Some material evidence remains, however, to provide an understanding of how even a seemingly anonymous product can be identified with its maker. Sarah (Brown) Sprague, an Indian woman also known as "Granny Sprague," made a living in the early nineteenth century by selling baskets and seating flag-bottomed

*Figure 14: Ladder-back side chair seated by Sarah (Brown) Sprague, also known as "Granny Sprague." Photo courtesy of Old Sturbridge Village.*

chairs for white families in and around Webster, Massachusetts. What little we know of Sarah comes from recollections written by Octavia Sweetser, who had been a good friend of Sarah's granddaughter, Angela Sprague. Mrs. Sweetser's recollections indicate that Sarah—a Nipmuc Indian—traveled quite a distance to market her wares, including the ten miles to Sturbridge where among her regular customers was the family of Samuel F. Bemis.

Sarah's son Israel and his wife, Sally White, died at early ages, leaving two young daughters behind. The youngest, Angela, was cared for by her Grandmother Sprague. So well did Granny Sprague come to know the Bemis family for whom she bottomed chairs that after her death sometime in the 1860s, Angela was sent to live with them.

Although raised in a white family and later married to a white man, Angela remained quite aware of her Indian identity as it had been passed on to her by her grandmother. According to Octavia Sweetser, another ward of the Bemis family, Angela accompanied Granny on her basket-selling/chair-seating circuit. Angela also *helped* her grandmother, for she well remembered handing her rush as she worked.

Granny Sprague's seating work must have seemed to Angela an important part of her grandmother's identity as a Native artisan, for following Granny's death, Angela asked to keep as her own two of the chairs that the old woman had seated. Years later, nearly a century after Granny's death, they were donated to the Old Sturbridge Village collections by Octavia Sweetser, to whom Angela had willed them [*Figure 14*]. These neatly seated chairs had been kept as a sort of memorial to Granny Sprague and were donated to the museum along with her story. Granny Sprague was just one of many Indian women who had bottomed chairs during the two hundred years prior to her death. A rare, early reference to a rush chair bottomed by an Indian woman appears in a 1672 account book and simply states, "woven by Indian squa[w] Hanna."44

Certainly not all Indians made baskets and bottomed chairs, but for many these trades became a means of subsistence and even resistance as their land and other traditional means of living were lost to European encroachment. The object of making these crafts wasn't just to supply the market, as it was for many non-Indian producers. For Indians, the use of local, natural materials to create objects that could be sold or exchanged for goods helped to maintain at least some element of their traditional economies. Even crafts that were virtually anonymous, like chair bottoming, helped some individuals—including, perhaps, Sarah (Brown) Sprague—to find an identity in a world that had seemingly turned on its head. One might argue that the mobility that accompanied such crafts allowed Indians the freedom to work at their own pace without being tied down by the demands of other forms of labor. Some Indians considered it a natural right to gather materials for their crafts wherever they might be located. Emily Allen Woods, who grew up in Brimfield, Massachusetts, recalled that Indians in that vicinity "never hesitated to cut a tree for basket stuff when they saw one they wanted, no matter whose land it was on."[45] This practice was common enough to prompt the author of a history of Windsor, Connecticut, to note in 1859 that there was still a "prevalent impression" among the people of New England that Indians had a hereditary right to cut trees for baskets and brooms within the domains once owned by their ancestors.[46] And, as Ann McMullen has demonstrated, the decoration on some Indian baskets suggests a culture of resistance.[47] The very practice of these crafts as a means of livelihood, then, might be seen as a form of resistance to the dominant Euro-American economic and social systems.

In *Oldtown Folks* (1869), Harriet Beecher Stowe describes the early nineteenth-century descendants of the Natick Indians as a "roving, uncertain class of people, who are always falling into want, and needing to be helped, hanging like a tattered fringe on the thrifty and well-kept petticoat of New England society."[48] This perception of Indians as needy and dependent made many white New Englanders feel superior to the Natives in their communities. Yet the products of these Indians and other marginalized workers were essential to the everyday economies of New England households. Indians, in fact, helped to maintain the "well-kept petticoat of New England society" with their baskets for keeping things orderly, their newly woven chair seats, their mats for wiping dirty feet, and their brooms for sweeping up. In the process, these crafts, among Natives and non-Natives alike, became associated with Indian cultural identity.

It was, ironically, the Indian as icon of tradition that some twentieth-century marketers used to help sell factory-produced baskets, the very wares that by the end of the nineteenth century had forced many Native Americans to find other means of economic survival.[49] The cover of an early twentieth-century catalog for the Shelton Basket Company of Shelton, Connecticut [*Figure 15*] presents a romanticized image of an Indian basket maker that helped to sell the factory's products because it suggested basketry as a time-honored craft—indeed, as "America's first industry." The image also helped to suggest high quality by implying handmade, Indian construction even though the items in the catalog were neither Indian nor hand made. Even after consumer demand for their handmade products had ceased, Indians continued to pass their craft traditions on to future generations, as part of their Native American identity if no longer as a means of existence.

*Figure 15: Cover of advertising pamphlet for Shelton Baskets, c. 1900. Photo courtesy of Connecticut Historical Society.*

# Notes

1. Ten of McKinstry's baskets were valued collectively at fifty cents, making them worth about five cents each. Joseph McKinstry inventory, 33, p. 129, Worcester County Probate Records, Office of Probate, Worcester County Courthouse, Worcester, Mass. (Worcester County probate records referenced in this essay were transcribed by Holly V. Izard).

2. McKinstry also owned a cheese basket for straining whey from cheese curds and a "knife and comb basket." An unmarried farmer, he did not apparently own many of the common household baskets such as sewing or clothes baskets.

3. *Documents Relative to the Manufactures in the United States* (Washington, D.C., 1833), 27.

4. Ellen D. Larned, *History of Windham County, Connecticut,* 2 vols. (Worcester: published by the author, 1880), 2:532.

5. Harriette Merrifield Forbes, *The Hundredth Town: Glimpses of Life in Westborough, 1717-1817* (Boston: Rockwell and Churchill, 1889), 174.

6. Emory Washburn, *Historical Sketches of the Town of Leicester, Massachusetts* (Boston: 1860), 267. Salem was remembered for having shot down Major Pitcairn at the Battle of Bunker Hill. Peter Salem's livelihood was, indeed, precarious. As he grew older, his resources grew smaller, and he was unable to supply his few wants. The overseers of the poor for Leicester, unwilling to provide charity for the old man, sent him to Framingham, Massachusetts, where his former masters had given a

bond to the town to support him during his life. He died in Framingham in 1816.

7.  David Foster Estes, *History of Holden, Massachusetts, 1684-1894* (Worcester, 1894), 333. It was not uncommon for the blind to make baskets and other handwoven articles. In 1841 the New York Institution for the Blind reported that its fifty pupils were employed in making baskets, mats, rugs, and carpeting and in braiding palm-leaf hats. See John Barber and Henry Howe, *Historical Collections of the State of New York* (New York: 1841), 328.

8.  Charles Carleton Coffin, *The History of Boscawen and Webster, from 1733-1878* (Concord, N.H., 1878), 653. Although Yankee basket makers mentioned in local histories are usually male, there are the occasional references to female basket makers as well. Betsey Colby of Weare, New Hampshire, was remembered as "an excellent basket weaver." It was a trade that she had reportedly learned from her father, Samuel, who made baskets in the 1820s. William Little, *The History of Weare, New Hampshire* (Lowell, Mass., 1888), 539.

9.  Sylvester Judd, *History of Hadley* (repr. Springfield, Mass.: Hunting & Company, 1905), 360.

10.  Esther Bernon Carpenter, *South-County Neighbors* (Boston: Roberts Brothers, 1887), 62. Carpenter's comment suggests that Indian men in the area peddled brooms, while Indian women peddled baskets.

11.  Judge Keyes Danforth, *Boyhood Reminiscences* (New York: Gazlay Brothers, 1895), 158. I am grateful to my colleague Frank White for bringing this reference to my attention.

12.  Danforth, *Boyhood Reminiscences*, 158.

13.  Arthur Lathum Perry, *Origins in Williamstown* (New York: Charles Scribner's Sons, 1894), 63.

14. Sometimes the race of basket makers and bottomers was difficult for local recorders to determine. Intermarriage between Native Americans and African Americans was common, and these "black Indians" were identified in public records at various times as "colored," "mulatto," or "Indian." Basket maker Barzaleel Mann was listed as mulatto in the Upton 1850 census, as was his five-year-old daughter, Emily. But Mann and his wife Nancy were described in the Shrewsbury town history as Indian basket makers, and their daughter Emily is listed in the Shrewsbury birth records as Indian. By 1860, following the death of her parents, Emily was living in the Mendon home of Francis Gunn, a bottomer who, along with his family, is described as "black." Emily, however, is described as "Indian."

15. *History of Coos County* (Boston: W. A. Fergusson & Company, 1888), 892.

16. Forbes, *Hundredth Town*, 171.

17. "Indian Families Who Have Lived in This Vicinity," *The Warren Herald*, June 18, 1897.

18. Among those who devoted most of their time to the craft were shop manufacturers. Although they existed in the early nineteenth century, basket factories became more common during the second half of the century.

19. *Fourth Annual Report of the Board of Managers of the Prison Discipline Society* (Boston: Perkins and Marvin, 1829), 311.

20. In 1831, for instance, the manufacture of nails was suspended at the Wethersfield Prison due to "the demand for these in the market having become less active." But the demand for chairs was up, and in that year the chair shop at the prison brought in more income for the institution than any other shop. *Sixth Report of the Board of Managers of the Prison Discipline Society* (Boston: Perkins and Marvin, 1831), 92.

21. See Nan Wolverton, "Bottomed Out: Female Chair Seaters in Nineteenth-Century Rural New England," in *Rural New England Furniture: People, Place, and Production*, The Dublin Seminar for New England Folklife Annual Proceedings 1998.

22. Kenneth M. Wilson, *New England Glass and Glassmaking* (New York: Thomas Y. Crowell Company, 1972), 154-56; *Fourth Annual Report of the Board of Managers of the Prison Discipline Society* (Boston: Perkins and Marvin, 1829), 317.

23. Gloria Teleki, *The Baskets of Rural America* (New York: E. P. Dutton & Co., Inc., 1975), 34.

24. Eva Butler, "Some Early Indian Basket Makers of Southern New England," addendum, in Frank G. Speck, *Eastern Algonkian Block-Stamp Decoration* (Trenton: The Archeological Society of New Jersey, 1947), 42, 48.

25. Nahum Tainter Account Book, December 16, 1806, Old Sturbridge Village Research Library. When Tainter settled his accounts with Salem in 1810, he had Salem leave his mark—a large X—near his name.

26. Potter & Rice Daybook D, August 27, 1834; Potter & Allen Daybook A, April 6, and May 9, 1835, Oakham Historical Society, Oakham, Massachusetts.

27. Alice Morse Earle, *Home Life in Colonial Days* (New York: The Macmillan Company, 1898), 303-4.

28. Not all products were peddled door to door. Some individuals sold their wares to local storekeepers. In the account book of storekeeper Jonathan Devotion of Windham, Connecticut, one Joseph Walton was credited for baskets, mats, and for bottoming chairs in 1798. Sarah Mooch, listed as a "squaw," was credited for four brooms in 1797 against her purchase of rum and sundries. Andrew Jackson, list-

ed as a "Negro," was credited in 1800 for a broom and ashes against his purchase of tea, rum, and fish. Jonathan Devotion and Co., Account Book, Windham, Connecticut, 1795-1800, Manuscript Collection, Old Sturbridge Village Research Library. Other store accounts such as those recorded by Potter & Allen of Oakham, Massachusetts, include entries for moccasins—used by Yankees as slippers as well as with snowshoes—and mats, suggesting the acquisition of such goods from Native Americans.

29. John Johnson, *Life of John W. Johnson* (Portland, 1861), 72.

30. Nathan Fiske inventory, 64, p. 159, Worcester County Probate Records, Office of Probate.

31. E. Victor Bigelow, *A Narrative History of the Town of Cohasset, Massachusetts* (Boston, 1898), 235.

32. Lydia Howard Sigourney, *Sketch of Connecticut, Forty Years Since* (Hartford: Oliver D. Cooke & Sons, 1824), 144.

33. Judd, *History of Hadley*, 360-61. Although Dickinson was told that broom making was for Indians, splint brooms were in fact also made by many Yankee farmers on winter evenings.

34. Ambrose Beardsley and Samuel Orcutt, *History of the Old Town of Derby, Connecticut, 1642-1880* (Springfield, Mass., 1880), l-li.

35. When Harriet Beecher Stowe describes the autumn activity of gathering chestnuts for the Cushing family in *Poganuc People*, she notes that the boys and their father prepared for this festive outing by excitedly gathering up the necessary baskets and pails for the harvest. Mrs. Cushing, becoming somewhat alarmed that her household arrangements were being disturbed by these preparations, pleaded "Now, father, *please* don't take all my baskets this time . . . ," (Boston: Houghton, Mifflin and Company, 1898), 157.

36  Miscellaneous probate inventories, Worcester County Probate Records, Office of Probate.

37.  Eel pots were used by both Indians and non-Indians alike. According to one account, when John Eliot was translating the Bible into the Indian language he sought help from the Indians as he tried to come up with the Indian word for lattice. Eliot's description of lattice, however, only prompted them to come up with the word for eel pot—a form with which they were quite familiar. William Biglow, *History of the Town of Natick, Mass.* (Boston: Marsh, Capen & Lyon, 1830), p. 85.

38.  Prudence Clark inventory, docket #12266, Worcester County Probate Records, Office of Probate.

39.  We know from inventories of Indian households such as those documented by Kathleen Bragdon that Indians used the products of their own manufacture in addition to selling them. The 1753 inventory of Nathanial Coochuck, for instance, includes among other items "his baskets." Bragdon, "Probate Records as a Source for Algonquian Ethnohistory," in William Cowan, ed., *Papers of the 10th Algonquian Conference* (Ottawa, Canada, 1979).

40.  Russell G. Handsman and Ann McMullen note this attribution in *A Key into the Language of Woodsplint Baskets* (Washington, Conn.: American Indian Archaeological Institute, 1987), 31. Handsman and McMullen also suggest that although this design may originally have been used to appeal to the Anglo market, it later was considered a traditional decoration by some basket makers.

41.  For more on the souvenir in Northeast Indian art see Ruth B. Phillips, *Trading Identities: The Souvenir in Native North American Art from the Northeast, 1700-1900* (Seattle: Univ. of Washington Press, 1998).

42.  John Avery, *History of the Town of Ledyard 1650-1900* (Norwich, Conn.: Woyes & Davis, 1901), 259.

43. Washburn, *Historical Sketches of Leicester*, 267.

44. Benno M. Forman, *American Seating Furniture, 1630-1730* (New York: W. W. Norton & Company, 1988), 112.

45. *The Warren Herald*, June 18, 1897.

46. Henry R. Stiles, *The History of Ancient Windsor, Connecticut* (New York: Charles B. Norton, 1859), 114.

47. Handsman and McMullen, *A Key into the Language of Woodsplint Baskets*, 114-23.

48. Harriet Beecher Stowe, *Oldtown Folks* (Boston: Fields, Osgood & Company, 1869), 19.

49. There were still some Indians trying to exist by making baskets and other crafts at the end of the nineteenth century. Jacob A. Riis documented the presence of a handful of Mohawk and Iroquois Indians in the west-side tenements of New York. Riis noted that they tried to "eke out such a living as they can weaving mats and baskets, and threading glass pearls on slippers and pincushions, until, one after another, they have died off and gone to happier hunting-grounds." Quoted in Phillips, *Trading Identities*, 263.

# Index

role of Indian churches and,
264–298
will and reason in, 235
women in, 183–185
Church, Benjamin, 121
Clapp, Elisha, 316
Clapp, Jonas, 346
Clinton, Bill, 16
Cobb, Peter, 147–148
Cogenhew, Hepzibath, 275
Cogenhew, Reuben, 276, 303, 304
Cogenhew, Samuel, 275
Coggeshall, Daniel, 125–126
Coggswell, Julia, 193–195
Cogley, Richard, 53
Cohen, Charles L., 78
Colby, Betwey, 363
Colman, Benjamin, 205–206
colonialism
censuses and control in, 149
consciousness and, 84–99
control over history and, 13–15
domination in, 214–215
dreams under, 95–97
land encroachment and, 195–213
pauper apprenticeships and,
139–140
power in, 235–239
resistance to, 20, 175–213
translation as power in, 56–60
women under, 180–181, 183–184
Colonial Society of Massachusetts,
15–16
Comaroff, Jean, 97
Comaroff, John, 97
Comer, John, 87
condensation, in dreams, 88

confession, 233–235
in letters, 244–246
power and, 236–239
Reformed doctrine and, 246–252
Congdon, Ailse, 344
congregationalism, 86, 260,
280–281, 339
consciousness and colonization,
84–99
Coombs, Isaac, 276
Cooper, Sarah, 346
Coquit, Judah, 276–277
Cotton, John, Jr., 271
creation stories, 174–176
Crocker, Jabez, 209–210
culture
disparagement of Indian, 199–201
intermarriage and, 279–283
women in, 180, 181–184, 220

Danforth, Keyes, 344
Davenport, Samuel, 108
Davis, John, 344
*Day-Breaking, if Not the Sun-Rising, of
the Gospel with the Indians in New
England, The* (Wilson), 72
Deake, Edward, 239
De Forest, John W., 189
Den Ouden, Amy, 20, 174–177,
195–213, 221–222
detribalization, 160
Devotion, Jonathan, 365
*Dialogues* (Eliot), 19
Diamond, Jared, 25
Dickinson, Levi, 349
diet, 47
disease, 90

# Index